EXPLORING THE NEW SOUTH AMERICAN REGIONALISM (NSAR)

The International Political Economy of New Regionalisms Series

The International Political Economy of New Regionalisms Series presents innovative analyses of a range of novel regional relations and institutions. Going beyond established, formal, interstate economic organizations, this essential series provides informed interdisciplinary and international research and debate about myriad heterogeneous intermediate-level interactions.

Reflective of its cosmopolitan and creative orientation, this series is developed by an international editorial team of established and emerging scholars in both the South and North. It reinforces ongoing networks of analysts in both academia and think-tanks as well as international agencies concerned with micro-, meso- and macro-level regionalisms.

Recent titles in the series (continued at the back of the book)

China's Diplomacy in Eastern and Southern Africa
Edited by Seifudein Adem

Regionalism and Regional Security in South Asia
The Role of SAARC
Zahid Shahab Ahmed

Comparative Regionalisms for Development in the 21st Century
Insights from the Global South
Edited by Emmanuel Fanta, Timothy M. Shaw and Vanessa T. Tang

Mapping Agency
Comparing Regionalisms in Africa
Edited by Ulrike Lorenz-Carl and Martin Rempe

Exploring the New South American Regionalism (NSAR)

Edited by

ERNESTO VIVARES
FLACSO, Ecuador

Routledge
Taylor & Francis Group

LONDON AND NEW YORK

First published 2014 by Ashgate Publishing

Published 2016 by Routledge
2 Park Square, Milton Park, Abingdon, Oxfordshire OX14 4RN
711 Third Avenue, New York, NY 10017, USA

First issued in paperback 2016

Routledge is an imprint of the Taylor & Francis Group, an informa business

British Library Cataloguing in Publication Data
A catalogue record for this book is available from the British Library

The Library of Congress has cataloged the printed edition as follows:
Exploring the new South American regionalism (NSAR) / by [edited by] Ernesto Vivares.
    pages cm.—(The international political economy of new regionalisms series)
  Includes bibliographical references and index.
  ISBN 978-1-4094-6959-9 (hardback)
1. Regionalism—South America. 2. Regionalism—
Economic aspects—South America. 3. Economic development—South America. 4. South America—Economic integration. 5. National security—South America. 6. Unión de Naciones Suramericanas. I. Vivares, Ernesto.

  HC165.E97 2013
  337.1'8—dc23

                                                                2013020851

ISBN 13: 978-1-138-27049-7 (pbk)
ISBN 13: 978-1-4094-6959-9 (hbk)

Contents

List of Figures and Tables   vii
List of Contributors   ix

Preface   xiii
Anthony Payne

Introduction: Contours of the New South American Regionalism   1
Ernesto Vivares

PART I: THINKING AND CONCEPTUALIZING ABOUT REGIONALISM IN THE AMERICAS

1   Toward a Political Economy of the New South American
    Regionalism   9
    Ernesto Vivares

2   The Origins of the Union of South American Nations:
    A Multicausal Account of South American Regionalism   29
    Carlos Espinosa

3   Washington and the New South American Regionalism   49
    Francisco Carrión Mena

4   East Asian Economic Cooperation: Lessons for South American
    Regionalism   65
    John Wong

PART II: ECONOMIC AND SOCIAL DEVELOPMENT

5   The Need for a New South American Economic Regionalization   91
    Renato Baumann

6   Incorporation and Regionalism in Latin America   113
    Juliana Martínez Franzoni and Diego Sánchez-Ancochea

7   Rescaling Responsibilities and Rights: The Case of UNASUR
      Health   129
      Pía Riggirozzi

8   Global Contexts and Challenges of Building a Regional
      Governance of Social Policy and Its Implications for South America 147
      Nicola Yeates

PART III: BROADENING REGIONALISM: CRIME, INTELLIGENCE, AND DEFENSE

9   Drug Trafficking and Organized Crime: UNASUR Perspectives   163
      Daniel Pontón

10   Defense and the New South American Regionalism: Exploring
      New Conditions and Perspectives on Defense in South America   183
      Germán Montenegro

11   Trends, Strategic Tension, and Cooperation in Security and
      Intelligence in the Andean Region   197
      Fredy Rivera Vélez

Conclusion   213
Bibliography   219
Index   243

List of Figures and Tables

Figures

4.1	Japan-Led "Flying Geese" Pattern for EA-I's Growth and Integration	70
4.2	China's Economic Growth and Inflation, 1978–2010	73
4.3	China's Trade Balance with Selected Economies	74
4.4	The Pattern of China-Led Regional Growth and Integration	74
4.5	Comparing East Asian Economies, 2010	76
4.6	GDP of East Asia, Japan, China, and the USA since 1980	78
5.1	Asia and Latin America—Intraregional Trade Intensity Index—Producer Goods—1992–2008	99
5.2	Asia and Latin America—Intraregional Trade Intensity Index—Other Goods—1992–2008	99
5.3	Asia and Latin America—Export Concentration Index—Intraregional Trade in "Other" Goods—1992–2008	100
5.4	Asia and Latin America—Export Concentration Index—Intraregional Trade in Producer Goods—1992–2008	100
5.5	Asian Spoke Countries—Export Concentration Index—Producer Goods—1992–2008	101
5.6	Latin American Spoke Countries—Export Concentration Index—Producer Goods—1992–2008	101
5.7	Asia and Latin America—HHI for GDP in Constant Prices—1992–2008	102
5.8	East Asia and South Asia—Relative Entropy Indexes of GDP in Constant US Dollars—1992–2008	110
5.9	Central America, Andean Countries and MERCOSUR—Relative Entropy Indexes of GDP in Constant US Dollars—1992–2008	111
6.1	Latin America—Change in the Gini Coefficient, circa 2000–2009	116
6.2	Public Social Spending (in Per Capita US Dollars of 2000), 2000–2001 and 2008–2009	122
6.3	Public Spending in Health (in Per Capita US Dollars of 2000), 2000–2001 and 2008–2009	123
8.1	Regional Social Policies in Practice on Four Continents	153

Tables

1.1	Major Perspectives in the International Political Economy of Regionalism	18

4.1	Performance Indicators for East Asian Economies (GDP–Population)	66
4.2	Origins and Destinations of East Asian Intraregional Trade	68
4.3	East Asian Socioeconomic Development Indicators	72
4.4	Comparing East Asian Economies, 1985–2010	76
4.5	Intra- and Extra-ASEAN Trade, 2009	82

5.1	Asia and Latin America. Trade in Producer Goods and Other Goods, 1992–2008	97
5.2	Asia and Latin America—Indicators of Convergence of GDP Growth Rates—1992–2008	103
5.3	Asia and Latin America—Correlation between Selected Pairs of Indicators	104
5.4	East and South Asia—Composition of Regional Trade, 1992–2008	105
5.5	East and South Asia—Composition of Regional and External Trade, 1992–2008	106
5.6	Latin America—Composition of Regional Trade, 1992–2008	107
5.7	Latin America—Composition of Regional and External Trade, 1992–2008	108
5.8	Relative Entropy Indexes of GDP, 1992–2008	109
5.9	Mean GDP Growth Rates, 1992–2008	111

6.1	Annual Average Rate of Growth of Real Average Earnings, 2003–2009	117

11.1	US Military and Police Aid, 2005–2010	200
11.2	US Military and Police Aid to the Region, 2005–2010	201

List of Contributors

Renato Bauman is currently Director of the International Unit of IPEA (Brazilian Government think tank) and professor at the Universidade de Brasília and the Brazilian Diplomatic Academy. He holds a DPhil in Economics from Oxford University and was former Director (1995–2010) of the UN/ECLAC Brasília Office. He has written over 10 books and tens of articles regarding trade and integration in Latin America.

Francisco Carrión Mena is a specialist in international issues and diplomacy, and is ambassador at the Foreign Service of the Ecuadorian Government. He has been Minister of Foreign Affairs (2005–2007), Ambassador of Ecuador to Spain (2000–2005), and representative of Ecuador before the United Nations (2009–2011). He is author of various publications about migration, foreign policy, and international rights.

Carlos Espinosa is Director of Research and Professor of History at FLACSO–Ecuador. He holds a PhD in History from the University of Chicago and has been Visiting Scholar at Harvard University and Visiting Professor at Middlebury College. His research has encompassed Andean history, Latin American diplomatic history, and contemporary international security issues.

Juliana Martínez Franzoni is Associate Professor at the University of Costa Rica. Her work on social policy formation and socioeconomic and gender inequality in Latin America has been most recently rewarded with fellowships by Fulbright, the Kellogg Institute for International Studies, and the British Academy. She has published in journals like *Social Politics* (2012), *Development and Change* (2011), *Global Social Policy* (2011), and *Latin American Politics and Society* (2008). With Diego Sánchez-Ancochea she also has a forthcoming article in *Latin American Research Review*.

German Montenegro is PhD at the National University of Quilmes, Argentina, and researcher at the Department of Social Sciences there. He has occupied different positions in areas of security and defense in Argentina and South America such as Under Secretary of Military–Technical Issues, Secretary of Military Affairs at the Ministry of Defense, Government of Argentina, and currently is director of the School of National Defense.

Daniel Pontón has a Bachelor's Degree in Sociology and Master's Degree in Public Policy; is an Associated Researcher at FLACSO Ecuador; is Director of the Metropolitan Observatory of Citizen Security of Quito; and is studying for a PhD at the National University of Cuyo Argentina. His has a vast trajectory in the field research and consultant in themes of organized crime, crime, security policy, and citizen security. He has published different research papers in this regard and currently is advisor of the National Secretary of Planning and Development of the Ecuadorian Government.

Pía Riggirozzi holds a PhD from the University of Warwick and is lecturer in Global Politics at the Department of Social Sciences: Politics and International Relations. Her research focuses on global governance and international institutions, political economy of development, and regionalism. Some of her most distinguish works are *Post-neoliberalism in Latin America* (2012), *Region, Regionness and Regionalism in Latin America* (2011), and *Social Policy in Post-neo-liberal Latin America*.

Fredy Rivera Vélez is currently coordinator of the PhD program in International Studies at FLACSO Ecuador. He holds a PhD in sociology from the National University of Cuyo, Argentina. His research focuses on defense, intelligence, security, and organized crime for the Andean Region. He was undersecretary of state for the areas of domestic and citizen security.

Diego Sánchez-Ancochea is University Lecturer in the Political Economy of Latin America at the University of Oxford and Governing Body Fellow of St Antony's College. His research focuses on state–society relations, industrial policy, income distribution, and public policy. Recent publications include papers in *Latin American Research Review* (2013), *Studies in Comparative International Development* (2012), *Global Social Policy* (2011), and *Economy and Society* (2009). He has also coedited three books and (together with Juliana Martínez Franzoni) a special issue on varieties of capitalism in Latin America in *Economy and Society*.

Ernesto Vivares holds a PhD from the University of Sheffield and is research professor and coordinator of the program of International Relations at FLACSO Ecuador. His research focuses on the international political economy of development, South American regionalism, and research methods. Among his publications is *A Political Economy of Regional Development Banks: Financing Regional Growth and the Inter-American Development Bank. The Case of Argentina* (Routledge, 2013).

John Wong is currently Professorial Fellow and Academic Advisor at the East Asian Institute (EAI) of the National University of Singapore. He was formerly Research Director of EAI, and Director of the Institute of East Asian Political

Economy (IEAPE). Prior to these, he taught economics at the University of Singapore. He obtained his PhD from London in 1966. Has written and/or edited 34 books and published numerous articles and papers on China and other East Asian economies, including ASEAN.

Nicola Yeates is Professor of Social Policy at the Open University, UK. She has published widely on diverse matters of global and regional social policy from an international perspective, including most recently *World-Regional Social Policy and Global Governance: New Research and Policy Agendas in Africa, Asia, Europe and Latin America* (Routledge, 2010; co-edited with B. Deacon, M. Macovei, and L. van Langenhove). Full details of her research and publications can be located on Open University's Open Research Online (http://oro.open.ac.uk).

Preface

South America remains a strangely specialist taste for students of political economy in the uncertain world order of the present. Of late, the European Union has dominated attention because of the crisis of the Eurozone and the Union's full embrace of German-led austerity. The USA is of course never ignored and the world has watched as it has successively faced a key Presidential election, a fiscal cliff, and something that has come to be known as a sequester. East Asia too is now always a center of attention, with ongoing debates as to whether the economies of China and India are slowing and, if so, at what rate and with what implications for them and everybody else. As for the rest of the world, Africa has moved back into fashion, with some observers seeing signs of an economic renaissance. In all of this chatter, both academic and journalistic, South America often tends to be, if not ignored, then somewhat under-noticed.

It should not be; for, arguably, it has been in South America over the last decade or so that some of the most interesting and progressive experiments in the conduct of political economy have been taking place. Think of Brazil, Argentina, Ecuador, and Venezuela, to name only the most prominent of South American countries wherein novel strategies of economic, social, and political development are being explored in the aftermath of long decades of neo-liberalism. South America is actually a region of hope within the global political economy and it is highly likely that there are lessons that should be learnt from the experience of these countries, and others, in the region and then applied in Europe, Asia, and Africa.

In this situation it is excellent news that we now have available this new study edited by Ernesto Vivares. It is the product of a seminar held by FLACSO in Ecuador toward the end of 2011 and is most timely in its appearance. Vivares and his collaborators explore what they call the New South American Regionalism (NSAR). This formulation has been deliberately chosen to connect the intellectual endeavors of the FLACSO team to a prominent strand of academic literature of the last several years that has generally come to be known as the study of the "new regionalism." The starting-point here was the observation that the shift toward a more intense globalization from the early 1980s onwards was also accompanied by a widespread embrace (and in the case of the European Union perhaps a re-embrace) of regionalism. What had often been considered to be opposites in political economy (globalization versus regionalism, as it were) now appeared as complementary. Regionalism was seen variously as a means of resisting globalization, but also of managing it and possibly deepening it at the same time.

At any rate, there began to appear a volley of new accounts of contemporary regionalism in all parts of the world which were later assembled by analysts into different schools of thought. Vivares describes the main contours of this literature very well in his chapter in this book and in fact identifies no less than six separable schools or approaches labeled, not necessarily all that clearly by their proponents: "neorealist," "liberal institutionalist," liberal economic integration," "world order," "new realist," and "new regionalist." This tide of writing has calmed a little of late, especially given that the core source for much of this thinking, namely Western Europe, has for some period of time seemed to be either stagnating or, more recently, fighting for its very regionalist existence. But the issues that gave rise to these debates have far from gone away and in any case, as implied above, South American regionalism remained under-studied by comparison with many other world regions.

Looking back into the new regionalist literature from a contemporary perspective, what appears to me to be most novel about it in retrospect was rather less what it had to say about how "new" regionalism was different to "old" regionalism, or indeed even what it had to say about regionalism as a form of regionalism. Its originality lay rather in the connection it made between regionalism and the much wider question of development, understood as the means by which countries (and regions) sought to insert themselves into the emerging global order on some basis that gave them opportunities to achieve at least a measure of well-being for some of their peoples. In other words, the focus on regionalism was a way of actually thinking about and addressing in a new era the longstanding, and entirely explicable, South American preoccupation with the core question of its development.

This book edited by Ernesto Vivares sits explicitly in this tradition of study. It seeks to analyze the new regional identity built up over the last few years in South America around the Union of South American Nations (UNASUR). It takes for granted that this emerging reality does not easily fit into existing models of regionalism developed in other regions. We know in short what it is not, even if we cannot yet see sharply and clearly what it is. The problem here (but also the source of the interest of the phenomenon) is precisely that South American countries are in the process of "building a heterogeneous path of regional development within a changing hemispheric and world order." I am quoting there from the book's Introduction, because that summary remark captures neatly and accurately the topic at hand. The issue is not just about region-formation as a particular piece of political architecture, but instead, and centrally, about how people live, about well-being and inequality, about who wins and who loses in the politics of development. These are big questions, without doubt, but they are the ones that need effort and thought from all of us.

Vivares and his colleagues rightly do not attempt to assert a single answer to them. The book has been deliberately constructed on the basis of multiple disciplines and methods. The authors do not all agree, but they do talk interestingly to each other. There are chapters that focus on the making of markets and the pursuit of social policy, as well as others that consider different sorts of regional matters, such as drug trafficking, defense, and cooperation in the gathering of intelligence. The diet offered is rich and varied. What holds it all together and what makes the book so palatable and so well worth reading is the conviction of all the contributors that something interesting and important is being constructed within the "New South American Regionalism." I am convinced by this claim and I think you will be too when you have finished the book.

Anthony Payne
Director, of the Sheffield Political Economy Research Institute (SPERI)
University of Sheffield, UK

Introduction
Contours of the New South American Regionalism

Ernesto Vivares

The political economy of globalization and regionalism in the Americas has been marked for a set of major historical events since the 1980s. In 1994, the US administration, with the support of Canada and Mexico, launched George W. Bush's "Enterprise for the Americas," a project to assemble a hemispheric area of free trade from Alaska to Tierra del Fuego, in the spirit of market-led development of the North American Free Trade Agreement (NAFTA) and engineered to absorb the South American Economies (2002). With the annex of Mexico into NAFTA and neoliberalism becoming the creed of development in the Americas, little doubt was initially cast on the supremacy of market enterprise on that continent. However, at the Summit of the Americas in 2004, set with the purpose of accepting the deal, a germinal association of South American governments unexpectedly brought to an end the North American's initiative, with Brazil, Venezuela, and Argentina refusing to accept the project. Since then the political economy of South America has historically turned in a sort of new regional identity which does not fit the model of the dominant ideas of regionalism in either the North American, the European, or the Asian projects. This regional identity was marked by the dynamic of new social forces that emerged in the last two decades of neoliberal reforms, with politics, the return of the state, democracy, and commodities becoming the central drivers of regional development.

Undoubtedly we know, in the light of the major streams of thought in global studies and regionalism, what this incipient regional configuration is not. Evidently, the embryonic regional South American experience is not the result of the agency of a socialist or neoliberal project. Beyond the wide range of studies dedicated to the region, integration, institutions, and regionalisms are only side of the coin. The other side to combine in the analysis is comprised of the different configurations of historical structures, social forces, and political orders building a heterogeneous path of regional development within a changing hemispheric and world order.

In South America, more than the overlapping of regional projects and their rationalities, we witness different structural configurations at the base of each regional project. The early experience has not been able yet to forge a regional union based on the session of national sovereign powers to major regional institutions such as the European Union or to equal the institutionality of the inter-American system. Nonetheless, it has been able to consolidate, quite remarkably, a democratic process of stability and reduction of inequalities considering the well-known history of political stability, inequality, and development in the region.

Anticipating a wave of research on the contours and outcomes of this new regionalism, Gasparini and Lustig (2011) analyze the trends in income distribution of the region in the period 1980–2008, with interesting results. They find a direct relation between the structural reforms of the 1990s with the increase in income inequality and a sharp decline of inequality after the 2000s, particularly in those countries following a heterodox path of development. The conclusion is direct: the unequalizing effect of market-oriented reforms in the absence of safety nets and social inclusion increase inequality; social spending and labour institutions cannot be market-oriented variables of development. Going further in that area of study, Birdsall, Lustig, and McLeod (2011) explore the relation between this sharp reduction of the inequality in the region and the type of political orders. Accordingly, they find that the countries with a major reduction of inequality are those whose development orientation combines a favorable external environment in commodities with a political order oriented to progressive social policies for workers and householders, and education upgrading. The clear conclusion is that the region is on the same path as most of the developing regions answering globalization and the shift of power, thanks to the new consolidated democracies via equality and education.

The new South American regionalism has not built regional structures under a unifying regional project, but the Union of South American Nations (UNASUR) proves to be the more effective regional tool to defend democratic political stability, instead of the Organization of American States (OAS), actively promoted by the US administration. The resolution of the Bolivian crisis in 2008, Ecuador in 2010, and the staunch opposition to the coups in Honduras and Paraguay speak clearly about the nature of UNASUR as an area of regional political coordination without the intervention of the USA. Clearly, the incipient NSAR does not fit the mold, although it delivers new answers to development and conflict beyond the dominant interpretation of regionalism, and it reflects diverse regional configurations. Dominant concepts of the past do no always explain present realities.

The renowned international political economy scholar Robert Cox (1981: 128) has long argued that, when the structures and problems of one era give way to new configurations and problems, theory and scholars are challenged to respond and explain these new realities of development. This book is a collective effort and attempt to move in that direction and, in doing so, it does not claim a universal answer, new concepts, or unifying methodologies, but just the start of an agenda of research for the future.

It is therefore not intended to assert that the way in which different South American democratic orders are facing the challenges of development since the beginning of the millennium has brought about a new regional configuration. Scholars from varying perspectives recognize and debate the extent of agreement about the major angles of the New South American Regionalism (Bonilla y Long, 2010; Riggirozzi, 2010; Tussie and Trucco, 2009; Phillips, 2004). Accordingly, scholars agree on the indissoluble link between the NSAR's political economy, the economic cycle of globalization and change, and the directions of its neopopulist, neodevelopmentalist, and market-oriented strategies of development. In this sense, we sought to explore the process of region formation of the NSAR in multidimensional levels of development with entrance sometimes by country other than by topics shaped by and shaping the dynamic between regionalism and regionalization (Söderbaum, 2012; Boas and McNeill, 2004).

Seen sometimes as a reaction to a decade of excessive market-led reforms in the 1990s and by others as new left-wing path of development, the identity of the NSAR lies in what it does, what it attempts to do, and who wins and who does not win. The exercise is not simple as it demands a deep and serious opening to research and reflection from a critical perspective and analytical eclecticism about the political economy of regional development. It is a critical perspective as it does not take the things and ideas as naturally given but as manmade, in a historical and geographical context. And it seeks to be analytically eclectic as it is open to different perceptions in order to explore key areas of development in a wide sense, build realistic questions, and find clues to tendencies in regional and national development in South America.

Accordingly, the project condensed in this book was the result of an open discussion that took place at the end of 2011 in FLACSO Ecuador from different perspectives of global and regional studies addressed to explore specific dimensions of the recent South American development. The meeting gathered 11 scholars who concurred to explore and discuss, from different perspectives and focusing on their own diverse areas, tensions and issues raised by the regional dynamics of development in South America. It was a conceptual and methodological challenge, not without its perils, as there was not a unique perspective and methodological approach that unified the collective effort and bridged the different perspectives involved.

The strategy thus was to open and build, from specific issues of development, something other than answers to why this new South American regionalist configuration of development is not emulating the European, North American, or Asian models. Or why this regional germinal identity lacks institutional strength or the resignation of national sovereign powers in favor of regional organizations. Or, moreover, why it is not pursuing the universal wisdom of trade and finance. Instead of that, the purpose of this exercise was to frame this regional phenomenon from its axes of development, conflict, and social change.

This kind of project is not new; Ashgate's publications by Professor Timothy Shaw and other similar authors have, for a long time, made important contributions to the comparative and empirical research about regionalism, regionalization, and region formation, with a particular focus on the global south. The approach is similar, although the focus here is the political economy of development of the South American regional formation. In view of that, the organization of this book expresses the way we approached our focus of study, the NSAR. It began with theoretical and conceptual revision of regionalism, regionalization, and region formation. Then it focused on a historical review in order to trace the hemispheric and global dynamic surrounding the NSAR, to finally move forward three major sets or contours of development in three sections: the global and regional changing context, the economic and social, and finally the conflict focusing on the state.

Thus, the first chapter analyzes the wide range of perspectives on regionalism and regionalization and their links with the major schools of political economic thought on globalization and development, the North American and British schools. There the aim is to identify the visions of development, globalization, and political projects underlying these perspectives in order to assess the extent to which they can inform regionalism in developing region such as South America and the political nature of its regionalism. The following section examines the origin of UNASUR as multidimensional, post-neoliberal, and institutionalized regionalism on the scale of the South American subcontinent and above all its political focus on development. As a historian, Carlos Espinosa does that in reference to five political economic dimensions: Brazilian leadership, the counterpoint between US hemispheric regionalism and Brazilian aspirations, the collective identity and/or territoriality of South America, models of development, and political coalitions. The chapter accounts for the emergence of regionalism on the scale of South America, and the role of the turn to the Left and populist political coalitions in the making of UNASUR is taken into account.

After that, from the experience of well-known South American diplomat Francisco Carrión Mena, explore the scope, collective leadership, and orientations of the NSAR and the complex relation with Washington in a context of global change, with the USA diverted from the region given security issues. It reviews the historical diplomatic path of regionalism and integration in Latin America in order to remark on the different features of the structure of UNSASUR and its relations with all minor blocs. Carrion concludes that a central feature of the NSRA is to go beyond the traditional focus on trade and finance, which marks a new relation between this nascent regionalist and the hegemonic decline of the USA. This chapter is followed by the chapter by John Wong, who seeks a contrast the NSAR with other new experiences of regionalism in East Asia (EA). The author analyzes how the historical political economy of integration led EA into of the most dynamic regions in terms of economic growth in the world. The work highlights the fact that many of the positive factors in EA economic integration are either absent or quite weak in South America. These include EA's successful export-oriented, industrialization-focused strategies which are the key to East Asian economic regionalism. In the next chapter, Renato Bauman argues the NSAR requires a pragmatic, differentiated approach for the preferences granted to different countries in the region, depending on their geographical proximity. The text shows that a well-designed process in this direction should pay off in terms of creating a degree of complementarity and hence a "regional multiplier" that allows all the participating countries to benefit in the upswings of the business cycle of the larger economies in region. This should contribute to reducing the disparities in the economic potential of the various countries; at the same time that might help preserve and improve the competitiveness of their exports.

Linking economic growth with the historical records of social inclusion, Juliana Martínez Franzoni and Diego Sánchez-Ancochea examine how Latin American countries have historically failed to secure market incorporation (e.g. people's participation in the cash nexus, which in turn requires the creation of a sufficient number of formal, well-paying jobs) and social incorporation (e.g. decommodification of rights) simultaneously. To answer this question, the chapter draws on the experience of Bolivia, Brazil, Chile, Peru, and Uruguay. It also discusses some of the challenges to secure further improvements in market and social incorporation in the immediate future and link our discussion to the process of regional integration. Continuing with the exploration of social and policy issues of the NSAR, Pía Riggirozzi's chapter argues that Latin America offers new grounds to evaluate symbolic, material, and institutional foundations defining a regional project, and at the same time the region's ability to interact autonomously as an international actor. By looking at the institutional and policy action of the newly established regional Health Council within UNASUR, this chapter explores first the linkages between regional integration and social development and, secondly, what regionalism through social policy means for how we theorize regionalism as a process and region as an actor. Following the social dimension of regionalism and development, the next chapter, by Nicola Yeates, addresses the contexts and challenges of building a regional governance of social policy given the growing interest in the potential of regional integration initiatives to advance social policy. This (re)turn to the possibilities of regional social policy in South America is situated in the context of longer histories of regional integration and in more recent histories of neo-liberal global social experimentation and struggles to forge alternative social models and modes of global governance. The chapter discusses the regional social policy in regional integration initiatives, and what this reveals in "practical policy" issues to be addressed in advancing the socialization of regionalism and the regionalization of social policy.

The next section starts with dealing with a downside of regionalization, narcotraffic. There, an expert in the matter at regional level, Daniel Pontón analyzes the relations between narcotraffic and organized crime in Latin America in the last 11 years. The study highlights the complex dynamics featured by it capacity to adapt to different economic, social, geographical, and political diverse configurations, and therefore the challenges that it represents for any regional project. The chapter represents an advanced political economy of narcotraffic and organized crime in South America and its capacity of infiltration in different levels of development and institutionality.

In the next chapter, German Montenegro explores and analyzes the new tendencies in matters of defense in South America. The work traces the historical dynamic and changes that define and reorient the concepts and orientations of national defense in the region such as the role of the state, the consolidation of democratic regimes, and the subordination of the military power to the democratic authority and the deactivation of conflicts with military derivation. In this regard, the author highlights that UNASUR has constituted a historical step in the regional defense integration because of it level of political democratic coordination.

Last but not least, in the final chapter of the book, a regional expert in strategic study, Fredy Rivera Vélez, analyzes the shift from the interstates' conflicts toward the redefinition of the perspectives and doctrines of national security in the region as an expression of the rise of the democratic authority over military rule. The author focuses on domestic and personal security, as well as cooperation in national matters of defense, particularly the capacity of UNASUR for that. The chapter also analyzes the institutional regional transformation accompanying that and the changes in regional cooperation that extend to other key areas of conflict, security, and development.

PART I
Thinking and Conceptualizing about Regionalism in the Americas

Chapter 1

Toward a Political Economy of the New South American Regionalism

Ernesto Vivares

Concepts

The recent events in world politics mark both the break of the world order that emerged post-1945 and a complex transition toward a new international configuration of social forces and power, with an increasing presence of regions as the forces reshaping the new contours and features of development. Today, crises and transitions, conflict and development are by large centered in regions as sociohistorical and politicoeconomic configurations that are limited to grasp by using the traditional, nation-centered empirical and functionalist approaches. Thus, the understanding of regionalism and development needs a closer analysis in order to bridge our understanding of development in global and national politics. Without doubt, regionalisms will not replace states as central actors in world politics, but it is out of question that they exist together with the structure of the Westphalian order.

As Hettne points out, this results in two projects, struggling to define the restructuring of the world and development beyond the balance of power, which rest on conflicting orientations that will define the transformation. That is a "neo-imperialism and 'hard' power of the sole superpower[s] versus inter-regionalism and 'soft' or 'civilian' power of a regional formation" (Hettne, 2005a: 269). On top of that, the global political landscape manifests a clear exhaustion and limits of both the Bretton Woods and the United Nations systems with erratic and insufficient responses to crisis, conflict, and development. On the other hand, the regional frontiers of nation states, as the result of formal (i.e. economy) and informal (i.e. organized crime) regionalization are surpassed by global and regional production networks and social forces building a development path that is no longer confined to frontiers of nation states (Payne and Phillips, 2010).

Today, regions are the platform where crises and conflicts emerge and spread, the crisis of the financialized model of development of the European Union or the power of organized crime in Latin America are two sides of the same coin, the relation between global order and the new regionalisms of development. Our point is that formal and informal regionalization is at the very base of the many regionalisms and it is a central political–economic concept to grasp the dynamic between global, regional, and national development. Regionalization goes faster than and beyond the formal top-down interstate and institutional processes of regional integration and cooperation, but complement s the agency and gives sense to its political nature (Söderbaum, 2012; Hettne, 2005; Boas *et al.*, 2004).

Thus, the study of regionalism and regionalization are pragmatically important as they speak about concrete issues of policy, practice, and change, particularly in cases such as the new South America phenomenon. This introductory, theoretical chapter aims then to provide an overview and examine the major perspectives and theoretical sources of regionalism and regionalization, at the international and regional levels, in order to define the major lines of thinking and key concepts necessary to build an eclectic and multidisciplinary approach able to comprehend the New South American Regionalism (NSAR).

To start with, we need to redefine the notion of development within the context of globalization in order to frame the debates on international political economy (IPE) and regionalism, hence to see the major lines that define its contours, extensions, and challenges today. A simple view of world affairs today shows that there are three major elements that cut across the major problems of development at global, regional, and national level: inequality, debt crises, and security conflicts as the result of current historical order (Payne and Phillips, 2010; Duffield, 2001).

These elements present two challenges to any scholar seeking to comprehend the political economy (PE) of development of a new regionalism such as the new South American phenomenon. The first is the lens through which we analyze them, which is the central ontological and epistemological matter, as it permits us to identify the relationship between knowledge, power, and history in the different interpretations of regionalism. Secondly is the matter of how to define and explore some of the key political–economic dimensions within an eclectic research approach able to grasp the relation between the different areas of development, from macro to micro and from well-being to conflict (Katzenstein, 2010; Payne and Phillips, 2010).

Nation-states and regionalization are important and different methodological and explanatory tools, but they can complement one another when they are tied to the same pragmatic research objective, in our case, development. Methodological nationalism and state-centrism has for a long time dominated our interpretation of world politics and development, but today can only be useful as long as these are contextualized in a pragmatic eclecticism with regionalization. That is our point in order to integrate in a critical PE the structural and agential issues of regions and development rather than seeking to fit theoretical paradigms (Sil and Katzenstein, 2010).

If, as Payne concludes, everything in world politics, regions, and nations is developing from the very moment that a collective well-being is sought, the analytical challenge is then to find its meaning and components in its own political–economic context of both nation-states and regionalization (Payne, 2005). For instance, monopoly market, finance, and trade are central elements that define North American regionalism; while financialized development, trade, and institutional rights are key drivers of the European Union. In the same way, South America counts for an identifiable core of components that delineate that region, substantive examples being inequality in commodities, politics, trade, geopolitics, and crime.

In a changing world order, South American regionalism has become a force contesting globalization, and the region the space where the PE of development with its inseparable outcomes of conflict and well-being takes place. South American regionalization thus emerges as complex and multidimensional social processes of region formation shaped by the neoliberal order of the past and the form of globalization today, but with a germinal regionalism contesting them. To approach that, we adopt two key ontological distinctions. The first is between agency and structure in the construction and dynamic of regions, assuming the different but complementary nature of the agency of regional political projects, regionalism (lead by state and non-state actors), and the structure and processes of regionalization. The second ontological distinction is the relation and dynamic between that sociohistorical regional construction (region) and the world order that we define here as regionalism, with its major outcomes of development defined by the two pillars of conflict and well-being. In other words, regionalisms are political projects addressed by the traditional research focus on "interstate integration," while regionalization alludes to processes and structures that cut across national state frontiers, shaping regional opportunities for—or constraints on—development, while shaping regions.

Equating the idea of globalization with market development, a great number of regional studies rest on the normative assumption that regionalism has to foster a growing economic interdependence, regional and international, through a state-led action. However, different is to think that if regions are a sort of middle structure between societies and world orders, the dynamic and developmental outcome of states, socioeconomic forces, and regional organizations are part of an open game rather than a normative one (Söderbaum, 2011). Coming from the time of the Cold War, the traditional idea of region, in its most basic notion, was seen as a set of states linked and in close association with, given their geography, a high level of interdependence (Nye, 1965). However, in a time of globalization, the concept has become more comprehensively used to explain the relation between regions with world orders, as well as with state and non-state actors. In any case the central and common academic idea is that every region is socially constructed in a context of development and politically contested by state and non-state actors through different political projects. The evidence shows then that every region always keeps a significant level of heterogeneity with imprecise and dynamic geographical limits, therein the importance of its relationships with regionalism and regionalization (Söderbaum, 2012). Regions are not naturally predefined by the international markets, but by social and heterogeneous historical constructions with unclear and active margins, shaped by processes of regionalization or different configurations of forces which generate diverse projects of regionalism. Latin

America is a typical case of that, where from the top we can see many regional projects overlapping, while, from the structure, different political–economic configurations. That is the point made by Nicolas Phillips, who, in order to understand the Southern Cone, had first to identify the PE of its different capitalist configurations (Phillips, 2004). The final distinction to adopt is that regionalism and regionalization can be driven by state and non-state actors; a key concept that allows us to integrate the notion of conflict and informal regionalization, thereby widening the notion of regionalism and development (Boas *et al.*, 2005).

Today the relation between regionalism and regionalization is somehow a key part of the debates in the IPE of development. Despite the fact that many still equate regionalism with interstate integration, a top-down event, certainly the debate about regionalism has moved to a bottom-up focus and, in particular, to the exploration of the relation between formal and informal regionalism, formal and informal coalitions, formal and informal economic actors, regional communities, and even organized crime. In that sense, the study of regionalism is attached to the study of development, world orders, and globalization.

We can say therefore that regionalism constitutes the body of ideas, values, and political projects that contribute to the creation, maintenance, or transformation of a region type or world order. Generally, regionalism leads into the creation of different kinds of regional institutional structures, which can imply cession or not of national sovereignty. To talk about regionalism as structures of formal governmental and economic integration is a narrow idea derived from the Cold War; the notion of regionalism is more comprehensive than integration but includes it. Regionalism includes state and non-state actors, formal and informal regional networks, all capable of building regionalization. Regionalization then is the structural process of regional formation. Regionalization can be caused by regionalist projects, but it can also rise in the absence of them (Söderbaum, 2012; Söderbaum and Shaw, 2003).

These conceptual distinctions are noteworthy, as they permit the assembling of a multidisciplinary research approach able to grasp different dimensions of regionalism and regionalization in agential and structural terms, including the elements of conflict and well-being. A typical example of this is the study of the complex orientations and configurations of political projects of regionalism in developing areas. Seen from the perspective of agency, they appear as a complex and even contradictory web of overlapping and opposing projects; however, when they are related to their different economic configurations and orientations, there emerges a new sense of the underlying PE. Something similar occurs with the study of conflict, which is usually associated in development studies to inequality. However, as shown by different studies in various developing regions, conflict might also be connected to organized crime and even defense and intelligence (Rivera, 2011a, 2011b).

Different scholars concur that the regional phenomenon taking place in South America is part of what is called the "new regionalisms," as it occurs within the new historical order of globalization (Bonilla and Long, 2010; Altmann and Rojas,

2008; Söderbaum, 2005). However, what there is not agreement about is how to academically grasp its international political–economic nature. There are several approaches to what the understanding and research of the new regionalism should be. They vary in many ways depending on what is understood by theory and its role in the research process (Burgess, 1982). For some, nation-state entries are the secure method; for others, regionalization–regionalism constitute a new reflectivist way to grasp globalization, power change, and development today.

For our case here we try to remain open to the construction of *ad hoc* and pragmatic approaches that frame specific research strategies for precise purposes taken from contextual case studies, some across regions and others focused on nation states (Katzenstein, 2010). In other words, the challenge is to build up *ad hoc* pragmatic perspectives and conceptual tools to bring together, in a multidisciplinary and coherent perspective, different premises that permit the generation of research strategies for specific case studies, avoiding falling into the political bias of the major perspectives (Katzenstein, 2010).

To achieve that, first it is necessary to understand the different roles of international political–economic theory in the research process of development and regionalism, with the goal of outlining and examining the advantages and limitations of the different perspectives on regionalism. The classifications of approaches to understand these research theories are extensive and range from orthodox to heterodox positions and from rationalist to reflectivist approaches, or they can be disciplinary or interdisciplinary. However, given the importance of departing from the delineation of the existent and dominant ideas of the present, we start with Cohen's distinction and characterization of the two major approaches of thought in IPE, the American and British schools (2011). The distinction is adopted here in a pragmatic way, to identify the main positive and negative elements of the different perspectives and theories on regionalism anchored in the major traditions of the two major epistemic communities of IPE; thus with the aim to open a research agenda anchored in the PE of South American development. We recognize that there is not a linear relationship or alignment between the two major schools of international political-economic thinking and the diverse theories on regionalism, although there is a vital distinction as to how different theories overcome the analytical and methodological distinctions and rigidities of different traditions of thinking in IPE.

Two Sources of Political–Economic Thought Permeating Regionalism and Regionalization

The first major school of IPE is the (North) American school (Cohen, 2011; Cox, 2009). Scholars of this school (Krasner, 2000; Keohane, 2002; Nye, 2004; Waltz, 2001; Frieden and Lake, 2000) conceived the IPE as a matter of articulation between two scientific disciplines—politics and economics—governed by their own independent ontologies, epistemologies, and methodologies. (North)

American realism and neoliberal institutionalism are its major theoretical sources' certainty in the unstoppable path of world trade and financial expansion on the basis of the British and North American experience. The North American IPE concerns itself with the compatible management of politics and economics, and its research agenda seeks to reveal how economics (usually trade and finance) impinges on political systems.

This concept of IPE here mainly addresses agency and political–economic behaviors, mostly of states and institutions, largely nurtured by traditional realist and liberal institutionalist approaches. For the (North) American school, regionalism is about states' actions, regional institutions, regional arrangements, and governmental regional projects oriented toward maximizing economic growth via trade and financial agreements, and more recently including security issues too. It is concerned with the stability and security of political systems impinged by economic dynamics of markets, focusing its research on the rationality and agency of regional integration projects led by state actors. Its starting point is the idea that there is an international system governed by the logic of cause–effect oriented toward the balance of its elements and the eradication of conflict. It conceives the international system as the sum of its components; national states, and national economies where political–economic behavior takes place and is interpreted mainly through the lens of rational choices or game theories, using orthodox positivist and functionalist methodologies.

The aim of this school is practical and realistic in its approach to examining how systems work (or not), seeking to predict political–economic behaviors. The aim is generally to prescribe solutions for the good functioning of institutions, states, and political orders in order to facilitate frameworks that positively or negatively stimulate the behavior of economic agents and markets. Actors behave on the basis of incentives and constraints to maximize benefits or avoid losses as a response to alterations in the pattern of an assumed universal logic of economic functioning (flows of trade and finance). Thus, economics becomes a one way *ceteris paribus* factor, or a level of material production of life, at the base of politics conceived as institutional systems, where political–economic behaviors take place and must be studied assuming the actors' rationalist choices, maximization of benefits, interests, ideas, and identities. Scholars working along the lines of the (North) American school are adept at its empirical positivist methodology because of its precision. However, its weakness lies in two central flaws. On the one hand, its overconfidence in institutional functionalism to inform power and conflict; and, on the other, in the limited range of factors that it can examine by leaving key elements in the reign of assumptions, usually expressed as *ceteris paribus* such as the conditions regarding how economics actors and market work (Cox, 2009).

The second major school of IPE identified by scholars is the British School, also named the "pluralist school," due to the multiple theories it refers to (Cohen, 2011; Cox, 2009). This school includes thinkers (Katzenstein, 2010; Strange, 1986, 1988; Gilpin, 2001; Cox, 1981, 2009) nurtured principally by neorealist, critical, and historical perspectives. The pluralist school of IPE is characterized then by the absence of a set of well-matched theories and their corresponding methodologies on the basis of a pre-established research agenda. The IPE is understood as a socially complex process that can only be grasped by assuming the inseparable nature of politics and economics, state and markets, and the international and domestic. Along these lines, the critical IPE does not present a common understanding of regionalism, but different critical, multidisciplinary perspectives concerned with how reality is produced and how to achieve desirable development outcomes (Cox, 2001: 76). Whilst one of its weaknesses is its absence of a predefined methodology, its strength is its openness to grasp strategic change, development, and conflict.

One of the central premises of IPE is that, if development has been and is constantly reframed by globalization and regionalism, then it is imperative to rethink development inside the IPE within them, from its historical structures. From this perspective, it concerns development and how it is affected by historical social processes, where the dynamics between the worlds orders and social forces struggle for its orientation, defining who gets what, how, and what for. As a result, the pluralist or critical international political-economic approach views politics and economics as two inseparable dimensions of historical and social constructions of power. The advantage of critical IPE is that it is a multidisciplinary field of theories and research that gravitated around the complex concept of development as understood in terms of change, conflict, and well-being produced in the world historical order.

Where Is It Heading?

In this sense the central challenge is to avoid the biases of the narrow focus on agency and empiricism of the (North) American school as well as the diverse structuralism and methodological limitations of the pluralist perspective. There are two central reasons for this. The first is that the research path of the former school usually fails to explain and is in conflict with the outcomes of heterodox strategies of development based on the prescriptions of the Bretton Woods perspective of development (Payne, 2005). The pluralist path, on the other hand, presents its major weaknesses in terms of producing empirical research, given its emphasis on conceptualizations and structural changes. For the purpose of this research therefore, the solution demands a multidisciplinary perspective that integrates four dimensions of analysis in a coherent conceptual and methodological framework. On the one hand, the dimensions of agency and structure of regionalism permit us to avoid the bias and dichotomy between analyses focused on projects of integration and those addressing the structures and process of regionalism. On the other, the richness of the processes of change and conflict will allow us to see regionalism beyond only institutionalism and economy.

The framework of this study hence aims to bring together different research methodologies that account for the specificity of key dimensions of the political economy of development and regionalism. There are different research strategies for that and many ways to see the role of perspectives and theories in research (Burgess, 1982). Therefore our research is heterodox and open to the refining of a multidisciplinary approach by critically exploring a bundle of initial research questions: How transformative is and what are the challenges of the NSAR in responding to a changing hemispheric and world order? To what extent do its dynamics of development reflect different orientations and structures ignored for two decades of neoliberalization, opening, and retreat of the state? To what extent are the new regional leaderships shaping the region? Is the NSAR raising the regional governance to deal with inequality and conflict? What is the nature of the major dynamics of conflict and security in the NSAR and what challenges do they present for the democratic regional governance of citizen security and against organized crime? What are the challenges imposed on the regional democratic governance in terms of the ever-sensitive areas of national security in South America? To what extent are we witnessing the configuration of new patterns in the production of well-being in relation to the challenge of inequality?

Approaching a PE of South American Regionalism

There is a great deal of debate and academic research concerning the political–economic nature of regionalism, most of them based on the North American, European, and Asian experiences (Riggirozzi, 2010). However, what we do not have yet is a line of research focusing on the political–economic nature of South American regionalism, with few exceptions such as the research of Tussie and Trucco (2009) and Bonilla and Long (2010). Beyond that, to an important extent the investigation produced around the theme features some noticeable characteristics such as a research focus on integration (agency), led by states and informed by actor-oriented IPE perspectives. As one might expect, the most-used perspective in the region with which to comprehend the PE of regionalism comes from the (North) American school of IPE and its key thinkers (Lake, 2009; Mansfield and Milner, 1997; North, 1990; Keohane, 1984; Krasner, 1976; Nye, 1965). There are, of course, a cluster of critical thinkers, some from the region and others from outside, who have studied South American regionalism from different perspectives of the social sciences—particularly economics and politics—but they are still a diffuse group of scholars.

Following the contributions, among others, of Cohen (2008) and Söderbaum (2005), we tried to typify and analyze the major perspectives in IPE that nurture a wide range of perspectives and theories on regionalism and regionalization. At the foundation of this effort is the underlying assumption that, as researchers, we are part of the object of study and have a position in relation to maintaining the status quo or in relation to answering how things are changing. As a result, we identify with the major sources of taught and epistemic communities in IPE, the North American and the British school. The importance of this distinction is that even though both of them present weakness and strengths to explain regionalism, they are the starting point to explore a global south approach regarding regionalism and regionalization within globalization. Noteworthy, in some cases there is no direct correlation between these schools of IPE and perspectives and theories about regionalism, in particular regarding some neorealist and constructivist approaches that bridge both international political-economic sides.

Fredrik Söderbaum is one of the only scholars to have carried out a thorough classification of the different trends in thinking on the IPE of regionalism (2005). According to him, there are important methodological relationships, research compatibilities and advantages to making use of the rationalist–reflectivist classifications about theories on regionalism and regionalization. The advantage of that is that it helps us to move from a focus on the existent experiences (Europe, North America, and Asia) as the basis of the normative assumptions in orthodox approaches to regionalism, to inter-regionalism such as in the new global south regionalism based on soft and civilian power. Secondly, it allows us to assess the experiences of developing regionalism in context and based on its outcomes, and the conflicts and orientations of development in a changing world order. Finally, it provides us with tools to balance agency and structure within a framework of development that prioritizes the comprehension of change, conflict, and well-being.

Before discussing the classification itself, it is important to define three concepts: regionalism, regionalization, and integration. We take the concept of regionalism to mean the broad process of change that gives rise to regional integration and as such is the way that a given region shapes and is shaped by globalization. Regionalism in this sense is understood today as "New Regionalism" and includes regional integration projects and the political–economic processes at their foundation. In other words, regionalism is agency and structure, defined by the dynamic between the whole (region) and the parts (nation). Hence, regionalism can be seen as a particular configuration of forces that are bounded, particularly, to economy and conflict given its cross-border nature in a globalized economy and reproduction of material life. Regionalism includes material structures and capabilities, processes, ideas, and institutions which do not determine the regionalization but define conflict and development the creation of opportunities and the imposition of constraints.

Regionalization, on the other hand, is "the substantive process [generated by] state and none-state actors that leads to patterns of cooperation, integration, complementarity, and identity within a particular cross-national geographical space" (Söderbaum, 2005: 22). Finally, integration refers to the outcomes of regional agency, as well as the encounters and dynamics between different regionalist political projects of regionalization, which can complement or oppose it according to the structures and substantive processes that give them sense and orientation. The three elements mentioned constitute the basis of the political economy of the new regionalism and none of them can be understood without the other or hold its own value as an independent particular research focus (see Table 1.1).

Table 1.1   Major Perspectives in the International Political Economy of Regionalism

Actor-oriented regional perspectives	Critical perspectives and main scholars
Neorealism (Waltz, 2001: Gilpin, 2001; Grieco, 1997: Haggard in Mansfield and Milner, 1997; Mansfield and Milner, 1997; Hurrell, 1995; Buzan, 1991) Focus: Existence of a regional hegemon that provides stability and direction to the rest. Limitations: State as unitary units, focus on core regions, narrow about conflict, normative assumption upon economics, inequality. Advantages: Issue of power in regional integration, security, focused on UE, NAFTA.	*World-order approach* (Payne and Gamble, 1996; Payne, 2005; Hook and Kearns, 1999; Breslin and Hook, 2003; Phillips, 2004) Focus: Nature of power and development, and relationship with neoliberal globalization. Limitations: Conflict and well-being, little research yet. Advantages: Regionalization and globalization, development, agency, and structure, domestic and regional.
Liberal institutionalism approach (Mitrany, 1966; Deutsch, *et al.* 1958; Hass, 1958; Mattli, 1999; Hurrel, 1995; Keohane, 1984; Mansfield and Milner, 1997) Focus: Absolute gains and how to solve distributional conflicts. Limitations: Normative neoliberal and rationalist assumptions, power, focused on UE, NAFTA, APEC, conflict, and inequality. Advantages: Issue of institutionalization of regionalism, interstate cooperation, security.	*New realist/regionalisms approaches* (Boas *et al.*, 1999; Shaw, 1988, 2000; Boas, Marchand, and Shaw, 2005) Focus: Social nature of power, conflict, and development. Limitations: Wideness, weak methodology, inequality. Advantages: Includes processes, regionalism from below, conflict.
Liberal economic integration approach (Balassa, 2011; Estevadeordal and Suominen, 2007; Cable and Henderson, 1994; Robson, 1993; Kuwayama, 2005) Focus: Regional market and progressive liberalization by trickledown effect reduce inequalities. Limitations: Conflict, informal economy, heterodox development. Advantages: Trade and security, focused on UE, NAFTA.	*New regionalism approach* (Hettne *et al.*, 1999, 2000, 2001; Hettne, 2003; Hettne and Söderbaum, 1999) Focus: Change unequal, and hegemonic power relations and patterns of dominance. Limitations: Conflict. Advantages: Non-state actors, regionalism as element of development under, and as response to, globalization.

North American and Actor-Oriented Regional Perspectives

To an important extent, neorealism, liberal institutionalism, and liberal economic integration perspectives share common theoretical and epistemological grounds. In brief, they dominate most of the interpretations of South American regionalism and are principally produced by the academy and multilateral institutions in North America. The marriage between these three perspectives is the dominant perspective in Latin American academia concerning the study of regionalism, with few exceptions given the influence of the US academy. Actor-oriented perspectives tend to examine South American regionalism from its institutional degree and trade variation of the "standards"—Europe, North America, and Asia-Pacific. The scholars utilizing this perspective disregard critical and pluralist perspectives as "non-scientific" (Mansfield and Milner, 1997) and speculative (Mattli, 1999). Its major advantage has been to put in the center of the research focus the agency, tensions, and challenges of regional political integration. Its major weaknesses lay in the limitations of these perspectives to deal with the governance of globalization out of their realist and liberal perspectives of development, and the tensions of what they assume are the developmental outcomes of heterodox strategies of development.

Neorealism focuses on the struggle and distribution of power within a particular region as the result of the links between security and growing economic interdependence (Gomez-Mera, 2008). The view defines as "structure" the anarchical system in which states are conceived of as unitary and rational egoists always tending toward competition and conflict. For neorealists, regionalism arises whenever cooperation is necessary for geopolitical reasons either to counter the power of a rising regional power or to restrict the behavior of conflictive small state members in the region (Grieco, 1997). A hegemon is a necessary element of regionalism as it promotes regional cooperation and institutionalization (Hurrel, 1995).

Given its neorealist assumption concerning the structure of conflict and zero-sum game, neorealism tends to neglect—or its analyses are in tension with—the observable at the level of current processes of regionalization and regionalism. The contribution of Barry Buzan (1991, 2003) is undoubtedly the most important for solving these shortcomings. He deploys the concept of the "regional security complex," defining it as "a set of states whose major security perceptions and concerns are so interlinked that their national security problems cannot reasonably be analyzed or resolved, apart from each one shaping desecuritization and securitization (Buzan, 2003: 141).

The concept is useful but not without limitations. Again strong states are regarded as indispensable to the control of subregional anarchy and conflict. The evidence of Buzan rests on the comparative analysis of the experiences of Western Europe and the European Union. The methodological limitation arises, henceforth, for our case study, in the dichotomy of holding the states as unitary actors in permanent conflict and competition, while at the same time examining the outcomes of the regional democratic governance of conflict and regional security. However, the central drawback here is conceptualization based on the great powers' experience, which, having been concentrated on the centrality of national power (Söderbaum, 2005: 225), tends to reinforce existing international structures, major institutions, and interests of the self-preservation of those powers and order.

Neoliberal institutionalism gathers, in an inside-out perspective, a group of functionalist and institutionalist theories emphasizing the importance of institutionalizing regional integration. It emerges from the central premise of liberal institutionalism which espouses that regionalism is the rational response of governmental cooperation for solving the problems of an increased regional interdependence, such as the European experience (Mitrany, 1966; Deutsch, *et al.*, 1958; Hass, 1958). The common ground of these theories is their normative nature, as most of them rest on a significant number of assumptions such as the rationality of actors, the technical nature of institutionalization, and pluralist environments. However, their central assumptions make a bridge between new functionalist and neoclassic approaches by conceiving that the ahistorical and universal liberal nature of politics and economics define a political–economic function that constantly follows interests (Mattli, 1999: 23).

Liberal institutionalism was considered a failure in the 1970s, but for a long time, and even today, its scholars have sought for it to be the model of regionalization for Latin America and Africa. For many, its central failure lies in its limited conception of power, narrow rational approaches, and neoliberal realist conclusions (Breslin and Higgott, 2000). Nonetheless, its major advantage is that liberal institutionalism is an excellent approach to understanding and improving agency in a given and stable order, but is unable to explain change except divested of its universalistic and ahistorical political and economic assumptions. After decades of absence, liberal institutionalism returned in its new version of neoliberalism institutionalism. It reemerged in the 1990s principally promoted by international and regional financial institutions as well as by academic epistemic communities bound to actor-oriented, problem-solving approaches.

Today neoliberal institutionalism is the dominant approach to regionalism in South America, marrying epistemologically neorealism and neoliberalism (Keohane, 1984; Mansfield and Milner, 1997). Neoliberal institutionalism is stronger than its predecessor concerning its assumptions regarding the relationship between politics and economics. Here politics is shaped and limited by the universal way that economics work. Hence states are constrained and, in order to reach development, limited by a globalized economy dominated by trade and finance, firms and markets. Regional trade agreements (trade regionalization) are the responses from states, as global and regional economic integration is unstoppable, giving rise to the importance of institutions and regimes (Keohane, 1984). Regional trade agreements constitute the cornerstone of regional public goods as they are part of an incremental problem-solving process defined by the level of institutionalization and trade complementarity (Söderbaum, 2005: 227).

Three elements can be identified as the central weaknesses of neoliberal institutionalism. The first is the idea that regionalism is defined by its level of institutionalization subordinated to the dynamic of trade and based on the major regional experiences (EU, NAFTA, APEC). Secondly, there exits the identification of regionalism as a state-led project of integration which confines the concept of regionalism and its research to state and governmental agency, leaving out not only strategic areas of analysis but also conflict and well-being. Finally, there is the reduction of regionalism to a trade phenomenon where institutions only play a role in creating incentives and constraints to given processes (Söderbaum, 2005).

The third most influential and dominant school of thinking on regionalism in South America is the body of economic theories called regional economic integration or liberal regional economic integration. This set of economic integration approaches generally cement the relation between—and are the basis of—the economic assumptions upon which neorealism and neoliberal institutionalism are founded. According to these approaches, regional integration proceeds through a sequence of trade and economic agreements that define a model of linear evolution in order to reach complete economic integration. According to the Balassa model (1961), the progression from preferential trade areas to free trade areas, with customs unions, common markets, monetary unions, and ending up with a complete economic area, generally is the basis of most of the research on regionalism in regional development banks (Estevadeordal and Suominen, 2007). These theories are concerned principally with the welfare effects as the result of trade creation, diversion, and integration (Cable and Henderson, 1994), although they present rigid limitations to integrally explain development given their disciplinary boundaries.

Liberal regional economic integration approaches are usually used in combination with actor-oriented theories, with the aim of generating models to predict and enhance paths of interstate cooperation (Estevadeordal and Suominen, 2007: 4). In this sense, there are two different lines of economic integration research. The first line of study concentrates on whether the impact of economic regionalism contributes to the world trading system. The second group, also created to explain economic integration in Europe, distances itself from orthodox economics by focusing more on investment, employment, infrastructure, and structural transformations, as well as market and government failures (Robson, 1993).

The advantage of the last approach is that it provides the conceptual grounds to explore regionalism in developing regions. Its major disadvantage is the absence of research regarding heterodox experiences and political–economic processes of regionalization such as those seen in South America. Certainly, regional economic integration still offers a vast and rich field of research that can integrate more heterodox perspectives on the impact of alternative strategies of growth based on the experiences of developing regions. The key in this regard is to bridge economics and politics by transcending the rigid disciplinary boundaries and unrealistic assumptions of problem-solving or actor-oriented approaches (Söderbaum, 2005: 231).

Critical–Oriented Regional Perspectives

There is a vast array of critical approaches to regionalism today and any attempt to summarize them would demand an analysis that exceeds the limits of this collective research project. In most cases, these approaches have developed under the disciplinary umbrella of critical IPE by the academy in developing regions as response to the theoretical and epistemological shortcomings of actor-oriented perspectives on regionalism and political and economic biases. They do not represent a unified body of theories, but rather multidisciplinary approaches and perspectives that, by seeking to comprehend development, assume and integrate conflict and well-being as inseparable parts of it. For a close analysis, we focus this section on the analysis of their three principal approaches: the world order approach (WOA), the new realist/regionalism approach (NR/RA), and the new regionalist approach (NRA).

This set of approaches can be defined as theoretical and methodological heterodoxies given the absence of a unified research agenda or unique methodology. Beyond that, they offer a solid platform to approaching development by integrating conflict and well-being into multidisciplinary approaches that seek to comprehend development within the framework of regionalism and globalization. Critical approaches are concerned with change and therefore move beyond the countless rationalist and economic assumptions of problem-solving theories. They are not incompatible with the use of actor-oriented theories but rather integrate them within contextual frameworks and tangible outcomes of development as a product of different strategies of development. They challenge the narrow conception of regionalism as interstate agency, trade integration, and security cooperation by widening the scope of the research in a multidisciplinary approach differentiating integration projects from regionalization and regionalism.

The WOA is a direct derivation of the critical IPE associated with the work of Robert Cox and is concentrated at the Universities of Sheffield and Warwick in the UK (Payne and Gamble, 1996; Payne, 2005; Hook and Kearns, 1999; Breslin and Hook, 2003). Following the Coxian and neo-Gramscian method of historical structures, the approach seeks to integrate the agency and structure, as well as the domestic and global dimensions of regionalism in a critical framework (Söderbaum, 2005). The central research focus of the WOA is exploring the relationship between regionalization, globalization, multilateralism, and world orders by analyzing the agency and processes of historical structures that define development (Payne, 2005). This includes state–society complexes, the social forces anchored in economic structures and types of world political orders (Payne and Gamble, 1996). The main concern of the WOA is how existent state–society complexes have sought to respond to globalization and, in doing so, their generation of different state-led regionalist schemes to manage countries' or regions' insertion into the current world order (Payne, 2005).

For scholars who utilize the WOA, regionalism is a response to the dominant form of globalization (neoliberalism) that must be understood as a historical and contextual manifestation of current power in the global political economy. Regionalism constitutes the complex management of development to deal with globalization "where there is no longer a single state with the authority and capacity to impose its leadership" (Payne, 1996: 252–3). It is originated and promoted by policy-making elites, within the framework of the dominant ideology of development, anchoring the process of interstate cooperation. Contrary to realist suspicions that regionalism would bring on trade wars and military conflicts between nations, the WOA argues that certain forms of regionalism, in particular in developing regions, show signs of addressing conflict, inequality, and uneven development, though the evidence is still focused on only a few places in the world (Payne, 2005).

In addition to actor-oriented perspectives, the WOA accounts for the limits and advantages of this collective research project. In terms of limits, the WOA does not distinguish clearly between state and non-state actors or complex cross-border political–economic processes given the incipient empirical investigations in this sense. Given this absence, there is a risk of narrowing research on the PE of regionalism to elite-led processes focusing on the study of the formal economy and security structures and limiting the study and integration of the political–economic relationship of conflict and well-being in development. An important advance in integrating well-being into development and regionalism are the contributions of Anthony Payne (2004) and Nicola Phillips (2004). Concerning its advantages, first, the WOA allows the analytical integration of agency of integration (interstate or elite-led integration projects) with the development of regionalization (political–economic processes) in light of the outcomes of regionalism (development, conflict, and well-being). Secondly, as stated by Fredrick Söderbaum, it helps us to go beyond "the rigid and problematic conceptualizations of states, regions and regional organizations inherent in neorealism and liberal institutionalism" (2005: 238). Last, but not least, the WOA is not biased with a particular type of regionalism at the core of the world order.

The label of the NR/RA gathers different critical approaches to regionalism and integrating into their framework diverse poststructural, political anthropological, realist, and postmodernist analytical trends (Boas *et al.*, 1999; Shaw, 1988, 2000; Marchand *et al.*, 1999). These approaches seek to develop a pluralist perspective on the basis of a historical, contextualized, and agency-oriented approach to regionalism able to comprehend its different dimensions, complexity, contradictions, and diversity, particularly in the developing world (Marchand *et al.*, 1999). They challenge actor-oriented approaches on regionalism by considering them too narrowly concerned with states and overconfident of the technical nature and capacity of regional multilateralism and institutions. The NR/RA stresses the need to focus the research about regionalism more on the "informal regionalism from below;" non-state actors and informal activities including informal economies and actors, smuggling, mafia, and organized crime (Marchand *et al.*, 1999: 905–6).

In the same way as the WOA, the NR/RA puts the emphasis on the relationship between globalization, regionalism, and multilateralism. Rather than be limited by the perceptions of regionalism as interstate processes or a top-down phenomenon, the NR/RA sees regionalism as the juxtaposition and opposition of complex processes of cooperation and conflict—"a weave-world" of formal and informal processes that define development and conflict (Boas *et al.*, 1999: 1062–3). Its central limitations are that it is sometimes methodologically difficult to group a wide number of perspectives into a coherent whole. Its major advantage is its view of regionalism as a bottom-up process that includes conflict, allowing research on regionalism to include perspectives beyond economics and institutions.

Last but not least is the NRA developed by the World Institute for Development Economics and Research within the United Nations University (UNU/WIDER). This approach departs from the assumption that regionalism is a qualitatively new phenomenon in the context of the current structural transformation of the global political economy (Hettne, Inotai, and Sunkel, 1999, 2000, 2001). The dynamics between globalization and regionalization shape the emerging world order rather than countries alone, which demands a rethinking of the conceptual framework able to grasp these new dynamics; as, along with the WOA, the NRA is particularly related to the critical perspectives of IPE, challenging the epistemological, ontological, and methodological assumptions of actor-oriented approaches on regionalism.

The NRA is concerned with processes and consequences of regionalization at different levels, including politics and economics, which it defines as the different characters of "regionness" (Hettne and Söderbaum, 1999). Regions are constructed, deconstructed, and reconstructed by collective human agency, whereas regionalism is a heterogeneous, comprehensive, and multidimensional phenomenon constructed "by a variety of state, market, society, and external actors both within and outside formal regional organizations" (Söderbaum, 2005). Regionalism emerges as a manifestation of globalization and the hegemony of the world order but, at the same time, shapes its political economy. In other words, regionalism is not a passive phenomenon but active, and represents the "return of the political" in development (Hettne, 2003: 53). Addressing Polanyi's ideas, Hettne (1997: 86) points out:

> The current phenomenon of regionalism could be seen as the manifestation of the second movement, the protection of society, on the level of the macroregion, as a political reaction against the global market expansion which gained momentum in the 1980s. Thus we can speak of a "Second Great Transformation."

For the NRA, regionalism redefines and improves regional multilateralism as it becomes an inherent element of development, in particular in developing regions (Hettne, 2003: 37). The NRA highlights that regionalism is more than the conventional idea of state-led projects, as states under globalization are limited in their ability to deliver development at the national level by themselves. Societies and social processes also play a political role in protecting the weak and the poor, delivering development, and dealing with conflicts and inequality. The extension of Polanyi's assumption is that societies move toward self-protection when the state is pulled out of development (neoliberalism), and get closer to the state when it returns to lead development.

Contours of the Framework

Actor-oriented and critical approaches of regionalism present different epistemological, ontological, and methodological assumptions, but they can also be combined to some extent if, in particular, problem-solving approaches are divested of their biased political and economic assumptions. The identification of these assumptions is central for this collective project, as it will help us to avoid being biased. The second methodological step is to adopt a critical framework able to dialogue with the multidimensional political economy of regionalism that by targeting development includes the structural and agential components of conflict and inequality.

To start with, the analysis presented above has identified four of these postulates whose identification is central to avoiding the bias of our collective research:

1. The state-centric ontology or the idea that states are unitary units living in an anarchic world;
2. The neoliberal economic postulate technically promoted by the Bretton Woods institutions and its regional sisters, that trade and finance have a universal way of functioning;
3. The idea that regionalism in developing regions has to be comprehended on the basis of the experiences at the core of the world order (EU, NAFTA, APEC);
4. The reduction of regionalism to the idea of interstate political projects and levels of institutionalization.

Critical approaches to regionalism seem to be the strongest methodological option as they provide a framework able to grasp the multidimensional nature of the political economy of regionalism by integrating embedded actor-oriented approaches to analyze the agency and structure of development, conflict, and inequality of regionalism. They have been designed to overcome the problematic conceptualizations of state, economics, and regionalism inherent in neorealism and neoliberal institutionalism. There are pros and cons in each one of the critical approaches presented here; however, the three present different and useful elements to a collective research approach, which needs to be flexible in order to grasp different dimensions of regionalism and development.

On the other hand, the WOA offers a critical flexible framework that allows integrated analysis of power by grasping agency and structure as well as domestic and regional characteristics, identifying the ideological nature of neoliberal economics and putting the notion of development in the center of its analysis. However, it is limited in its ability to contain conflict given its focus on state-led processes. The opposite happens with the NRA which facilitates the framing of conflict in its complex political–economic nature as it focuses on regionalism from below. The combination of the NRA elements with institutionalism may allow us to approach the agency and structure of conflict; that is, security and conflict. In other words, we can combine a political–economic approach on regionalism with security studies in all its areas even from the point of view of what today can be defined as the new national interest (Rivera, 2011a, 2011b). Finally, the methodological virtue of the NRA goes beyond the notion of regionalism merely conceived as interstate projects including non-state actors.

As shown above, the shortcomings of actor-oriented and critical perspectives on regionalism in order to explain the agency and structure of the regional political economy is clear. However, in order to keep the focus of a multidisciplinary research on common grounds, we also need a concept that helps us to go beyond the three major dominant disciplines informing the political economy of regionalism. The first is the neoliberal economics, which assumes that the same rules of economic development and regionalism can universally be applied to every country and region. The second is the traditional paradigms of international relations (IR) that considers regionalism as an expression of interstate relations and must follow the experiences of Western states. Finally, it is the discipline of development studies, which clearly regards development as the agency of limited aid work for the poor and disadvantaged, independent of the structural factors and unequal politics of development that produce it.

A multidisciplinary and comprehensive political economy of regionalism can only be founded by putting in its center a multidimensional notion of development, which must include the two major outcomes of how life, conflict, and well-being are produced in our societies. In other words, it is about what type of development occurs, for whom and what, who wins and who loses. By doing so, the political economy of regionalism becomes something more concrete and real, including the formal and informal world, what is produced from the top but also what is produced from below as results of different forms of development. Thus development takes a new, wider integral and critical sense as defined by the dynamic of change, structural causes of conflict, and production of well-being collectively generated by societies at the regional level through interstate projects of integration and regionalization. It implies thinking of production of well-being as going beyond the conventional top-down, state-centric, and economist conception of welfare and instead to approach it as inherent to development and regionalism. What happens to one country happens to its neighbors. Well-being in regionalism and development is therefore a process, its outcomes are seen as a whole, and the constructions of everyday life always imply tension for the distribution of power and resources in a given order.

Development is more than orthodox economics and institutions, whereby unorthodox economic views make the difference in understanding trade, financing of development, and even the strategic importance of natural resources in developing areas (Falconi, 2005; Acosta and Martinez, 2010). For decades the Washington-sponsored regional multilateral system has promoted the ideas that growth, trade, and finance can only be understood in one way, but the last ten years undeniably prove something different. In short, alternative economics has been perhaps the most fecund academic area and source of construction of new perceptions about the relations between growth and new regionalism.

Probably the most distinctive feature of the new regionalism in developing areas is the issue of dynamics between conflict and security. All conceptions of security refer to how to comprehend and define conflict by state and non-state actors. Historically, in developing areas conflict has been conceived as related and motivated by inequality and poverty; however, the dominant conflicts today are more connected to organized crime, refugees, and weak civil democratic governance of security. If conflict is the structure and security the agency, it necessarily follows that both must be regarded in relation to the notion of development and its civil governance within a democratic framework. If historically societies have needed to build their own systems of welfare production to temper economic growth, conflict has been the other inherent part of development. The other side of security in developing regions is its strategic importance concerning the need for the protections of democratic order as defined in the new arena of security and the construction of security complexes around the regional protection of civil democratic governances (Buzan, 2003; Bonilla and Long, 2010).

The final component derived from the debates presented above is the complex political–economic nature of regionalism and the bias of conceiving that regionalism as intergovernmental projects of regionalization is led by states perceived as unitary actors. Regionalism is more than the sum of states and top-down projects in movement. As we have seen, it refers also to the complex relationship between globalization and social constructions from below in a whole process of development, featuring continuous tensions between conflicts and the collective construction of well-being (Hettne, 1997; Hettne *et al.*, 1999; Payne, 2004, 2005). In this sense, it is useful to recognize the diverse political–economic nature of the different and complementary elements of regionalism as a whole.

The first element is the essence of projects of integration for regionalization, which can be led by state and non-state actors, which are mostly about interstate agreements, institutionalization, trade, and narrow issues of security such as narcotrafficking and terrorism, all militarized in its governance. Interstate projects or regionalization are by nature the top-down agency of regionalization led by states and powerful economic actors and increasingly open to the participation of nongovernmental organizations. These prioritize either economic or political dimensions of integration. The second element is the regionalization which emerges as outcomes and processes launched and led by projects of integration, but that turn into social processes that cut across all geographical and national boundaries, becoming themselves strategic for development, collective construction of well-being and resolution of conflicts. And finally, the last element is regionalism which refers to double dynamics that frame development and its major outcomes: the first is the intertwining between globalization and regionalization; the second is the context of socially constructed regionness. The NSAR world order and the Americas as a hemisphere host the US hegemony.

Chapter 2

The Origins of the Union of South American Nations: A Multicausal Account of South American Regionalism

Carlos Espinosa

This chapter examines the origin of the Union of South American Nations (UNASUR) defined as a multidimensional, postneoliberal, institutionalized regionalism on the scale of the South American subcontinent. UNASUR is accounted for with reference to five key variables: Brazilian leadership, the counterpoint between US hemispheric regionalism and Brazilian aspirations, the collective identity and/or territoriality of South America, models of development, and political coalitions. This multicausal explanation eclectically draws on realism, constructivism, and political economy models.

Introduction

Since 1980 there has been a sustained boom in regionalism throughout the world. On all continents, nation-states have joined together in a variety of regionalist projects, ranging in scope from commercially oriented free-trade zones without much institutionalization to more ambitious multidimensional "communities" and "unions" that include common financial, monetary, and security institutions. Some regionalist projects have been built upon a high level of preexisting "regionness"; that is, a significant level of economic interdependence, web of transnational networks, and sense of a common identity, while other regionalist projects have attempted to jump-start regions without much underlying economic or sociocultural convergence. Latin America has, of course, not been exempt from this world-wide drive toward regionalism. From Southern Common Market (MERCOSUR) and the North American Free Trade Agreement (NAFTA) to the Comunidad Andina de Naciones (CAN) and UNASUR, integration schemes anchored in geographic proximity have proliferated in recent decades in Latin America.

UNASUR is surely one of the most significant of these regionalist experiments in Latin America. Forged in 2008 with membership of 12 South American states, it is intergovernmental in its exercise of authority and multidimensional in scope.

Although its institutional density is still modest, it has a panoply of agreements, forums, and administrative organs. UNASUR encompasses a presidential summit that coordinates foreign policy stances and addresses political and security crises, a South American Defense Council (SADC) that seeks to construct a regional security community, an incipient financial architecture turning on a regional development bank, specialized councils dedicated to health and education, and a soon to be elected parliament. UNASUR even possesses prodemocracy and, very likely in the future, human rights collective governance mechanisms.

In the long history of Latin American regionalist initiatives, UNASUR stands out for several reasons. It revolves around one of the world's new rising powers, Brazil, it is pitched at a novel scale, that of the South American subcontinent (Malamud in Riggirozzi, 2012), and it has been driven by governments who have been highly critical of neoliberalism (Peña, 2009). UNASUR, in other words, diverges from the US-dominated hemispheric mold of integration that informed the Organization of American States (OAS) and the Inter-American Treaty of Reciprocal Assistance during the Cold War, as well as from post-Cold War initiatives inspired by neoliberal open-regionalism, such as MERCOSUR or NAFTA.

As a historian of international relations, I will focus on the diachronic "process" of crystallization of UNASUR between 1990 and the present, as well as contextualizing UNASUR vis à vis prior cycles of integration in Latin America. I describe the formation of UNASUR with reference to a cluster of key variables: Brazilian leadership, the interplay of a regional power (Brazil) with the global hegemon (the USA), models of development, political coalitions of the governments of member countries, and the regional identities enabling UNASUR. The intersection of these multiple causal variables accounts for the emergence and shape of UNASUR. What these variables account for are not only the rise of a regional institution, but the scale at which it was pitched, its scope, its institutional make-up, and its ideological orientation. As some of these variables have already been identified in the literature as pertinent for understanding UNASUR, for example models of development (Riggirozzi in Riggirozzi, 2012), my contribution is limited to integrating these variables in an eclectic, process-oriented, and explanatory account of the formation of UNASUR.

The burgeoning literature on regionalism has been over the years inspired by various "paradigmatic" and "mid-range" theories. These include functionalism (Vieira, 2005), realism (Mohammeddinov, 2006), neoinstitutionalism (Mittelman, 1996), and constructivism (Väyrynen, 2003). Accordingly, regionalist projects have been seen as germinating under the umbrella of a global hegemon or regional power, as a spiral of cooperation spilling over from low politics to high politics, as rationalist collective action in pursuit of common interests, or as founded upon a preexisting cultural identity. Among the causal variables associated with each of these models, the role of global or regional powers in regionalism, and the importance of a shared regional identity are especially apt for understanding the emergence of UNASUR. These notions, drawn respectively from realism and constructivism, must, however, be complemented by two additional explanatory variables that are often underscored by political economy: national-level models of development in both their structural and ideational dimensions (Leftwich, 2006), and the domestic political coalitions that sustain them.

A discussion of regionalism that brings together the variables I want to emphasize is Peter Katzenstein's well-regarded work on Asian regionalism, which provides a viable eclectic model that accounts for regionalisms in the post-Cold War epoch. In *Regionalism and Asia*, Katzenstein looks at how Asian regionalism is being shaped by competing visions of Asian identity, by the leadership of one or another rival regional powers, either Japan or China, and by the external global hegemon's, that is, the USA's, engagement with Asia (Katzenstein, 2000). Katzenstein even pays attention to models of development as a shaping force in regionalism, pointing to competing visions of "Asianness", pointing to neoliberalism or the Asian development state. What is missing in his work and must be addressed for South American regionalism are the domestic political coalitions behind models of development.

Formulated in schematic terms, this historical chapter will turn on the following explanatory axes:

- UNASUR has sprung from the leadership of South America's most powerful state and largest economy (Morales, 2010). Brazil has led the way toward UNASUR at key moments, and the participation of a state of Brazil's structural weight and soft power have been indispensable for the formation and consolidation of UNASUR. The Brazilian regionalist drive has been anchored not only in state-level agency and capabilities, both material and symbolic, but also in the interests of Brazilian transnational corporations interpenetrated with the Brazilian state in a developmentalist model.

- The formation of UNASUR on an unprecedented scale, that of the South American subcontinent, has been conditioned by notions of South American identity originating in ideas of a Brazilian-centered, South American "theater of operations" developed by Brazilian strategic visions.

- The efforts of the global hegemon, the USA, to assure itself a captive market in Latin America and so reinforce the mold of US-dominated hemispheric integration have contributed to the crystallization of UNASUR by way of negative reactions among South American states to North American regionalist initiatives.

- UNASUR has been shaped by postneoliberal development models, whether developmentalist or redistributionist (Riggirozzi, in Riggirozzi, 2012).

- UNASUR has been molded by governments anchored in political coalitions strongly based on popular forces, which consistently exhibit a corresponding political style defined by popular mobilization, friend–enemy politics, and presidentialist leadership.

Cycles of Latin American Regionalism

In the thrall of US dominance and endowed with a discourse of Hispanic American or Latin American unity, Latin America has been a fertile ground for integration initiatives. Several cycles of regionalism pitched at various levels have transpired since the early nineteenth century. These cycles were molded by distinct identities, interplay between regional powers and US hegemony, models of development, and political coalitions. They have also shown variations in the scope of regionalism, sometimes focusing on political coordination and at other times on trade and/or investment convergence.

Regional initiatives over time have been pitched at multiple geographic scales. The USA has consistently preferred the hemispheric scale in regional integration, as a way of asserting US dominance over a broad zone of influence that runs from Mexico to Tierra del Fuego. Latin American regionalism, in turn, has been scaled at the level of Hispanic America or Latin America, at the same time that it has often been complicit with the US aspiration of continental hegemony. Concomitantly, integration has also taken place at a subregional level in subregions defined by either subregional security complexes, such as the Southern Cone, or by US foreign policy or economic strategies, such as in the Andes and Central America.

Surprisingly, before UNASUR, South America was not regarded as an appropriate candidate for regionalism, whether of economic or multidimensional scope. No regional initiative was pitched on the scale of the South American subcontinent prior to the advent of UNASUR. What explains this remarkable absence? The US worked in favor of a hemispheric level of integration, while the discourses of Bolivian or Hispanic American and Latin America unity looked toward broad continental integration without the USA. At the same time, until the late 1990s Brazil did not have the regional or global weight it now possesses, so that it could not serve as the axis of a regionalist project, pitched at a subcontinental scale.

Cycle I: Hispanic American Regionalism (1820s–1870s)

Hispanic America was the collective identity underlying early manifestations of regionalism among Latin American states, beginning in the first half of the nineteenth century. Sprung from the Bolivian discourse of unity in the face of European and US threats, and underpinned by a linguistic and cultural identity, Hispanic American regionalism was the dominant paradigm of integration in the mid-nineteenth century. It underwrote the periodic holding of Inter-American Congresses that attempted to formulate common political and foreign policy principles, such as a shared republicanism, and made some attempt at cooperation on pragmatic matters, such as postal standards (Espinosa, 2010). Significantly, cooperation efforts associated with the Hispanic American identity failed to include the USA or Brazil. The USA was outside of the cultural and linguistic community assumed by early Hispanic American multilateralism, while Brazil was an outsider both because of its monarchical regime and its somewhat different cultural matrix, Portuguese and Afro-American, rather than Hispanic and *mestizo*. Sometimes Peru, sometimes Chile provided the impetus for political coordination between Spanish-speaking republics, although no single regional power consistently led Hispanic American regionalism. Ruled by merchant and landowning elites committed to agroexport strategies, Hispanic American countries had little interest in economic regionalism (Bulmer-Thomas and Knight, 2003). While bilateral trade treaties underwritten by most favored nation clauses were signed between some dyads in Latin America, trade-driven regionalism made little sense, as most economies in the region were oriented toward external markets, located mostly in Europe (Espinosa, 2010).

Cycle II: Pan-Americanism (1870s–1930s)

In the late nineteenth century and early twentieth century, regionalism took the form of Pan-Americanism, which was continental in scale and included the USA and Brazil. Pan-Americanism differed from earlier Hispanic American regionalism in that it was a vehicle for the exercise of regional hegemony by the USA and by its inclusion of Brazil. The inclusion of Brazil presupposed a Latin American identity which encompassed the Hispanic American states plus Brazil.

The concept of Latin America was floated by France in the age of Napoleon III (1850–1870), as it sought to project its imperial influence across the Atlantic (Mignolo, 1991). Its legacy was that it allowed for the inclusion of Portuguese-speaking Brazil in regionalist efforts. Pan-Americanism resulted from a fusion of the identity of Latin America and that of the "Western hemisphere" promoted by the USA.

In its nineteenth- and early twentieth-century visions of regionalism, the USA consistently mobilized the geopolitical notion of "the Western hemisphere". This geographic identity was elaborated under the Monroe Doctrine in an effort to carve out a sphere of influence, lying under US domination and free of European meddling. Although US hegemony exercised through the Roosevelt Corollary (1905) was most pronounced in the circum-Caribbean area (Smith, 1986), the USA insisted on hemispheric-level projection and so preferred hemispheric integration schemes. In addition to the workings of a Latin American identity, US ambitions coalescing around the term Western hemisphere engendered Pan-Americanism.

Pan-Americanism (1880s to 1930s), promoted by the USA and presupposing the notion of Latin America, served as the identity on the basis of which the Union of American Republics was set up in 1889–1890 and continued in operation until World War II. The Union of American Republics or Pan-American Union was a forum for political coordination and the construction of norms of regional interaction (Smith, 1986). Although some tariff agreements were considered at the continental level in the 1890s, the dominance of commodity export economies geared toward European and US markets discouraged economic integration across Latin American economies.

In the context of Pan-Americanism, Brazilian elites reversed their earlier policy of not joining regionalist efforts and cautiously espoused regionalism (Turcotte and Mostajo, 2008). Brazil's acceptance of Pan-Americanism in the late nineteenth century was driven not only by an identity logic, focusing on the concept of Latin America, but also by a strong interest in a special relationship with the USA (Turcotte and Mostajo, 2008). The so-called loyal bargain with the USA could be comfortably inserted within a regionalist framework organized around the figure of Pan-Americanism.

Subregional-level integration efforts made some headway under the cover of hemispheric or Latin American regionalism. At the start of the twentieth century, Argentina, Brazil, and Chile, middle powers seeking to defuse tensions between them, established political coordination mechanisms through the ABC pact and talked about drawing down tariffs. The so-called ABC powers were recognized by the USA as an interlocutor, as shown by their role as mediators in the dispute between the US and the Mexican state during the Mexican revolution. The cooperation between the ABC states, however, was rapidly undermined by underlying territorial disputes and by Brazil's preference for a special relationship with the USA.

Cycle III: The Inter-American System and Developmentalism (1945–1980)

With the end of the Second World War, Pan-Americanism transmuted into the so-called inter-American system, which entailed not only political coordination through the OAS, but also a collective defense system known as the Inter-American Reciprocity Treaty (IART). Inter-Americanism brought together the US state and Latin American elites in a Cold War alliance to guard against radical nationalist or left-wing political movements, who favored neutrality in the Cold War. Economic ties between Latin American states remained weak in the immediate Post-War Epoch, dampening economic regionalism. US economic hegemony, in contrast, was consolidated between the 1920s and the 1950s, but required only bilateral trade treaties between either the Latin American state or the USA. Only Peronist Argentina, with its doctrine of the Third Way was skeptical of the inter-American system in the 1950s, a skepticism that led it to propose, although without any effect, Latin American regionalist alternatives to US-led hemispheric unity. Brazil, meanwhile, accepted the inter-American system, as result of the community of values in the context of the Cold War (Hirst, 2007), as Brazilian elites saw Brazil as a bulwark against communism in the 1940s and 1950s, and again during the military dictatorship between 1964 and the early 1980s.

It took the convergence of Latin American developmentalism or *Cepalismo* with the US-led Alliance for Progress in the 1960s for economic regionalism in Latin America to take off. Developmentalism, with its emphasis on import substitution industrialization (ISI) and state direction of the economy, sought regional markets for industrial goods among regional economies at similar levels of industrial competence (Grugel in Gamble and Payne, 1996). Often underwritten by populist coalitions joining a national bourgeoisie with a growing middle class and unionized labor, developmentalism combined nationalism with regionalism (Morales, 2010). At the same time, the US-led Alliance for Progress worked to forge regional markets in Latin America for US transnational corporations that had located in Latin America by way of tariff wall-jumping strategies (Thorp, 1998). The Latin American Free Trade Association (LAFTA) , established in 1961, which joined together Mexico with several South American economies, was the regional correlate of internally oriented industrialization. Although consistent with the goals of the US Alliance for Progress, LAFTA did not include the USA, as the USA was satisfied with the captive markets that protectionism in Latin America afforded its transnationals who engaged in on-site production. The trade benefits and spillover effects of LAFTA were extremely limited as the economic interaction among South American countries and between South America and Mexico failed to gain traction.

In the late 1970s, Brazilian foreign policy shifted in ways that would become path-defining for the rise of UNASUR. The Brazilian military regime opted for its own repressive brand of developmentalism, after the 1964 coup, as a strong state was viewed as playing a crucial role in industrialization at the same time that popular demands were brutally suppressed. While short on idealism regarding Latin American unity, the military regime in Brazil believed that regional integration was functional for opening up markets for Brazil's industrial goods, as shown by Brazil's entry into SELA (Sistema Económico Latinoamericano and del Caribe) in 1976. Meanwhile, Brazil went from a policy of seeking a special relationship with the USA to one of living with unresolved tensions with the USA that forced a more autonomous posture. The Brazilian military regime disagreed with the Carter administration on human rights issues and on adherence to the Nuclear Nonproliferation Treaty. These squabbles led the military regime to downplay Brazil's long-term propensity to seek a special relationship with the USA (Grabebdroff, 1979).

While LAFTA was struggling to be born, a subregionalist experiment known as the Andean Pact was crafted. It was intended to render viable ISI among the small and mostly undeveloped internal markets of the Pacific coast of South America. Spurred by the ISI model, the Andean Pact managed to mount a common market and even a dispute resolution mechanism known as the Andean Tribunal of Justice. The USA tacitly gave its seal of approval to a subregion it had nourished in its counterinsurgency strategies in the early 1960s, when it had sought to defuse tensions over land reform in an area marked by old-fashioned landowning classes and a largely landless and restless peasantry.

The Origins of UNASUR I: From Open Regionalism to Strategic Regionalism 1980–2002

The historical trajectory that led to UNASUR in the 2000s may be seen as beginning in the late 1980s and early 1990s. South American regionalism was born in a new cycle of regionalism in Latin America, initially at least characterized by the hegemony of neoliberal open-regionalism. As stated at the outset, the interplay between a regional power and the global hegemon, as well as a sense of common identity, served as key conditions of possibility for the formation of UNASUR. Concomitantly, the dominant models of development and the political coalitions behind them were also influential.

With the waning of ISI during the debt crisis in Latin America in the 1980s, developmentalist regionalism was supplanted by "open regionalism" associated with the neoliberal project. Like the prior spurt of regionalism linked to developmentalism, the new configuration of regionalism sought to bring down tariff walls and foster specialization, at a regional level. What distinguished the new regionalism in Latin America from the previous generation of regionalism informed by ISI was that it sometimes took place between asymmetrical economies (Bouzas, 2005), that it was not closely bound to industrialization programs (Casas, 2002), and that it was seen as complimentary not contradictory vis à vis extraregional trade and investment (Bowles in Rosamond *et al.*, 2002). Both the inauguration of MERCOSUR in the early 1990s and the launching of the Andean Pact as the Andean Community of Nations in the mid-1990s were strongly marked by neoliberal open-regionalism.

In the course of the 1990s, however, neoliberal open-regionalism began to slowly give way in South America to a more strategically oriented regionalism turning on Brazil's economic and geopolitical interests as a rising power. After 2002 South American regionalism in turn slid toward a postneoliberal model of integration that encompassed developmentalist and welfare perspectives, together with a vision of a security community. While a security community was not really postneoliberal, it was a departure from neoliberal open-regionalism, because neoliberal open-regionalism had been largely oblivious to security issues.

Open regionalism in Latin American began in the 1980s and early 1990s, as is well known, at the two geographic poles of the continent, with NAFTA and MERCOSUR. MERCOSUR presupposed a prior defusing of geopolitical tensions between Argentina and Brazil in the late 1970s, as they sought to move beyond balance of power politics. That was the spirit of the Integration Act signed in 1985 by Brazil and Argentina. Nevertheless, MERCOSUR, joined by Brazil, Argentina, Uruguay, and Paraguay, ultimately crystallized in the 1991 Asunción Treaty as a trade and investment-oriented, open regionalist bloc, rather than a multidimensional regional entity with strong political and security institutions (Dabene in Riggirozzi, 2012). Self-identification was not much in evidence in the formation of MERCOSUR, as the southern cone had never developed much of a cultural or political identity. While Brazil was crucial to the making of MERCOSUR, Brazil's role was not necessarily preponderant, as Argentina was also a key actor. What was decisive in the creation of MERCOSUR, in causal terms, was the convergence of broadly neoliberal economic policies among its members. The neoliberal governments of Collor de Mello in Brazil and Carlos Menem in Argentina, with their relatively narrow social basis, shaped MERCOSUR in an open-regionalist cast.

NAFTA, crafted between 1990 and 1994, meanwhile, fitted even more closely than MERCOSUR with the definitions of new regionalism. Bringing together a middle-income economy, that is, Mexico with two developed economies, the USA and Canada, NAFTA was asymmetrical at the same time that it presupposed openness toward nonmembers and was almost devoid of formal institutions. At a basic level, NAFTA was a pact between the elites of the USA and Mexico to turn Mexico into a special economic zone, where American investment was channeled toward labor-intensive *maquiladora* production marketed in the USA.

The passage from MERCOSUR to UNASUR was mainly driven by the counterpoint between US plans of expanding NAFTA into a hemispheric-scale economic bloc and Brazilian efforts to parry US ambitions and assert itself as a regional economic and geopolitical power (Bowles in Rosamond *et al.*, 2002). With the world increasingly divided up into rival trade blocs, especially after the Maastricht Treaty of 1991, the USA wanted to replicate NAFTA on a larger scale, initially through the Enterprise for the Americas proposal and subsequently the negotiations over the Free Trade Association of the Americas (FTAA). As in prior cycles of integration, the USA opted for hemispheric dominance, this time through a neoliberal framework that was narrow in scope and limited in its institutional makeup, although ambitious in terms of broad economic norms. FTAA was to encompass not only trade liberalization, but also World Trade Organization (WTO)-like neoliberal investment and property norms, such as the opening up of service sectors to privatization and the stiffening of intellectual property rights (Morales, 2010).

While FTAA was limited to economic issues, it was to take its place within a broader regional-security and political-governance complex dominated by the USA. The unspoken political and security correlates of FTAA were the USA promotion of liberal democracy in Latin America and US-led security cooperation to face so-called new threats such as drug trafficking and human migration. US-dominated governance in these areas was to be operated through US leadership in the OAS and bilaterally through security partnerships. Colombia would emerge in the late 1990s as a fulcrum of US security policy, as the USA staked out a major military initiative, known as Plan Colombia, to combat illicit drug traffic there.

Brazil responded with skepticism to US post-Cold War hemispheric proposals for economic integration, both the Enterprise for the Americas and the FTAA, and began to canvass alternatives already in the 1990s. Brazil's opposition to US initiatives was in part driven by divergence of interests on specific aspects of the FTAA negotiation agenda. Liberalization proposed by US hemispheric proposals was not reciprocal, as the USA would not curb its agricultural subsidies at the same time that it insisted on trade liberalization by Latin American countries. Divergent negotiation stances also emerged with regard to WTO style norms. Brazil favored a narrow, trade-oriented agreement and disagreed with US intentions to introduce intellectual property and privatization clauses that went beyond those agreed upon multilaterally in the context of WTO.

Yet the reasons for Brazil's skepticism about FTAA in the 1990s were ultimately strategic in nature, rather than having to do merely with specific disagreements with US hemispheric trade proposals. Brazil's leaders quickly saw that the country would be foregoing an opportunity to assert regional influence if MERCOSUR, and by extension South America, were subsumed within a US-dominated economic integration scheme (Bowles in Rosamond *et al.*, 2002). The US challenge led Brazil's leaders to move toward a strategic perspective that envisioned Brazil as the axis of a subcontinental region receptive to Brazilian investment and industrial exports (Briceño, 2006). Such a region would be strategic in a double sense, not only economically but also geopolitically. A region revolving around Brazil both economically and geopolitically would boost Brazil's status in the eyes of the international community.

A strategic perspective on regionalism was adumbrated as early as the administration of Itamar Franco (1992–1993), who took distance from the neoliberal enthusiasm of his failed predecessor, Flor Collor de Mello. In the face of US intentions of hemispheric economic integration, Itamar Franco together with his visionary foreign minister Celso Amorim, later Lula's foreign minister, came to see MERCOSUR as the nucleus of a broader South American market that would strengthen the Brazilian economy and impede the USA from achieving economic dominance on the subcontinent (Turcotte and Mostajo, 2008). ALCSA or South American Association of Free Commerce was the name given to the proposed South American market in 1994 (Sennes and Tomazini, 2006). South America was also seen by Itamar Franco as pertinent to Brazil's bid for a permanent seat in the UN Security Council, an aspiration that encountered stiff opposition from the P5+1. If Brazil managed to credibly present itself as the interlocutor of the subcontinent vis à vis the UN Security Council, its chances of being granted a seat at the Security Council would be bolstered.

Subsequently, Fernando Enrique Cardoso (1994–2002), while enthusiastically partaking in the neoliberal consensus, grew wary of FTAA's flagrant lack of reciprocity and prioritized conserving and extending MERCOSUR. As he famously stated, "FTAA is an option, MERCOSUR is destiny". In 2000, Cardoso decided to forge a South American economic bloc clearly revolving around Brazil. For the Cardoso administration a South American bloc was not only a default option vis à vis a scenario in which FTAA would fail to materialize, but also a strategic complement to MERCOSUR, an expanded field of expansion for the Brazilian economy.

Apart from the counterpoint between the USA and Brazil on economic issues, there were other impulses that led to the definition of a South American space of integration. One was Brazil's tradition of geopolitical thinking, where the notion of South America as a distinct geopolitical "theater of operations" was often alluded to (Kelly, 1997). During the era of military developmentalism, in the late 1960s and 1970s, Brazilian military strategists saw South America as Brazil's first "concentric circle" of influence. Indeed Brazil's military regime interfered in the internal politics of its smaller neighbors, especially Paraguay and Bolivia, in the late 1970s in support of client military dictatorships. Brazil's idea of a South American region in which Brazil held a major stake was also prefigured by its geopolitical discourse about the Amazon. One of Brazil's self-proclaimed missions was to exert sovereign control over the Amazon and protect it from First World-led internationalization initiatives. Brazil feared in the 1980s and 1990s that a coalition of metropolitan states, transnationals, and NGOs would wrest control over the Amazon on the grounds that it was for international public good. The Treaty of Amazonian Cooperation entered into with the other states of the Amazonian delta in 1978, but reworked in 1992, had already sought to assert the sovereignty of South American states over the Amazon and encourage the construction of infrastructure nexus across Amazonian national borders, as an extension of Brazil's conquest of the Amazon (Kucinski, 1978).

Brazil's geopolitical definition of South American space as a Brazilian sphere of interest was reinforced by the Colombian imbroglio. As the US military initiative in Colombia, known as Plan Colombia, took off in the late 1990s, Brazil began to define the USA as a geopolitical interloper in a region where Brazil felt it should be the primary power and lead the resolution of political and security crises. The turn that Brazil had taken in the 1970s from a policy of seeking a special relationship with the USA to seeing the USA as an unreliable partner opened up the possibility of defining the USA as an external competitor who impinged upon Brazil's regional prerogatives. Plan Colombia not only implied a direct US military presence in a region that Brazil saw as its theater of operations, but also posed a direct threat to Brazil's strategic objective of exerting control over the Amazon. Arguably, the epicenter of the Colombian conflict was located in the western Amazonian hinterland of Colombia. Plan Colombia, Brazilian strategists, feared would not serve to stabilize the Amazon delta, but rather to exacerbate the prevailing disorder of an area of strategic value for Brazil.

Another key underpinning of South America as a Brazilian-dominated theater of operations goes beyond the notion of the state as unitary actor, namely the role of Brazil's infrastructure and energy multinationals in propelling regionalization on a subcontinental scale. While heavily concentrated in MERCOSUR states, especially Argentina and Uruguay, Brazilian foreign investment in the South American subcontinent expanded toward 2002 and remained important throughout the decade (O'Connor, 2010). Brazilian transnational enterprises were and are closely tied to the Brazilian state, which strongly supports their expansion in South America as well as in Africa. A Brazilian public development bank, BNDES for example, engages in large-scale project finance for Brazilian investments in other countries. BNDES in turn works through the clearance house mechanisms of the ALADI, originally designed to facilitate trade, so as to channel loans through the Central Banks of other countries for the purchase of Brazilian imports associated with Brazilian investment ventures. In spite of Brazil's adherence to the neoliberal consensus in the 1990s, the developmentalist and even state-capitalist model, crafted in the 1960s and 1970s, survived in residual fashion in the 1990s, and would undergo something of a revival in the 2000s (O'Connor, 2010).

By 2000, these trends converged in the first steps toward the creation of UNASUR, although UNASUR was not proclaimed until 2008. In September 2000, in Brasilia, was held the first South American presidential summit leading up to the formation of UNASUR, chaired by Brazil's president Fernando Henrique Cardoso. The closing declaration of the summit made explicit the "geographic continuity" and "community of values" of South America, clearly casting integration on a South American scale (Declaration of Brasilia, 2000). Later documents associated with UNASUR were more emphatic in referring to a "South American identity" and even to "South American citizenship".

Clearly, it was Brazil that defined the scale of integration by turning a geopolitical space, that of South America, which it identified as its theater of operations, into a focus of collective identity. Thus the South American scale was not the outcome of rationalist collective action by the 12 member states based on a coincidence of previously defined state interests or identities; for the discourses of the other states involved in South American integration lacked a concept of South America. Venezuela, for instance, had always looked toward the Caribbean as its zone of influence, rather than the South American subcontinent. Even Chavez's newly minted Bolivian discourse did not specify South America as a distinct geopolitical zone, as it tended either to focus on the Andean countries or envisioned the unification of the whole of Latin America. Brazil, in other words, was able to control the terms of discourse and engender a consensus in favor of specifically South American integration. A kind of "band-wagoning" took place on the part of other states vis à vis the quintessentially Brazilian project of South American integration. While other states would balance Brazil in many contexts, in the formation of UNASUR they largely abetted Brazilian objectives and strategic visions.

Apart from defining South America as a space of integration, the declaration of the first summit of South American presidents in 2000 emphasized that integration efforts would seek market convergence between MERCOSUR and the Community of Andean Nations, and infrastructure connections between member countries (Sennes and Tomazini, 2006). The latter objective was pursued by the establishment of the Initiative for the Integration of the South American Regional Infrastructure (IIRSA) at the Brasilia 2000 summit. IIRSA was a policy-coordination mechanism designed to promote energy and infrastructure connections between South American countries (Herbas and Molina, 2005). IIRSA was no doubt designed with the interests of Brazilian infrastructure companies in mind, as it was these emerging corporate giants who alone in the region had the capabilities and financial backing to undertake major infrastructure projects. For example, energy connections proposed by the Energy Ring component of IIRSA canvassed at the Brasilia 2000 presidential summit clearly served Brazilian corporate interests, as Petrobras, was becoming a major player in the global energy market. Thus regionalism came to be seen not so much as a magnet for extraregional foreign direct investment, but as a vehicle for intraregional FDI at a time when Brazil took its place among the other BRICS (Brazil, Russia, India, China, and South

Africa) countries as a powerhouse in project finance and green-field construction of hydroelectric plants, natural gas pipelines, highways, bridges, and canals.

The Origins of UNASUR II: Toward a Postneoliberal and Multidimensional Regionalism

After 2000, South American regionalism, on track toward UNASUR, became increasingly detached from its open-regionalist, neoliberal origins, and even from the relatively narrow scope and institutional minimalism foreseen in the Brasilia Declaration of 2000. Together with the Venezuelan-led Bolivian Alliance for the Peoples of Our America (ALBA), UNASUR would take its place in yet a new cycle of regionalism in Latin America, marked by a turn away from neoliberal open-regionalism.

It was not only that South American regionalism was, after 2000, enmeshed in a strategic vision of Brazilian subcontinental economic and geopolitical ascendance, as it had already been since the 1990s, but also that it acquired a broader scope, a more complex set of institutions, and a distinctly postneoliberal profile (Phillips in Rosamond *et al.*, 2002; Riggirozzi in Riggirozzi, 2012). Security and welfare issues, as well as a renewed developmentalist perspective became part of UNASUR's vision and institutional design. While Brazil under Lula retained and even amplified its leading role in South American regionalism, the other left-wing or populist governments that emerged in the region in the 2000s, especially Venezuela, Argentina, and Ecuador, attempted to actively mold regional integration, in ways that mirrored their models of development and popular-based political coalitions. Venezuela was especially important in introducing a welfarist dimension in UNASUR, a vision that would turn into the cornerstone of the Venezuelan-led ALBA. In spite of Venezuela's petrodiplomacy, Venezuela did not displace Brazilian leadership in UNASUR, in part because Hugo Chavez retained Venezuela's traditional orientation toward the circum-Caribbean sphere, where, not coincidentally, most of ALBA's membership is found.

UNASUR took shape incrementally after the first Summit of South American Presidents in Brasilia in 2000. In 2004, at the Third Summit of South American Presidents in Cusco, Peru, the Community of South American Nations (CSAN) was created with 12 members (Declaración del Cusco, 2004). CSAN inherited from the Brasilia founding summit the triad of periodic presidential summits, the IIRSA initiative and plans for market convergence between the CAN and MERCOSUR. In 2007, CSAN agreed to the establishment of Banco del Sur, a regional development bank pushed by Argentina, Venezuela, and Ecuador, which is viewed as an alternative to Bretton Woods International Financial Institutions (IFIs). In 2008, CSAN then transmuted into UNASUR. When it was established in 2008 by the Constitutive Treaty, UNASUR included not only the preexisting triad of South American integration, that is, periodic summits, IIRSA, and market convergence between CAN and MERCOSUR, but also a

General Secretariat based in Quito, Ecuador. Between 2008 and 2012, several other institutions were added that broadened the scope and institutional density of UNASUR. A welfare component developed around specialized councils for education, health, and social development forged between 2008 and 2010. A security dimension, in turn, took shape with the creation of the SADC and a separate council devoted to the issue of illegal drugs. In 2010, UNASUR adopted a democracy clause that called for sanctions on member governments that came to power by coups d'état.

Between 1999 and 2007, political movements critical of the neoliberal status quo triumphed in electoral contests throughout much of South America, many of them by overwhelming margins (Touraine, 2006). These postneoliberal movements, propelled by the financial crisis of the late 1990s and the crisis of political representation, stitched together electoral agendas drawn, in many cases, from the multiplicity of single-issue social movements of the 1990s, such as those that had been oriented toward indigenous rights, land reform, the environment, or gender (Ramirez, 2006). Once in power, the postneoliberal governments pursued reform programs that distanced themselves from neoliberalism and in many instances swept away existing political parties. The move away from neoliberalism carried over into regional integration. Indeed, regionalism has been a prominent shared value among the entire cohort of postneoliberal governments, as they have understood the role of regional integration as either an alternative to or buffer from vis à vis globalization.

Identified as socialist in Venezuela, Ecuador, and Bolivia, populist in Argentina, and democratic socialist in Brazil and Uruguay, postneoliberal governments reveal substantial variations. Yet as a family of governments under the banner of antineoliberalism, they have exhibited three broad traits: developmentalism, welfarism, and a confrontational politics of a populist sort, with popular mobilization and an agonic, friend–enemy logic. Yet these three broad ideological or policy trends have erupted with varying intensity in each of the postneoliberal governments.

Developmentalism, of course, had a long and venerable tradition in Brazil, dating back at least to the 1950s, when it was identified with ISI, dirigisme, and the alliance of the state with national entrepreneurs (O'Connor, 2010). In the context of the postneoliberal moment, Brazilian developmentalism has been redefined as state backing for science and technology and a policy of promoting national champions, large firms deemed to be strategic for development and the transnational projection of influence (Sorj and Fausto, 2011). Among the postneoliberal governments of Ecuador, Argentina, and Bolivia, commitment to developmentalism has translated into state activism, especially a powerful regulatory role for the state vis à vis the economy and state-led construction of infrastructure. The long wave of the commodities boom since 2002 has rendered developmental state activism compatible with economies focused on agricultural and mineral exports to China. Industrialization, in other words, has taken a back seat to economic regulation and redistribution in the new mode of developmentalism.

Welfarist policies, meanwhile, run through all the country cases under discussions from Lula's *hambre cero* to Rafael Correa's cash transfers, to Venezuela's Bolivarian subsidized food outlets. Enabled by the long cycle of the commodities boom, redistributionist measures have supplanted the forced austerity of the neoliberal years. Confrontational politics driven by popular mobilization in turn may be defined as a friend–enemy division of the political field, where a virtuous people or citizenry are counterpoised to corrupt economic and political elites. Chavez in Venezuela and Correa in Ecuador have been perhaps the most clear-cut instances of this matrix of politics, as popular coalitions, whether electoral or oriented toward street demonstrations, have confronted traditional elites, transnational corporations, and external powers. Popular coalitions exhibit varying centers of gravity depending on the country: indigenous peoples in Bolivia; the poor in Venezuela; middle classes and popular sectors in Ecuador; unionized labor and the unemployed *piqueteros* in Argentina; and unionized labor, rural workers, and middle sectors in Brazil (Ramirez, 2006).

All three strands of the postneoliberal governments in Latin America have inflected regionalism in South America since 2000. Welfarist and developmentalist languages have traversed the declarations of the CSAN and also have been prevalent in UNASUR's discourse since its founding in 2008. References to social inclusion, social cohesion, and the need to address asymmetries between South American states may be read as indices of transnational welfarism. Indeed, UNASUR's institutional design includes at least three councils related to social issues. More significantly, Banco del Sur's brand of developmentalism, since the earliest proposals, translated into assurances that its lending practices for development projects would promote social inclusion for vulnerable groups. While welfarist principles were clearly encoded within UNASUR, enforceable norms turning on welfarism were not adopted, so that a lock-in effect has not been secured. Neoliberal open-regionalist projects in contrast by agreeing upon tariff reductions and intellectual property norms had been more effective at constraining legislative and policy options of member countries.

IIRSA, meanwhile, incarnates the public–private nexus associated with Brazil's model of developmentalism, as it envisions interstate cooperation for the pursuit of public–private infrastructure ventures. These are likely to be assigned to intraregional firms, especially Brazil's highly successful transnational corporations. As will be shown below, popular mobilization and the confrontational politics accompanying it impacted UNASUR not only by pushing redistribution and a welfarist agenda at the regional level, but also by provoking political crises that opened up opportunities for regional mediation. Whenever left wing or populist governments found themselves under pressure from their domestic opponents, UNASUR lent its support to guarantee the democratic order, a dynamic that ultimately led to the adoption of a democratic governance clause that sought to deter the overthrow of incumbents, whether left wing or populist.

Security Dynamics and Political Instability in the Formation of UNASUR

While UNASUR took a turn toward welfarism and developmentalism, security challenges and political instability rose, forcing closer regional cooperation and driving regional institution-building. It was mainly Brazil who acted upon the security and political crises, as it sought to assume the role it had defined for itself as regional stabilizer. Indeed, Brazil prioritized its global agenda of a multipolar order over its regional agenda (Malamud in Riggirozzi, 2012; Hettne, 2006). Pursuing international recognition of its role as a rising power and seeking to erode the stranglehold that established powers had on international multilateral institutions were more important for Brazil than regional integration. Yet in as much as South American regionalism materialized, it was because Brazil drove it forward.

Political instability in South America over the last decade has encompassed clashes between neoliberal governments and antineoliberal social movements, and the reverse dynamics of conflict between reformist popular governments and their pro-status-quo rivals. The ascension and indeed long reign of popular governments with a distinctly confrontational politics have engendered hostile reactions by entrenched elites. Security crises in turn have largely revolved around the combustible mix of internal conflict and proliferation of transnational illicit activities in Colombia.

The origins of UNASUR in concerns about security and political instability undermine any economist reading of UNASUR's emergence that privileges market convergence as the core causal variable. Since 2003 bouts of regional insecurity and political instability have grown and the responses, often led by Brazil, have been to find ways of addressing them by means of regional crisis management and security cooperation (Wagner, 2010). A brief trajectory of political instability follows.

In 2002, the government of Hugo Chavez defeated a coup attempt supported by a coalition of business groups and factions of the Venezuelan military. In 2003, in Bolivia, an array of social movements forming part of Evo Morales' MAS (Movimiento Al Socialismo) managed to force the removal of neoliberal president Gonzalo Sanchez de Losada from office. In Ecuador, in 2005, the *Forajido* revolt, which combined protests against the corrupt political class with criticisms of neoliberalism and of US policies in nearby Colombia, overthrew neoliberal president Lucio Gutierrez. This civic uprising paved the way for Ecuador's turn to the Left and the electoral victory of Rafael Correa in 2006. In 2008, Evo Morales, after two years in power, beat back a major challenge from business elites in the eastern lowlands, the so-called Media Luna (or 'crescent'), who intended to shield themselves from egalitarian reforms by pushing for regional autonomy. In 2010, Rafael Correa, in Ecuador, personally defied a police uprising that sought to conserve corporate privileges, leading to Correa being held captive briefly. More recently, in 2012, President Fernando Lugo in Paraguay was deposed by a congressional coup led by traditional parties and business elites.

Several of these bouts of domestic political instability have provoked attempts at multilateral crisis resolution. Such efforts have reflected Brazil's willingness to assume the role of regional stabilizer and deprive the USA of opportunities to intervene diplomatically or covertly in South America (Sorj and Fausto, 2011). The 2002 coup attempt in Venezuela against Hugo Chavez led Brazil to join up with the USA, Spain, Portugal, Mexico, and Chile, in the Friends of Venezuela group that sought to mediate between Hugo Chavez and his right-wing adversaries (Turcotte and Mostajo, 2008). While the group was composed of mostly extraregional actors, it demonstrated Brazil's willingness to play the role of stabilizer in South America. Brazil was also a key actor in defusing the 2008 internal crisis in Bolivia, now through the vehicle of UNASUR. A recently constituted UNASUR strongly backed Evo Morales, and at the UNASUR presidential summit in Chile in 2008, warned that UNASUR would not consent to the rupture of the democratic order or the dismemberment of Bolivia and called for an investigation of a massacre that took place during the faceoff between Morales and his rivals (Declaración de Santiago, 2008). Confronted with the September 2010 police revolt in Ecuador, UNASUR convoked an emergency meeting in Buenos Aires that called for the maintenance of the constitutional order in Ecuador and expressed the need for a democratic clause in UNASUR to deter "institutional ruptures" (Declaration of Buenos Aires, 2010). The democratic clause of UNASUR was adopted in December 2010.

The subcontinent's security concerns have, meanwhile, as mentioned above, largely revolved around Colombia's chronic intrastate conflict between governments backed by Colombian elites and putatively left-wing insurgencies deeply engaged in Colombia's sprawling drug-trafficking networks. The spiraling of Colombia's security crisis has combined with Brazil's intent to become a regional stabilizer to drive a current of regionalism oriented toward security maintenance. The impulses coming from the global hegemon, the USA, have also inadvertently played a role in the growth of security regionalism in South America. By militarizing its assistance to successive Colombian governments, the USA has triggered Brazil's aversion to a strong US presence in the region as well as efforts to reverse it by pursuing intraregional solutions to insecurity in Colombia. At the same, overall US neglect of South America, beyond the Colombian vortex, engendered an opportunity for intraregional cooperation, as the USA was in some way disengaged from the region.

The Colombian crisis' impact on the construction of UNASUR can be briefly charted. In late 2007, Venezuela, Brazil, France, Argentina, Ecuador, and Bolivia joined in the humanitarian Operation Emanuel. An ad hoc multilateral initiative, Operation Emmanuel attempted to address Colombia's hostage problem by mediating the release of high-profile hostages in the hands of FARC guerrillas. This amounted to a search for autonomous intraregional solutions to the Colombian security crisis by way of cooperation among South American countries. The Uribe government in Colombia, of course, was uncooperative, as it was content with its special relationship with the USA and worried that left-wing governments in the region might push for a negotiated settlement with FARC. While the mediation efforts of Operation Emmanuel failed, the initiative set a precedent for intraregional cooperation in security vis à vis the Colombian crisis. A few months later, in March 2008, border tensions flared between Colombia and Ecuador, as Colombia executed a well-planned raid on a FARC camp on the Ecuadorian side of the Colombian–Ecuadorian border, justified in terms of the Bush doctrine of preemptive war. The Ecuador–Colombia dispute that followed demonstrated the urgency of closer security cooperation to prevent a regionalization of the Colombian conflict and the need to diminish the USA's role in Colombia, as it was promoting not only militarization of the Colombian crisis, but also the adoption of destabilizing norms that diverged from the mainstream interpretations of international law favored by the legalistic diplomatic culture of South America. The Ecuador–Colombia dispute was the immediate antecedent to the establishment of the SADC within the recently created UNASUR in December 2008. In 2009, soon after the formation of the SADC, another bilateral dispute arose, now between Colombia and Venezuela, over a Colombian–US agreement to provide the USA with several airfields in Colombia. Venezuela saw the agreement as setting up a staging ground for a potential US intervention in Venezuela. The Presidents of UNASUR gathered together in Bariloche, Argentina, to resolve the row, with Lula pressing Colombia to tender a guarantee that the airfields would not be deployed against other countries of the region.

The SADC, founded in December 2008, was promoted by the Lula government, as a vehicle for Brazil's role as regional stabilizer. By way of a regional security organization, Brazil could promote stability in its zone of influence. At a time in which Brazil was upgrading its military, the SADC was also viewed by Brazil as a way of unifying the military industries of the region, presumably around joint ventures with Brazilian firms (Declaración de Santiago, 2009). The SADC would thus serve the needs of Brazil's burgeoning military industrial complex, in which private firms produce military hardware on order by the Brazilian military. This constitutes another example of how Brazil's model of development or variant of capitalism has molded South American regionalism.

While the hidden agenda of Brazil's SADC is to prop up Brazil's intended role as stabilizer, the explicit objective, according to the founding Santiago Declaration is to craft a peace zone or security community in which interstate war is no long imaginable (Wagner, 2010). The SADC proposes to achieve the ambitious goal of a peace zone through confidence-building measures such as transparency in reporting of military expenditure, exchanges of officers, and a regional military academy among other measures. South America's unique defense identity would turn on three pillars: the peace zone, respect for the traditional norms of sovereignty and nonintervention, and the condemnation of ruptures of the democratic order.

Conclusion

UNASUR developed as a subcontinental, multidimensional, postneoliberal, and institutionally complex integration framework through a historical, multicausal process. This process built upon and detached itself from prior cycles of integration in Latin America.

The role of Brazil as regional power, the counterpoint between US hegemony and Brazil's balancing of US hemispheric initiatives, the models of development of left wing/populist governments, whether developmentalist or redistributionist, and the popular based political coalitions and attendant political styles of left wing/ Populist governments have all driven and shaped South American regionalism.

South American regionalism thus cannot be understood as a strictly economic phenomenon or a result of a process propelled overwhelmingly by economic calculus. Only a multicausal and multidimensional approach can grasp the complex trajectory and the present, multidimensional configuration of UNASUR. As many studies have pointed out, UNASUR also cannot be seen as an expression of neoliberal open-regionalism. Strategic, welfarist, and developmentalist notions have had a decisive influence in its normative and institutional make-up. Moreover, South American regionalism has been shaped by political coalitions quite different from those that crafted neoliberal open-regionalism. Popular coalitions with centers of gravity lying squarely among popular actors, whether the poor, indigenous groups or massive electoral majorities, have molded UNASUR; whereas open regionalism was always propelled by elitist neoliberal governments with narrow social bases closely aligned to IFIs.

The variables that the present account sees as relevant for the formation of UNASUR will continue to be significant for its consolidation. If Brazil does not exercise leadership in UNASUR because of its commitment to its global agenda, it will be difficult for UNASUR to obtain greater depth. Likewise, if the USA manages to regain its prior levels of influence in South America or refuses to grant recognition to Brazil as regional interlocutor, South America would not be able to assert its autonomy by means of UNASUR. Without further experimentation in the direction of transnational welfarism, UNASUR would stagnate, as market convergence between MERCOSUR and CAN is not making progress.

Popular coalitions and regional identity will also continue to be crucial for UNASUR's progress. In the absence of a coalition of left-wing/populist governments, neither shared visions nor the need to shield incumbents from "counterrevolutionary" bids would continue to drive UNASUR. If Brazil and other members of UNASUR decide to strongly back CELAC (Comunidad de Estados Latinoamericanos and Caribeños), which brings together South and Central America, South America would lose cohesiveness as a means of integration and collective identity.

Chapter 3

Washington and the New South American Regionalism

Francisco Carrión Mena

Introduction

While it has not always been successful in its initiatives to do so, Latin America has been a pioneering region in promoting integration processes and encouraging efforts aimed at regional unity to confront the demand for development from its people within changing circumstances that characterize the international arena.

As opposed to the crisis that has affected the global multilateral mechanisms for the past few decades, in Latin America there have emerged novel and ambitious signs of new regionalisms or new multilateral integration systems. From the previous integrationist proposal of the Andean Community of Nations (formerly the Andean Pact), the Latin American Integration Association (formerly the Latin American Free Trade Association) and the Latin American Economic System have appeared along with new alternative initiatives such as the Southern Common Market (MERCOSUR), the Caribbean Community and Common Market (CARICOM), the Union of South American Nations (UNASUR), the Central American Integration System (SICA), the Bolivian Alliance for the Peoples of Our America (ALBA), and recently Community of Latin American and Caribbean States (CELAC). All of these organizations have their own identities with their respective geographic scopes, with particular characteristics and even different geopolitical visions, but with equal shared commitment to constructing options to strengthen their capacity to answer to regional and global challenges.

After a quarter-century of political and economic changes in Latin America, particularly in South America, the region has undergone alternative integration processes undertaken for different causes and circumstances. These alternatives present proposals that tend toward increasing negotiating capacity with the intention of changing the paradigm of this liberal, asymmetrical, and clearly insufficient commercial and economic integration for one oriented toward development in its broader sense, which includes the social and political cooperation based on respect for the environment.

The obvious decline of the USA as the single hegemonic world power that emerged after the Cold War implies a fundamental change in the international order. Its economy has suffered visible deterioration as a consequence of irresponsible financial speculation and decadent capitalism. This fact is one of the principal global changes that influences the new world order in a decisive way. There are those who maintain that this American decadence is temporal or cyclical, while others say it is permanent. Whatever the case may be, it is undeniable that there exists a decrease in its traditional hegemonic power. Washington no longer determines the equilibrium of world power in a decisive way as it did after the Cold War. There are new and influential players to take account of.

As the principal global actor with planetary influence, it is indispensible to analyze the relationship of the USA with this new South American regionalism that positions itself with strength and ambition to rethink this traditionally unequal and submissive relationship from a position of lesser asymmetry. Without a reflection on this relationship, the understanding of the consolidation process of the new South American regionalism would be incomplete and would not allow one to appreciate its scope and viability.

Does this new united attitude, which is the most autonomous and probably most mature in Latin America—especially South America—and this new world order in which Washington has decreased it predominant power, convenience, disturb, or favor the relationship with the potential world power hegemon that just happens to be located in its geographic and historical area of influence? Does it turn out to be more practical to have a regional dependence on Washington or does it pose new difficulties that compel Washington to have a different type of rapprochement with its neighbor to the south? What is more, does this new reality require Washington to reexamine its continental foreign policy or finally dedicate itself to creating one? It is probably time that it does so.

Integration and Regionalism in Latin America

Regionalism as a historic phenomenon that proposes integrating states not only economically but also politically and socially in order to increase their negotiating capacity and drive their development has gone through a fundamental change in Latin America. From the integrationist concept in which the priorities were commerce and the exchange of goods and services within the interregional environment in opposition to outsiders, and eventually policies of common industrial development, it has evolved into a notion that incorporates strategic themes that involve transversal axes key to the existence of the State and its development. The new regionalism, as a dynamic process and in no way static, goes beyond previous approaches under the premise that commerce is an important factor of integration, but it is not the only one nor is it sufficient. It adds strategic factors such as security, conflict resolution, the defense of democracy, fair socioeconomic development, and environmental protection, as well as physical integration and energy resources. It becomes a multidimensional and alternative phenomenon to the traditional commercial integration despite having developed in a context of marked globalization—particularly economic, commercial, and financial—before the political and social.

The old regional integrationist proposals cited, whose authors are called "the first generation", have not managed to establish themselves for various reasons: lack of political will, institutional, and democratic instability, bilateral differences of opinion among its members, incompletion of its obligations, weakness of the States, and unfavorable international situations. Faced with these frustrated or feeble integration processes in Latin America that have prioritized the commercial, there have appeared new processes called the "second generation" regionalism that seek to replace the causes for the lack of success of their predecessors and take advantage of a more favorable international situation. I refer to the principal processes.

MERCOSUR, which is on the line between first and second generation, was formally created in Asunción more than twenty years ago. After intermittent blockades due to mistrust, noncompliance, and discord principally between Brazil and Argentina, and disagreements between those countries and weaker countries, it seemed as if there is a timid resurgence of the process although it still remains to be seen if there is true political will for some of the countries that are still interested in other free trade mechanisms with extraregional countries. A relevant factor to keep in mind is that, in any case, the auspicious appearance of UNASUR, of which MERCOSUR could be the formulating and executing agency of the commercial and regional economic integration policies along with the Andean Community of Nations (CAN) that would cover the northern countries of the subcontinent.

After a long and dubious gestation process started in Cusco at the end of 2004, UNASUR came to light in Brasilia in May, 2008, and its establishment treaty became valid in March of 2011. All the South American countries form part of the organization under Brazilian leadership, accompanied by some degree of enthusiasm from Argentina and Venezuela. They seek to construct a participative and consensual integration between the peoples of the subcontinent in the diverse settings of their relationship. It attempts to reach a fair connection that eliminates social and economic inequality, strengthens democracy, achieves social inclusion, eliminates asymmetries, and encourages sovereignty and independence of the member states. Its identity is geographic rather than ideological, as there is room for all the countries in the region, with complete respect for the free determination of each nation.

The constitutive instrument that UNASUR adopted ended up being much less ambitious than that which its developers proposed. It gave the impression that some countries wanted to lower the profile of the nascent organization. For example, the initial idea of incorporating both MERCOSUR and CAN into the institutional system within UNASUR was not accepted. The hierarchy and attributes of the Secretary General were slowly diminished to mere administrative levels without political authority as would have been desirable in order to take the initiative to face situations that demand quick responses and greater political representation.

However, UNASUR has shown its effectiveness in the areas of security and defense, natural disasters, social politics, and, above all, political dialogue. It is probably the initiative with greatest potential as it goes into the future, although there are still doubts about its impact due to the excessive areas they propose covering, the ambitiousness of the proposal, and, as always, the true political will of its members.

There exists little optimism, for example, regarding the advances that can be achieved in the area of commerce. There have not been any new ideas proposed on this matter that without a doubt constitutes one of the pillars of a conventional integrationist process. One of the arguments is that there are no modifications to the preexisting commercial structures that have presented few effects, such as CAN and MERCOSUR, in order to make it more active within the region and in regard to third markets (Bennett and Jackson, 2008).

Another sign suggestive of regionalism is SICA, which is made up of all of the countries of the subregion in addition to the Dominican Republic as an associate member. SICA was formally born at the start of 1993, after a founding treaty had been signed in Tegucigalpa two years beforehand, and was considered as a process that went beyond complementing its economies and the development of commerce, with objectives such as defense of human rights and democracy, the struggle against drug trafficking, corruption, and violence, the promotion of sustainable development, and environmental preservation. It seeks to establish itself in a region of "peace, liberty, democracy, and development", as its statute declares, which is conceptually a significant advancement for a process of this nature in a region so politically convulsive, economically slow, and with an extremely high rate of citizen insecurity. With the implementation of this mechanism, Central America has given a qualitatively important step in its integration, its institutional strengthening, and regional politics. Its strengthening will depend to a large extent on its dialogue with the USA, a decrease in its subordination, and capacity to make its subregional identity more autonomous in terms of not only economics but also democracy and institutional.

ALBA, for its part, is the most alternative and ground-breaking of the new processes of regionalism in Latin America, although not because of that is it the most successful nor the more promising in the immediate future. It emerged timidly at the end of 2001 as a proposal of President Chávez given his comparisons of the Caribbean as an alternative to the Free Trade Area of the Americas (FTAA, or ALCA in Spanish), which was encouraged by Washington and gained momentum when nationalist and progressive governments came into power in the region during the middle of the first decade of this century.

As Briceño Ruiz maintains, ALBA has gone through various phases in its search for consolidation. It made it up as it went along. From a few poorly articulated ideas at its beginning, and passing through the disorderly publication of official Venezuelan documents with the intention of defining the scope of the proposal centered on the necessity for endogenous and multidimensional development and positioning itself in contradiction to the exclusionary free market advocated by the ALCA, the ALBA has evolved into an atypical regionalism proposal. When Bolivia formally joined in 2006, the Nations

Commerce Treaty was included in Alba's structure, at the initiative of the Bolivians (Briceño, 2011: 19–84).

Alba's purpose is to develop a supportive and complementary integration concerned with the well-being of the nations, cooperation, fair trade, and the struggle against poverty, keeping in mind sustainable development and natural resources. Their identity, although heterogeneous, comes from an ideological affinity—the so-called "socialism of the 21st century"—more so than from a regional perception, as is the case with UNASUR, in which various ideological concepts fit in a geographical space (Legler and Santa Cruz, 2011: 18–20).

The Venezuelan leadership in ALBA is not discussed in the operational sphere along with its customer mechanisms, particularly oil companies; but in its ideological content it is Cuba that takes the lead. Its socialist and "anti-imperialist" bias defines its political path and at the same time reduces its options for expansion and connection with other countries that do not follow the same line of thinking. Its proposal has been clear from the beginning: opposition to the traditional integration based exclusively on commerce, incorporation of new alternative political and social pillars, and rejection of the imposing and unequal international relations of Washington. Its principles, its discourse, and pronouncements have led to a confrontation, at least rhetorical,[1] with the USA.

The new Latin American regionalism reflects a distinct, active, and purposeful dynamic that contrasts with the crisis of global multilateralism characterized by immobility and entanglement. While at the global level there is disappointment with the ineffectiveness of the traditional mechanisms, a lack of connection to reality, and only the primacy of the interests of the great powers, in Latin America there are a deluge of proposals and efforts to confront the regional and global changes. While it is true that the results of this effervescence are yet to be seen, as there is still a great deal of rhetoric, there is no lack of initiatives, and it seems that the political will to make them a reality exists. On the global level, none of this exists except to maintain the status quo that favors the traditional great powers, and that they in turn create ad hoc antidemocratic mechanisms that favor them to make up for the shortcomings of the global system.

The new regionalism, particularly that of South America, has as a common denominator the aim of going beyond the traditional approach of strictly commercial and economic integration. It proposes, ambitiously to be sure, a political integration based on the need of the nations and a broad multidisciplinary agenda that addresses not only economic themes but also social issues, cooperation, political dialogue, the environment, energy, and food, and that calls upon direct societal actors and the responsible authorities whose power is sustained in a participative democracy.

---

1 I say "rhetorical" because Venezuela continues to export oil to the USA, and even maintains a system of commercialization of combustibles in that country, while Ecuador, Bolivia, and Nicaragua continue to hold the USA as their principal market for exported goods.

To what do we owe the appearance of this new South American regionalism? Bonilla and Long correctly identify three reasons: "the end of the effectiveness and of consensus surrounding the current inter-American system" evident in the weariness of South America when faced with the inefficiency of the Organization of American States beginning in 1948; "the weakening of traditional axes of regional integration in South America" such as the exhaustion of CAN and the continuous functionality and identity crisis of MERCOSUR; and the "return of the State" as an expression of overcoming neoliberal politics and the introduction of governments with leftist and nationalist styles in various important countries in the region (Bonilla and Long, 2010).

To the three factors cited, however, we should add others that are also relevant: first, the tendency to create blocks and/or the consolidation of those that already exist as a mechanism for increasing the negotiating power of the member States, increasing their markets, and in some cases to impose policies and mechanisms of domination or at least in some way to offset the more powerful blocs. The formation of blocks is related to globalization whose conditioning factors have not been discussed in this chapter. It is a concrete manifestation of the will that these actors show of the international community in strengthening themselves by uniting their interests and objectives that are sometimes economic and at other times geopolitical.

Second, global multilateralism has become ineffective. This has been another determining factor that has fostered the emergence of the new South American regionalism. Hijacked by the exclusionary interests of the great powers, the multilateral global mechanisms have been incapable of responding to regional requirements that have their own identity and characteristics and do not always have a global impact. To this antiquated and ineffective multilateralism, South America has responded with alternatives that seek to reply to its problems and defend its interests.

Third, the influence of globalization has been an inducing factor for the formation of these regionalisms. The current global world in its different manifestations, both positive and negative, has encouraged countries in various regions, in this case South America, to look for links that strengthen them to face global problems with greater negotiating capacity. The small or medium powers have correctly assumed that by uniting not exclusively around commerce but also on other matters that interest and concern the region they belong to and to the planet as a whole they have a greater capacity to act in defense of their aspirations.

And, finally, there exists a fourth factor that is more circumstantial but equally important, related to the policies of the USA toward the region: the failure of the FTAA. Brazil, Argentina, Venezuela, and other countries did not accept the imposition of conditions based exclusively on free markets to encourage regionalism, and they promoted as an alternative a more advanced South American integration process, enriched by new areas of international relations of a political, social, and cultural nature. This posture started developing with the political modifications adopted by some countries that were incorporated during the process of establishing UNASUR.

All of these well-intentioned processes have come up against a reality that, in order to be successful, must be overcome or diminished: there is not a single Latin America, just as there is not a single South America. The difference of interests and realities has led there to be numerous regional visions with regard to global problems and ways to face them using effective homogeneous integration mechanisms. It is incorrect to consider Latin America to be a single uniform region. On the contrary, it is a heterogeneous, diverse, unequal region that, while there are historical, cultural, and religious similarities between the countries that make it up, does not constitute a block with similar interests.

In the region, there exist different perspectives and needs that are created according to the characteristics, interests, objectives, and even the threats to each country. Some coincide with the geographic or historical similarities or proximities, but there is not a single regional attitude, which obviously makes the formation of compact and homogeneous regionalisms according to their priorities and actions more difficult.

It is necessary to point out the role of Brazil in the regional context when analyzing the new South American regionalism. There is no doubt about its natural leadership with hegemonic intentions not only in South America but in all of Latin America, and its aspiration, which is increasingly close to becoming a reality, of establishing itself as a global player with influence on extraregional decision-making. Brazil is an emerging power that already has an influence on the G20 due to its economic, demographic, and strategic resources; it is the sixth largest economy on the planet, its manages to establish its influence in a wide range of sectors in other continents such as Africa and Asia, it legitimately insists on holding a permanent seat on the Security Council, and, for all this, requires the firm backing of Latin America and especially South America.

Notwithstanding these facts, the current Latin America is a region very distinct from that which existed only 20 years ago. There is, without a doubt, a democratic consolidation and institutional strengthening accompanied by sustained growth and consistent economic growth. They confirm greater relative political stability and a greater continuation of socioeconomic development politics that has had success in the last decade. The great curse of the region continues to be, however, the profound inequality in the distribution of wealth and, as such, in the continued existence of elevated indices of extreme poverty in some population segments in almost all of the countries. A well-understood and better implemented regionalism could be a contributing factor in diminishing this painful distributive difference.

The USA and Latin America

For various reasons, the history of relations between the USA and Latin America has been plagued with disagreements and confrontations as a result of a clear asymmetry that is not only economic and commercial but also political and military; in sum, a difference of power. The USA also had and has different objectives: global and regional ambitions of hegemony, the imposition of policies that benefit it, and combating threats that are not necessarily similar or proprietary for the rest of the countries in the region. There has been, and there continues to be, the typical relationship of a strong power with a group of subdominant powers, and others that are frankly weak, within the same geographic region. Such a relationship creates not only economic but also political subordination that creates a subordination of power.

As Connell-Smith reminds us, the Monroe Doctrine was always the "nucleus of US policy toward Latin America" and the guide for its actions to, under the original pretext of preventing European intervention on the continent, consolidate its own. This concept—although it was outlined in 1823 by President Monroe to refer to his country´s rejection of the traditional extracontinental powers although they were already in a process of decline—has not varied and is still in force (Connell-Smith, 1977, 300).

This vision and the increasing eagerness of the USA to secure its regional, and later global, imperial power led the USA to intervene not only with economic and commercial pressures—easy to implement thanks to its economic penetration in all the Latin American countries—and with the threat of the use of force, but also with direct military interventions and the overthrow of governments that jeopardized its interests and the subsequent establishment of regimes submissive to Washington. There are numerous examples, each one under different circumstances: Nicaragua, Dominican Republic, Panama, Cuba, Guatemala, Granada, and Haiti. In each of these, the pattern and the motives were similar: to confront risks to the public or private interests of the USA, the hegemonic power exerted, under veiled or open bilateral or multilateral mechanisms—such as the inter-American system of Human Rights in some cases—its force to protect them. The imposition of its power by any means or reason prevailed over any principle.

This hegemonic power exercised by the USA, with varying intensity depending on the period, has conditioned and even distorted the regional integration processes or those of regionalism undertaken in Latin America. Since the Pan-American Union of 1910, and including the "International Union for American Republics" before that, in 1890, under the control of the Secretary of State in Washington, until the formal creation of the Organization of American States in 1948, passing through multiple inter-American conferences and the cynical "Good Neighbor" policy, as well as the later requirement of being "associates" in the war, the USA was always careful of tending to its interests and imposing its power in the region that it has always seen as subordinate.

One example follows: In the area of security, the Inter-American Treaty of Reciprocal Assistance of 1947 reflects the supposed policy of pseudo-protection of the USA toward its neighbors, when in reality what it is is the conventional solidifying of hegemonic power of Washington in the region. In summary, the sadly famous expression that summarized the Monroe Doctrine, namely "America for the Americans" whose real meaning, as is well known is "America for the *North* Americans", by which they claimed the right to intervene in any country on the continent to defend their interests, has become obsolete. There have been many situations in which it application has been not only ineffective but pointless. The most pathetic, and perhaps the final blow for this instrument, was the Falkland Islands War in 1982, when Washington supported the UKagainst Argentina. Precisely due to the practical nonexistence of inter-American instruments that bind them in matters of security and mutual defense, there has opened a space for the creation of subcontinental mechanisms such as UNASUR´s South American Defense Council.

The twenty-first century starts in a historic period of division that is essential to this analysis. Starting with the Al Qaeda attack on the Twin Towers and the Pentagon in September 2001, which laid bare its vulnerability, the USA prioritized during the following decade a war on terrorism wherever it may be. The Middle East, Africa, and Asia became the focus of its attention. The reasons: the activities and operation centers of Al Qaeda and other terrorist groups had concentrated there, where ideas and doctrines were incubated, and there was a fear that they could launch new attacks. Latin America fell off the radar of Washington´s priority concerns as it did not represent an imminent danger nor was it relevant in terms of security except in terms of the border with Mexico and drug trafficking (Boniface, 2011: 100–104).

On the other hand, maintaining two ongoing wars at the same time, in Iraq and Afghanistan, for such a long period of time, and other hidden yet no less onerous commitments, has leveled an heavy economic cost and political expense that has not been able be recovered. The enormous solidarity and even sympathy that the world showed toward the USA after the attacks were not only not taken advantage of but arrogantly wasted and used as a pretext for the most reactionary and belligerent neoconservative theories to impose by force its global hegemonic ambitions. This visible waste due to inaction, misunderstanding, and limited global vision has produced a marked deterioration in its politics—including influence— with respect to Latin American, demonstrating scarce interest toward the region which it had considered as its natural sphere of influence.

The misunderstanding of the USA with regard to its zone of predominance has produced a vacuum that has been taken advantage of by emerging powers that until recently did not have a major presence in Latin America, positioning themselves as economic, financial, and even commercial alternatives to the USA. Particularly China, although also Russia, India, South Africa, and in some cases Iran have come to occupy spaces that were previously unquestionable territories subject to the hegemony of the USA. One just has to look at the numbers: China is, according to CEPAL (2011), aside from being the largest exporter of goods to the world, the principal commercial partner of Brazil, Chile, Venezuela, Cuba, and Peru. It is also the third country in terms of investment in Latin America whose final destination is the exploration and exploitation of primary materials, in particular petroleum.

Washington and the New South American Regionalism

South America has become aware of its potential in the last decade; its economic, political, and democratic development, its great natural resources, and its geographic and demographic dimensions, as well as of the changes produced in the world order—including globalization—from its excessive dependence on the USA and of the failure of the attempts of policies and formulas imposed from abroad. As a result of this awareness, they have launched innovative regional integration proposals. It could even be said, paradoxically, that they have also take advantage of—or they have benefited from the apparent disinterest of—Washington with regards to the region and the concentration of its focus on other regions from which security and interests have been put at risk. Latin America and especially South America is no longer the "backyard" of the USA. There is an irreversible paradigm shift in the relationship that the traditional hegemonic power has with its neighbors to the south.

Once the East–West conflict was overcome and the regional effects of the Cuban Revolution were tempered after almost half a century of shaping the foreign policy of Washington to impede a communist invasion on the continent, the motivation for maintaining the USA's interest in Latin America has shifted not toward areas related to development, the eradication of poverty, fostering education and health, or the strengthening of democracy and human rights, but essentially toward security, the struggle against drug trafficking and counteracting migration. That is, Washington's motivation is to maintain this agenda that is eminently negatively linked to the interests of hegemonic power and not to the needs of the weaker powers whose economic and political strengthening has, paradoxically, favored the very agenda of the USA in terms of strengthening commerce, weakening drug trafficking, and diminishing flows of immigrants.

In the recent history of the American continent and as an apparent reply to the new multidimensional regionalism (Hettne and Inotai, cited by De Lombaerde and Garay, 2006), during the Clinton administration, and followed with more enthusiasm under George W. Bush, Washington proposed in 1994 the creation of the FTAA, persuaded that the exchange of goods and services, in its purely neoliberal concept, would replace antihegemony sentiments and promote development. Despite the initial interest of some countries, the proposal did not take root. The wind of change blew in various important countries in South America. Brazil, Argentina, and Venezuela, among others, opposed the plan and dismissed the proposal, convinced of the strength that a broader and more inclusive regionalization would bring to promote their development and attend to the diverse needs of their nations. In other words, they rejected the market and commerce as the only factors that could lead to economic growth and development, and instead laid out a proposal that included other transversal factors that had a more effective and autonomous multidimensional influence.

When one analyzes the new South American regionalism, there is a tendency to do so based on the leadership Brazil exercises in South America. Washington and specialists in the USA are inclined to give this interpretation, but they are not entirely correct. There is no doubt that Brazil, as has been pointed out in previous paragraphs, has an important influence in the subcontinent, but it has not been a determining factor in the process of the creation and consolidation of this new regionalism. And of its own will, Brazil would appear to not be interested in fully exercising such leadership. It sees itself as a power that does not necessarily represent South America and is not making itself strong in the region as some would seem to believe. It expands its sphere of influence in other continents, in Africa, for example; it strengthens its global presence in a unilateral way and without assuming regional representation; it intervenes in a direct way in the search for solutions to global problems—as is the case of development of nuclear energy in Iran—to which the larger powers did not seem to have viable diplomatic options; but it does not appear to be a true leader in the region that has given it credibility, supported by its economic development and its democratic institutional consolidation that allows it to have greater international influence.

Aside from a few isolated efforts with some of its neighbors, Brazil remains with its back turned to other South American countries, especially those on the Pacific. It has launched road-infrastructure projects with Peru, but they still have not had the desired results. With Ecuador there is nothing concrete aside from well-intentioned declarations to open routes to the Pacific Basin. If Brazil aspires, as it has stated, to position itself as a global actor, from a geostrategic perspective, it would be imperative to have presence and access to the west of its regions and from there project itself in the Pacific Basin.

The roles that Venezuela and Argentina play as protectors of this regional leadership are not to be underestimated. Caracas has developed client relationships and ideological ties with various countries with vulnerable economies through oil and social cooperation; it has promoted, at least rhetorically, a belligerent attitude regarding the USA, accompanied by its allies in the ALBA; and it has established strong ties with nations that are declared antagonists of Washington such as Cuba, Iran, Russia, Belarus, and Syria, among others. However, they continue to provide crude oil and its derivatives to the US market with reciprocal complacency. To what extent is the belligerent and ideologized Venezuelan foreign policy consistent rhetoric, or is it simply a provocative façade?

Something that must be recognize about Chávez's government is its innovative, instigative, and ground-breaking character. Every integrationist process in Latin American should keep the thinking of Caracas in mind. Its approach is usually postliberal, with few commercial, supportive, anti-imperialist, and sovereign components, and much of the rhetoric is taken from so-called "twenty-first century socialism".

Buenos Aires joined the South American cause in a slow and steady way with the sad episode of the Falklands invasion in 1982. During that tragic incident, it received unanimous Latin American support and condemnation from the USA. Argentina then realized that belonging to and participating in Latin American regionalism projects was more advantageous and legitimate than bilateral rapprochement with the USA or the European Union. After a period of economic disaster and political instability, this approximation to the region has deepened since the arrival of Kirchner into power and has been reflected in the full support of the efforts to design and encourage a new South American regionalism in its multidimensional conception. A concrete demonstration of this commitment was the final blow given to the FTAA in Mar del Plata in 2006 during the Summit of the Americas in front of President Bush himself, and the election, not devoid of difficulties to be sure, of ex-President Néstor Kirchner as Secretary General of UNASUR, whose short period of office would only last until he died suddenly in October of 2010. He had shown his support for Venezuela in some causes along with ALBA in certain positions. There had been no shortage of controversies with Washington and he participated actively in the Non-Aligned Movement, and especially in the G77, where he became its president.

Furthermore, it is clear that the foreign policy of the USA and the prioritization of its objectives vary radically after 9/11. Latin America went on to occupy an even less important place and the few signs of interest in the region were mere ways of keeping up appearances. There was not a real interest—the real interest was in other regions. This fact was most evident with the Bush administration, but it did not change substantially with President Obama.

A few months after Obama took office, in April of 2009, the Fifth Summit of the Americas was held in Trinidad and Tobago. The President of the USA arrived at Puerto España making the remarkable and even promising statement "I have much to learn and I'm eager to listen".[2] Obama hoped to make his first multilateral contact with his neighbors into a special occasion to define what his administration proposed in the area of Latin American foreign policy and to hear what his colleagues had to say about that relationship. North America's neighbors hoped for a realistic and committed pronouncement that would propose novel elements and reflect a change in inter-American relationship. Obama did not make any significant announcements, as he had done in other regions, although it could have been a historic opportunity to do so from the perspective of his country and that of the Latin American and Caribbean region.

While few concrete results came out of the Summit, it was more of a symbolic act for the new President of the USA to have a first meeting with his colleagues from the continent as the first African–American Head of State and the first democrat in almost a decade. There were so many expectations in the world and, of course, Latin America was no exception. The Summit in Trinidad and Tobago

---

2   In a meeting of the leaders of UNASUR prior to the Summit of the Americas on 18 April 2009, the President of the USA showed signs of cordiality and affirmed that he "has much to learn and I'm eager to listen," offering a passive and harmonious setting for relations with the South American countries united there. El Mundo de España in: http://www.elmundo.es/elmundo/2009/04/18/internacional/1240076577.html

fell into the rhetoric of good will that is traditional in similar meetings and the usual stories that only serve to get the attention of public opinion.[3]

In this context of the plenary meeting of Latin America and the Caribbean, plagued by illusive hopes on the part of some countries, Obama met in separate meetings and in a parallel fashion with the presidents of the countries of UNASUR, which was under the presidency of Chile during that time.

The meeting signified clearly the political legitimacy of UNASUR on behalf of Washington as a valid regional representative. The gesture was even more significant if one keeps in mind that the statute of the organization had not been ratified by the members, that is to say, the statute was not yet in effect and had been drawn up a year beforehand by its plenipotentiaries. Formally, the organization did not exist legally or politically, and there were those who questioned it and called into doubt its usefulness. It was important confirmation that UNASUR, as representative of South America, would be the organization that the hegemonic power would choose to meet with.

As could be foreseen, the USA wanted to establish the framework for its priority interests. "UNASUR is doing an excellent job in its efforts in the areas of energy and security in the region", Obama said in an informal announcement during his visit with some of the leaders of UNASUR in the White House. So that the difference of opinion on the issues that were of greater concern would not be as visible, he also pointed out the need to work together on economic development and problems related to climate change. However, these topics were not mentioned again afterwards.

Obama gave the impression that he wanted to start from scratch with the region and leave behind the faded image left by his predecessor. His conciliatory and conversational style with some of the leaders who were open opponents of his country such as Chávez, Morales, and Correa, probably gained him sympathy and trust in some parts of South America, although at the same time it received critique from conservative sectors of the USA. But Obama did not manage to maintain this trust—soon the friendly rhetoric evaporated and the reality of his interests came through.

Washington has not made any significant new gestures toward UNASUR except for the declarations of its officials. Secretary of State Hillary Clinton made a short visit to Quito in June of 2010 when Ecuador had the Presidency. Assistant Secretary of State for Latin America Arturo Valenzuela stated on various occasions the will of his country to cultivate "a permanent dialogue with UNASUR as it plays a relevant role in preventing regional conflicts".

From the Senate, a fundamental body for the formulation of Washington's foreign policy, the influential Senator Richard Lugar publicly exhorted his government to invite UNASUR, including Venezuela, to join efforts in the

---

3   President Chávez, for example, showed a copy of the well-known work by Eduardo Galeano *Open Veins of Latin America* to his colleague Barack Obama to illustrate the exploitation the region has been subjected to.

struggle against drug trafficking, despite the deterioration in their relationships. He even managed to suggest that UNASUR could take on the role of the (rather ineffective) Organization of American States in addressing regional problems such as democracy and financial problems. His was an isolated voice, to be sure, which reflects the interest of the USA in this process.

Security and defense, in concordance with Washington, have been issues of great concern for South America and for the new regionalism. The constitution of the South American Defense Council (CDS in Spanish), for example, was created at the request of Brazil and is a concrete example of the possibilities that the process offers. Even before UNASUR's formation treaty came into effect, the CDS had shown its effectiveness. The serious internal problem in Bolivia that in the middle of 2008 almost led to a secession was interrupted in time, thanks to the rapid and effective actions of the CDS under the Presidency of Chile at that time. The same can be said for the conflicts between Columbia and Ecuador and Venezuela.

This is perhaps the area that most interests the USA. UNASUR could constitute a suitable mechanism for deactivating and preventing intraregional conflicts that the USA traditionally entered to defend its interests. Washington could possibly validate the CDS as a delegate, with Brazil taking the lead, to preserve South American security without the need to intervene directly. It would be bold but cannot be ruled out. Also, this instrument could be a possible future alternative to the Inter-American Treaty on Reciprocal Assistance on the subcontinent.

However, the case of the North American military bases in Columbia, under the pretext of improving success in the wars on terrorism and drug trafficking, and the subsequent rejection from all of South America (President Uribe of Columbia being the obvious exception) with Brazil, Venezuela, and Ecuador leading the charge, put to test the policy that had been habitual in Washington of intervening openly or underhandedly in continental security matters that affect it, according to its interpretation. That decision, accompanied by the suspicious and unexpected launch of the Fourth Fleet in the Caribbean, created a lot of friction between the region and the USA. It was not the usual imperial imposition of the system and a military contingent in the region according to a bilateral agreement with an unconditional ally. This time the opposition was firm and determined. The heads of state that make up UNASUR met in Bariloche in August of 2009 and, in a tense environment, demanded that the two countries provide detailed information about the terms of the agreement, the impact it would have on the entire region and in particular on the neighbors—among them Brazil, the most powerful, and Venezuela, the most confrontational—and called for a suspension of the agreement. On this occasion, things were not as easy as they usually had been in the past. The regional condemnation was strong, and both Columbia and the USA were isolated given the massive South American reaction channeled through this new unified regional mechanism.[4]

---

4   The incident was resolved with a declaration of unconstitutionality made by the Constitutional Court of Columbia.

The question that comes up after these incidences is whether Washington has a defined global policy with a strategic vision and a large scope, not only in Latin America, but also in South America, and in particular with regards to this renewed regionalist subcontinental proposal. The different events that have recently put it to the test, like the Honduran crisis, the acceptance of the return of Cuba to the Organization of American States, frictions with Venezuela, misunderstandings with Brazil, and the collapse of the FTAA confirm that the USA does not have a coherent and predictable policy.

On the other hand, there is sufficient reason to believe that the consolidation of a South American block that consists of a counterpart or that at least reduces the asymmetry in a space that was traditionally dominated by Washington makes it uncomfortable or causes resentment. And the fact that the block is led by a subhegemonic power with global aspirations could further irritate the world hegemon. But there could also be, at least speculatively, explanations that make one think that they would see in a positive light the creation of a new block of countries with which they could have more fluid exchanges. As cited in this chapter, there is no lack of declarations from high authorities in the USA about their positive assessment of the creation of UNASUR and of the benefit it will have in terms of working on themes that interest Washington.

Some may consider, as some authors do, that there is a hegemony voluntarily delegated by the USA to Brazil to give it the responsibility of the new block. However, this alternative seems very unlikely to me in the sense that there is not always agreement on the interests of these two countries. The firm Brazilian position on the installation of the US military bases in Columbia, the opposition to the ALCA, and the disagreement surrounding the intervention of Brazil and Turkey to reduce tensions regarding the Iran nuclear plan are, among others, signs of antagonistic positions that a delegated hegemony could not easily hold. On the contrary, the discrepancies have been visible, and it would seem that the tendency continues.

The manifestations of rhetorical confrontation, of confusion in some cases, of apparent good will in others, and of the imposition of force reflect the nonexistence of a foreign policy of the USA with regards to Latin America and even more so for the new regionalism that has emerged in South America. Washington does not have a defined policy toward its neighbors in the region. There are items on its agenda that have it concerned and that guide its international conduct: drug trafficking, terrorism, and illegal migration are among the highest priorities. But it has not managed to define a broad global medium- or long-term policy that will lead it to concentrate on a stable relationship that does not include only the negative aspects but also those topics that matter to Latin America that, on the contrary, prioritize development, the struggle against poverty, strengthening democracy, education and health, increasing fair trade, security, and the protection of human rights.

The USA did not seem to understand that precisely by addressing and strengthening these proprietary matters for Latin America they could be instrumental in diminishing the impact of those themes that are of greatest concern for Washington. In as much as there is more interest, investment, and equality in promoting socioeconomic, institutional, and democratic development, the spending destined to the struggle against insecurity, the restoration of peace, and illegal immigration have to decrease. However, we have to be realistic; this inconsistency does not mean that the USA will stop having the will and necessity to impose its power in this region that has traditionally submitted to its designs and imperial control.

De Lombaerde and Garay regard with benevolence the "ambiguous" position of Washington regarding the new South American regionalism in as much as "sometimes they support it, and other times they prefer bilateral or multilateral instruments" for their negotiations, especially on commerce or economics (De Lombaerde y Garay, 2006: 14–15).

There still exists from Washington the simple intention of imposing its power within a realist conception of its international policy without having essential aspects present. That is to say, by making the State of central importance as the only actor in a world of anarchy, the balance of power should lean toward the strongest, who is also using those instruments and mechanisms at its disposition given its will to survive, dominate, and propagate. The current policies that it adopts are guided by its own eagerness to consolidate and extend its power in the region, which at the same time address its interests and not that which a good part of the US public opinion believes are the ideals of democracy, liberty, and independence that guide its international governance.

However, the deterioration of this hegemonic power, which until recently was unthinkable in Washington, is not the same, and inevitably those weak and vulnerable spaces are being taken over by new powers with equally hegemonic ambitions, but they will have to face a region with greater response and negotiating capacity. This new relationship will probably be more equal in as much as there will be healthy competition and a better variety of commercial, investment, and even strategic options. They will not have done away with the dependence on external factors, but it will be distributed among various powers with which it will create an increased interdependence without submission to one in particular. And the USA will no longer be the undisputed hegemonic power; it will have to compete with others.

Two questions are appropriate at this point: What awaits the new South American regionalism in its relationship with the USA? And what awaits the USA in its relationship with this new South American regionalism? There are not any definitive answers yet.

Chapter 4

East Asian Economic Cooperation: Lessons for South American Regionalism

John Wong

East Asia as a Dynamic Economic Region

Geographically speaking, East Asia (EA) as conventionally defined is made up of two regions: Northeast Asia and Southeast Asia. In economic terms, EA comprises Japan, South Korea, and China (which also comprises Taiwan and Hong Kong) in the Northeast and ten Southeast Asian countries—Indonesia, Malaysia, the Philippines, Singapore, Thailand, Brunei, Cambodia, Laos, Myanmar, and Vietnam—which together constitute the Association of Southeast Asian Nations (ASEAN). The four economies of South Korea, Taiwan, Hong Kong, and Singapore used to be called the East Asian "NIEs" (newly industrialized economies), also dubbed the "Four Little Dragons". ASEAN was originally formed in 1967 by the five countries of Indonesia, Malaysia, the Philippines, Singapore, and Thailand. Others became ASEAN members much later.

Most of these EA economies, especially Japan, China, and the NIEs, were high-performance economies, having attained high growth at near-double digit rates for a sustained period (Table 4.1). Because of this, EA has been recognized as the world's most dynamic economic region since the second half of the twentieth century.

Situated on the western rim of the Pacific, EA is predisposed to be a diverse economic region. Japan, being the most advanced economy, started off as the economic leader of the region and has been the prime source of capital and technology for other EA economies, first the NIEs and then China and ASEAN. The resource-based ASEAN economies complement well the manufacturing-based NIEs, while both these groups of "late-starter" countries also complement the more developed Japanese economy. In addition, the huge potential of China, with its vast population and diverse needs, offers additional opportunities for all.

Not surprisingly, the EA region has already developed a fairly high level of intraregional trade. As shown in Table 4.2, the EA region in 2008 absorbed 47 percent of Japan's total exports, 50 percent of China's, 45 percent of Korea's, 56 percent of Taiwan's, 59 percent of Hong Kong's, 52 percent of Singapore's,

Table 4.1   Performance Indicators for East Asian Economies (GDP–Population)

Countries	Population (Mn) 2009	GDP Per Capital (US$) 2009	Total GDP (US$ bn) 2009	Growth of GDP (%)						
				1960–70	1970–80	1980–90	1990–2000	2000–08	2009	2010
China	1,335	3,734	4,984	5.2	5.5	10.3	9.7	10.4	9.2	10.3
Japan	128	39,727	5,068	10.9	4.3	4.1	1.3	1.6	-5.3	3.9
South Korea	49	17,078	833	8.6	10.1	8.9	5.7	4.5	0.2	6.2
Taiwan	23	18,500	423	9.2	9.7	7.9	5.7	4.1	-4.0	10.5
Hong Kong	7	30,065	210	10	9.3	6.9	3.8	5.2	-3.0	7.5
ASEAN–10										
Brunei	0.4	26,486.0	10.8	–	–	–	2.1	1.8	-0.5	1.0
Cambodia	15.0	692.6	10.4	–	–	–	6.4	9.2	0.1	5.5
Indonesia	231.4	2,363.6	546.9	3.9	7.2	6.1	3.8	5.2	4.5	6.1
Laos	5.9	910.5	5.6	–	–	–	6.1	6.9	7.6	8.0
Malaysia	28.3	6,822.0	193.1	6.5	7.9	5.3	6.5	5.5	-1.7	7.2
Myanmar	59.5	419.5	25.0	–	–	–	6.1	12.6	4.8	3.3
Philippines	92.2	1,749.6	161.4	5.1	6.0	1.0	3.3	5.1	1.1	7.3
Singapore	5.0	36,631.2	182.7	8.8	8.3	6.7	7.4	5.8	-1.3	14.5
Thailand	66.9	3,950.8	264.3	8.4	7.1	7.6	3.8	5.2	-2.2	7.8
Vietnam	87.2	1,119.6	96.3	–	–	–	7.3	7.7	5.2	6.8

Note: For Growth of GDP (%), the figures for Brunei, Cambodia, Laos, Vietnam and Myanmar for the years 1990 to 2008 had been computed from the data retrieved from Asian Development Bank website. The data for 2009 are from the ASEAN website. The data for 2010 are authors' compilation from Economist Intelligence Unit, China Daily, Singapore Statistics and The Star.

Sources: ASEAN Website http://www.aseansec.org/19226.htm; Asian Development Bank website, http://www.adb.org/Documents/Books/Key_Indicators/2010/ Country.asp; Economist Intelligence Unit website; China Daily; Singapore Statistics; The Star.

and 43 percent of the average of the ASEAN-4. Their trade dependence on the region in 1988 was generally much lower. Apart from its increasing intraregional trade, intraregional foreign direct investment (FDI) flows have also operated as a powerful integrating force for the EA region, especially since a great deal of regional FDI is trade-related in nature. Essentially open and outward-looking, the EA economies are highly dependent on foreign trade and foreign investment for their economic growth. In particular, both China and ASEAN have devised various incentive schemes to vie for FDI, which is generally treated not just as an additional source of capital supply but, more importantly, as a means of technology transfer and export market development.

Initially, Western capital dominated the EA region's FDI scene. Then Japanese capital flowed into the region in a second wave of investment, particularly after the early 1980s. In the 1990s, the region witnessed a new but no less significant trend associated with increasing FDI flows from the NIEs to ASEAN and China. The NIEs, having transformed themselves from capital-scarce to capital-surplus economies, comprised the third wave of investors when they became a new source of capital outflow to other less-developed EA economies. Driven by rising costs and higher wages, the NIEs were relocating their labor-intensive manufacturing facilities to ASEAN and China with lower production costs, much like what Japan had done earlier. In this way, trade and FDI (often closely interrelated) have operated as a powerful integrating force for the EA region.

The Flying Geese

Historically speaking, the EA growth process, as shown in Table 4.1, is marked by three waves. Japan was the first non-Western country to become industrialized in the region. The origin of the country's high growth rates dates back to the rapid post-war economic recovery of the 1950s, and the continued growth momentum during the 1960s and much of the 1970s. Japan's economic growth engine was initially based on the export of labor-intensive manufactured products; but due to rising wages and increasing costs it lost its comparative advantage for labor-intensive manufacturing to the four NIEs, which had started strengthening their industrial capacities in the 1960s. These four NIEs were arguably the most dynamic economies in the world at that time, as they had sustained near double-digit rates of growth for more than three decades, from the early 1960s to the early 1990s. The rise of the NIEs constituted the second wave of the region's growth and integration.

By the early 1980s, high costs and high wages had similarly caught up with these four NIEs, which had to restructure their economies toward more capital-intensive and higher value-added activities by passing their comparative advantage in labor-intensive products to the late-comers—China and other ASEAN economies— thereby spreading economic growth to the latter. In particular, China was able to register double-digit rates of high growth for over three decades since 1980. Many

Table 4.2   Origins and Destinations of East Asian Intraregional Trade

Origin of Regional Exports*	Year	Total Exports (US$ Million)	Share of Regional Exports Designated For (%)							
			Japan	China	Korea	Taiwan	Hong Kong	Singapore	ASEAN-4*	EA SUM
Japan	1988	264,856		3.6	5.8	5.4	4.4	3.1	4.9	27.2
	2000	479,249		6.3	6.4	7.5	5.7	4.3	9.5	39.7
	2004	565,675		13.1	7.8	7.4	6.3	3.2	9.1	46.9
	2006	649,931		14.3	7.7	6.8	5.6	3.0	8.1	45.5
	2008	782,049		16.0	7.6	5.9	5.2	3.4	8.8	46.9
China	1988	47,540	16.9		—	—	38.4	3.1	2.8	61.2
	2000	249,203	16.7		4.5	2.0	17.9	2.3	3.7	47.1
	2004	593,439	12.4		4.7	2.3	17.0	2.1	4.1	42.6
	2006	969380	9.5		4.6	2.1	16.0	2.4	4.0	38.6
	2008	1,020,778	11.4		7.2	2.5	18.7	3.2	7.0	50.0
Korea	1988	60,696	19.8	—		1.6	5.9	2.2	2.8	32.3
	2000	172,268	11.9	10.7		4.7	6.2	3.3	7.2	44.0
	2004	253,845	8.5	19.6		3.9	7.1	2.2	5.8	47.1
	2006	325,465	7.4	19.4		3.6	5.3	2.7	5.1	43.5
	2008	422,007	6.7	21.6		2.7	4.7	3.9	5.8	45.4
Taiwan	1988	60,667	—	3.7	—		—	—	—	—
	2000	148,321	11.2	16.9	2.6		21.1	3.7	7.4	62.9
	2004	182,370	7.6	19.9	3.1		18	3.7	7.4	59.7
	2006	243,801	7.3	23.2	3.2		16.6	4.2	7.3	61.8
	2008	256,255	6.9	26.2	3.4		12.8	4.6	7.3	61.2

Hong Kong	1988	63,163	5.2	34.4	1.0	2.5		2.3	0.3	45.7
	2000	201,860	5.5	34.6	1.9	2.5		2.3	0.5	47.3
	2004	259,314	5.3	44.0	2.2	2.4		2.2	3.3	59.4
	2006	316,816	4.9	47.0	2.1	2.6		2.0	3.2	61.8
	2008	362,675	4.3	48.5	1.7	1.9		2.0	3.4	61.8
Singapore	1988	39,306	8.6	3.0	2.0	2.8	6.2		20.3	42.9
	2000	137,804	7.5	3.9	3.6	6.0	7.9		24.9	53.8
	2004	179,615	6.4	8.6	4.1	4.6	9.8		21.7	55.2
	2006	271,799	5.5	9.8	3.2	3.5	10.1		28.3	60.4
	2008	338,176	4.9	9.1	3.6	2.8	10.4		21.4	52.2
ASEAN-4	1988	80,080	19.5	2.2	2.8	2.0	2.9	9.0		38.4
	2000	269,099	16.0	3.4	3.7	4.2	4.2	12.6		44.1
	2004	334,108	15.6	6.8	2.9	3.5	5.1	10.4		43.7
	2006	442,265	13.7	8.3	3.9	3.3	4.7	11.3		45.2
	2008	571,346	13.3	9.1	4.0	2.2	4.4	9.6		42.6

Source: Directory of Trade Statistics Year Book 2009, IMF. Taiwan's data from Bureau of Foreign Trade website. ASEAN-4 denote Malaysia, Indonesia, Thailand and the Philippines.

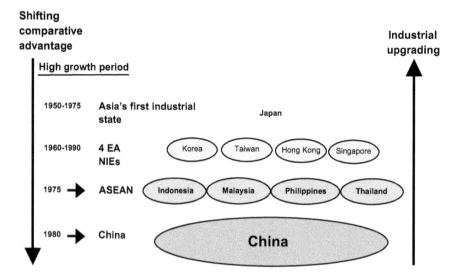

Figure 4.1   Japan-Led "Flying Geese" Pattern for EA-I's Growth and Integration

Japanese scholars like to depict this pattern of development in Asia as the "Flying Geese model" (originally coined by a Japanese economist, Kaname Akamatzu, in 1962), which for all its simplicity still provides a highly instructive and intuitive explanation of EA's process of successful economic growth from the rise of Japan to the rise of China. Figure 4.1 gives a graphic expression of the flying geese.

Suffice it to say that, in the process of growth, the EA economies have increased their economic interaction with each other, resulting in their growing economic interdependence. Despite their inherent political, social, and economic divergences, the EA economies can actually economically integrate quite well as a loosely constituted and market-driven regional grouping. This is essentially the underlying meaning of the flying geese principle.

The underlying economic theory for the flying-geese growth pattern is associated with the concept of shifting comparative advantage. Most of the EA economies are open and outward-looking, with their economic growth heavily dependent on exports, particularly labor-intensive manufactured exports in their early phases of industrialization. The theory of comparative advantage is therefore critical for these export-oriented economies.

To achieve high growth, most of these EA economies had devoted a high proportion of their GDP to domestic investment, which was generally matched by equally high levels of domestic savings. In fact, high investment and high savings provide the single most important neoclassical explanation of the high growth of the EA economies. Most EA economies had generally committed more than 30 percent of their GDP to domestic investment during their critical phases of industrial take-off.[1] This high investment propelled a "virtuous circle" in these economies: high rates of investment induced high export growth, and then high GDP growth, high savings and finally high investment again.

In terms of development policy, most EA economies shared the salient common feature of operating an effective export-oriented development strategy, as reflected in their generally high export–GDP ratios and their relatively high shares in the world export markets. Exports not only provide the economies of scales for production, but also facilitate technological progress and productivity growth. In this way, the overall export orientation of the EA economies had propelled them to high growth by reaping the gains from international trade and specialization (Wong, 1996). In contrast, many countries in Latin America and South Asia were long plagued by relatively low economic growth, mainly because they had failed to make a successful transition from their import substitution industrialization to export orientation, as EA had.

By and large, the ASEAN economies in Southeast Asia (except for Singapore) are well-endowed with a wide variety of primary commodities and natural resource products, which had played an important role in their early phases of economic growth. In contrast, the Northeast Asian Countries of Japan, China, and Korea are basically resource poor and land scarce. However, these EA countries have managed to overcome their natural resource constraints by intensifying their human resource development through education and training, as reflected in the social indicators of Table 4.3. Viewed from a different angle, rapid human capital formation actually constitutes the endogenous source of growth for many EA economies.

Furthermore, the institutional structure of EA has also been crucial for its economic growth. The basic development policies in EA are pro-growth and pro-market. Beyond its basic role of providing education and infrastructure, most EA governments generally (except in Hong Kong) actively participate in promoting growth, particularly for export promotion and industrial upgrading. Important government intervention is often undertaken through the market. In short, all these pro-growth institutional factors constitute what some development economists have referred to as the "East Asia Developmental State" model. The World Bank has referred to this high-growth phenomenon as the "East Asian Miracle".

China's Economic Rise

China's economy has chalked up spectacular performance since the start of its economic reform in 1978, growing at an annual rate of 9.9 percent for well over three decades (Figure 4.2). It did not suffer from the 1997 Asian financial crisis. It

---

1   See World Bank, *World Development Report* (various years) and Asia Development Bank, *Asian Development Outlook* (various years), which provide data on investment and savings rates of the EA economies for various years.

Table 4.3   East Asia Socioeconomic Development Indicators

	Per-capita GDP (US$) 2010	Total Fertility Rate (Births Per Woman) 2010	Average Life Expectency (Male) 2010	Average Life Expectancy 2010	Mortaility Rate at Birth (per 1,000 live births) 2009	Adult Literacy Rate (above 15 in age) 2005–9 Female	Male	Primary School Female	Male	Higher School Female	Male	Tertiary Education Female	Male	Year	HDI 2010	Human Development Index (New Scale) Ranking 2010
China	3,556	1.4	72	76	20	87	95	111	112	78	77	23	23	2008	0.663	91
Japan	32,600	1.2	82	85	2.8	99	99	100	100	101	10.1	54	62	2008	0.884	11
NIEs																
S. Korea	16,491	1.2	76	82	4.3	98	99	104	105	94	98	69	65	2008	0.877	12
Taiwan	15,552	1.2	75	81	5.4	89	96	102	100	99	98	85	79	2008	–	–
Hong Kong	24,626	1	79	85	2.6	91	97	105	111	86	86	34	33	2008	0.862	21
Singapore	35,022	1.1	77	81	2.3	91	97	95	96	73	75	40	47	2008	0.846	27
ASEAN-4																
Indonesia	2,142	2.3	68	73	30	89	95	116	112	74	73	32	19	2007	0.6	111
Malaysia	8,065	3	71	76	16	86	93	100	101	72	70	33	27	2007	0.744	59
Phillippines	1,639	3.3	68	74	21	94	94	109	110	87	79	32	25	2007	0.638	100
Thailand	4,036	1.7	71	76	18	92	96	108	108	88	79	45	38	2007	0.654	87
India	946	2.7	65	67	51	51	75	109	114	49	53	10	14	2006	0.519	122

Note: Human Development Index combines life expectancy, educational attainment and income indicators to give a composite measure of human development.

Source: CIA World Fact Book (2011), United Nations Database, Asian Development Bank

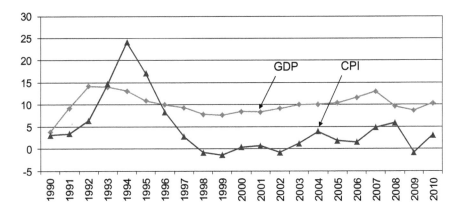

Figure 4.2   China's Economic Growth and Inflation, 1978–2010

was also relatively unaffected by the recent global financial crisis, which had dire consequences for most economies. China's economic growth for 2009 remained at 9.2 percent and went up to 10.3 percent growth for 2010. In fact, China's economy had not only quickly bounced back from the global financial crisis with high growth, but was also leading the global economy to recovery.

With its total (nominal) GDP just over US$5 trillion, China has recently succeeded Japan as the world's second largest economy. In purchasing power parity (PPP) terms, China has long been the world's number two economy, after the USA. For a few years now, China has already been the world's largest exporting country. In the post-crisis world, China has further distinguished itself as the country with the world's largest reserves (US$3.2 trillion) and as the only large country not burdened by huge domestic and external debts.

China's economy is set to continue with its high growth rate (around 8 percent) at least throughout this decade, while at the same time undergoing rebalancing and restructuring. China has just started its 12th Five-Year Plan (2010–2015), which is aimed at speeding up restructuring its growth pattern by reducing its dependence on exports in favor of greater domestic demand. This will render China's long-term economic growth more sustainable.

China's rise has radically altered the region's trade and investment patterns, operating as a source of the region's economic growth while also accelerating the process of regional economic integration. Regionally, as shown in Figure 4.3, China's overall trade pattern with the EA region is such that it incurs trade deficits with its regional trade partners and in turn chalks up trade surpluses with the European Union (EU) and USA. In this way, China's economy has become an important engine of growth for other EA economies, which are making use of China's huge domestic markets (for both manufactured products and primary commodities) as a source of their own growth.

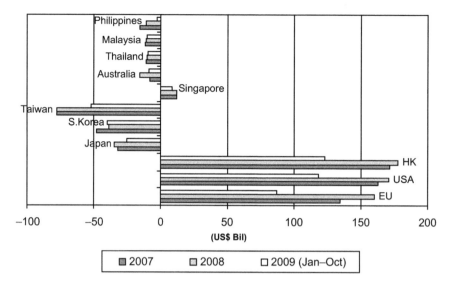

Figure 4.3   China's Trade Balance with Selected Economies

Furthermore, China's economy has also facilitated the region's economic integration. As shown in Figure 4.4, China imports high-tech parts and components from Japan, Korea, and Taiwan; raw materials and parts and components from ASEAN; and services from Hong Kong and Singapore. China then processes them

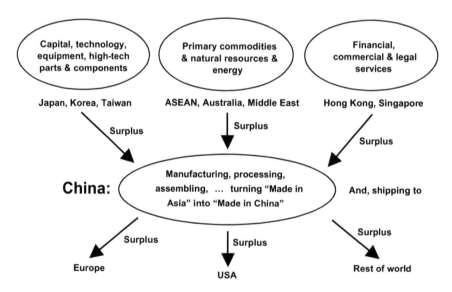

Figure 4.4   The Pattern of China-Led Regional Growth and Integration

and turns "Made in Asia" into "Made in China" for exports to the world markets at large. This is because China is the home of many regional and global supply chains (or regional production networks).

As China's economy today already has a large base, further high growth will certainly produce its own dynamics of "speed being compounded by scale". The next phase of China's economic rise is therefore set to produce an even more profound regional and global impact, altering the geoeconomic and geopolitical landscapes in both EA and the world at large.

Japan-led EA-I versus China-led EA-II

EA owed its first few decades of dynamic growth to the economic rise of Japan. That was the "first rise" of East Asia (or EA-I), which was clearly associated with Japan's economic growth. By the mid-1980s, when Japan's economic growth was at its peak, there was frequent talk of the rise of EA as the world's most dynamic economic region. Soon after this, however, particularly following the Plaza Accord in 1985 (when the Japanese yen was forced to revalue sharply), Japan as the "leading goose" not just lost its economic growth momentum, but also plunged into a prolonged recession, the so-called "lost decade". Meanwhile, the economic growth of the NIEs had also come down considerably, partly because their economies became mature. It looked as if EA was losing its luster as a dynamic economic region.

By the turn of this century, the notion of EA as the world's most dynamic economic region had revived, this time because of the economic rise of China. The "second rise" of East Asia or "EA-II" is clearly China-led. In fact, EA's third wave of high growth, heavily gravitating toward China, has proved to be economically far more significant than the previous two waves.

China's relentless high growth has been far more "dynamic" than Japan's past process of growth because of China's huge size and diversity, which situates the country in a position to generate a lot of growth potential both for itself and for the region. With greater internal dynamics, China promises to sustain its high growth much longer than Japan did. China's role as an engine for EA's growth is also far more powerful than that of Japan's during the previous period of economic growth. As shown earlier, China has played a much larger role in integrating the EA economies than Japan had, thanks to the operation of the many global and regional supply chains that are centered in China.

Not surprisingly, China has eclipsed Japan's economic leadership role in EA as the region's largest economy. In short, the China-led EA-II is quantitatively and qualitatively different from the Japan-led EA-I. As shown in Table 4.4, the China-led EA-II in 2010 accounted for 23.4 percent of global GDP, much the same as the USA (23.5 percent), though slightly smaller than that of the EU as compared to the 15 percent of the Japan-led EA-I (1985). For exports, EA-I accounted for 29 percent of the global market share, compared with the 24 percent of the EA-I.

Table 4.4   Comparing East Asian Economies, 1985–2010

	Japan-Led EA-I, 1985		China-Led EA-II, 2010	
	World GDP Share (%)	World Export Share (%)	World GDP Share (%)	World Export Share (%)
East Asia	15.2	24.2	23.4	29.0
Japan	(11.1)	(11.6)	(8.8)	(5.1)
China	(2.2)	(1.8)	(9.5)	(10.1)
USA	33.0	23.7	23.5	8.5
EU	–	–	25.9	12.0

While Japan's past growth potential has dissipated, with little chance of recovery because of a demographic shift toward an aging population, China is still able to sustain its high growth rate far longer. In the wake of global financial crisis, most developed economies—including Japan—are saddled with significant structural problems like high unemployment and serious household and government debts. They are also facing a looming public finance crisis. China's economy, in contrast, is still steaming ahead with high growth, backed by strong fundamentals and good internal and external balances. China is widely expected to continue with its high growth for the next 10–15 years.

In fact, with the relative decline of the developed economies in the aftermath of the financial crisis, the China-led EA-II will, in a few years, become the world's

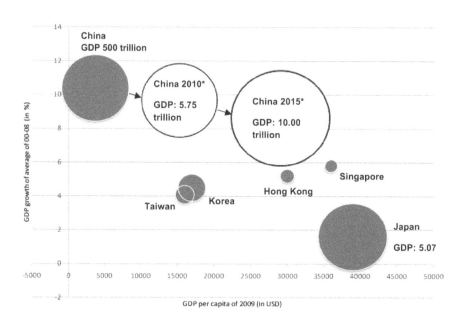

Figure 4.5   Comparing East Asian Economies, 2010

largest economic entity. This explains the clear shift of global economic gravity toward East Asia. Figure 4.5 highlights China's expanding economic size in EA.

Toward a China-Centric Regional Economic Order

China's basic development strategies will remain pro-growth while undergoing rebalancing gradually and addressing its many domestic economic and social issues at the same time. Overall, China has started to exert strong geoeconomic influence on the EA region as a whole, with its economic activities increasingly drawn to China. China's growth will affect the growth of other EA economies, and China's pace of economic restructuring will also set the tone for other EA economies to rebalance themselves. For example, if China's economy were to reduce its exports to the world, other EA economies will first feel the pinch by also cutting down their exports to China. As stated recently by Singapore's former Prime Minister, Lee Kuan Yew "None of the economies on its periphery can resist the attraction of China's market. Slowly, but inexorably, we are being drawn into China's economic orbit". In short, a China-centric East Asian Economic Community is slowly taking shape.

While EA's emerging geoeconomic pattern is sufficiently clear, its geopolitical landscape is much more complicated. On account of its size, the rise of China can be considered, in geopolitical terms, disruptive to many of its smaller neighbors, not all of which have unequivocally accepted China's message of "peaceful rise". China also lacks effective "soft power" to sell such messages (Information of the State Council in China, 2011).[2] In particular, Japan still has problems coming to terms with its relative decline and the rise of China.

It is easier for the region to embrace China's economic leadership because economic relations are basically market driven, with clear mutual benefits. It is far more difficult for the region to accept China's political leadership without having settled its many outstanding issues of regional geopolitical conflict. China's recent positions on the territorial disputes in the South China Sea are certainly not helpful in this regard. This means that EA-II will not be an effective and cohesive political grouping. Unless significant political shifts occur, it will remain "hot in economics, but cold in politics".

A more complicated issue is how the EA-II will integrate itself into the existing global order dominated by the USA. Evidence of this problem is seen in the recent shift of US strategic focus back to EA, promptly in response to the shift of global economic gravity toward the region. The presence of such extraregional political forces is likely to further "muddy" the region's geopolitical water. Figure 4.6 highlights the changing economic strengths of China, Japan and the USA since

---

2 The White Paper on China's peaceful development further reaffirms China's intentions of pursuing peace and stability in its approach to foreign policy.

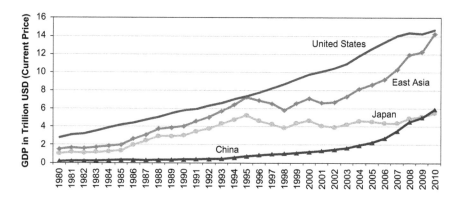

Figure 4.6   GDP of East Asia, Japan, China, and the USA since 1980

1980. It shows the total GDPs of EA and the USA converging and those of China and Japan also converging.

Historically, all established hegemonic powers strive to prevent the rise of another new power. The rise of Japan-led EA-I posed no threat to the existing US geopolitical interests because Japan's economic rise was under the US security umbrella. However, the current rise of the more China-centric EA-II will clearly be considered a challenge to the established global order dominated by the USA, partly because China is perceived to have far greater economic potential and partly because China's political and social systems are so much at odds with those of the West.

Great Britain at one time attempted to prevent the rise of Germany, but it did not make an effort to prevent the rise of the USA, largely because of the countries' political and social similarities, which in turn gave rise to mutual trust. In the case of China's rise, the factor of trust is missing; but it is an important factor that will complicate the acceptance of the China-centric EA-II in the existing global system.

ASEAN's Road to Regional Economic Cooperation

While the Northeast Asian countries of Japan, China, and South Korea have been "calling the shots" as far as EA's economic growth and integration is concerned, it is Southeast Asia that is taking the lead in terms of formal regional economic cooperation, as ASEAN is the only formal regional grouping in the whole of EA. Without a doubt, Japan and China can exert strong economic influence on the global economy; but politically ASEAN has strong international clout on account of its various programs of cooperation and dialogues with countries outside the region.

The following provides a succinct review of the ASEAN process of economic cooperation. It highlights the special methods that are employed by the ASEAN leaders to organize their regional activities, commonly known as the ASEAN Way.

ASEAN Vision 2015

At the 9th ASEAN Summit in Bali, Indonesia, in October 2003, ASEAN leaders adopted the Declaration of ASEAN Concord II, presenting a vision to bring about an ASEAN Community by 2020. This comprehensive program of regional cooperation for the ASEAN Community is comprised of three pillars: the ASEAN Economic Community, the ASEAN Security Community, and the ASEAN Socio-Cultural Community. The Vision 2020 was actually first proposed by the ASEAN leaders in December 1997 in Kuala Lumpur.

At the 12th ASEAN Summit in Cebu, Philippines, in January 2007, ASEAN leaders resolved to accelerate the completion of the ASEAN Economic Community (AEC) by 2015. The AEC is envisaged as a kind of single market that will bring about freer trade in goods, freer movement of labor and capital, and freer flow of services broadly similar to the European style common market. Admittedly, Vision 2015 is a highly ambitious target.

With the rise of China and India, ASEAN is facing many formidable economic challenges, including its loss of economic growth momentum and declining productivity. ASEAN is badly in need of new initiatives to boost its economic growth and greater economic integration. ASEAN leaders, in accelerating economic integration from 2020 to 2015, apparently wanted to reinforce ASEAN's central role in promoting regional economic growth and integration. Accordingly, they are following an ambitious agenda in order to galvanize ASEAN's efforts toward this common goal.

In a way, the AEC is a logical extension of ASEAN's previous economic cooperation initiatives such as the ASEAN Free Trade Area (AFTA), the ASEAN Investment Area (AIA), and the ASEAN Framework Agreement on Services (AFAS). The implementation of AFTA in 2003 has brought down tariff barriers significantly in accordance with the Common Effective Preferential Tariff (CEPT). For foreign direct investment (FDI), ASEAN investors have been given national treatment starting from 2010. As a result, the intra-ASEAN trade share has also grown to reach 24 percent of ASEAN's total trade. Viewed from this angle, ASEAN has already laid some important groundwork for its future economic integration endeavor.

However, a single market is a significant goal with correspondingly difficult challenges for ASEAN. ASEAN is economically and institutionally not ready for something like a single market within five years. Will that happen in 2015? Admittedly, there is a great deal of uncertainty.

ASEAN's Humble Beginning

ASEAN celebrates its 45th anniversary next year (2012). It came into being in 1967 when the Foreign Ministers of Indonesia, Malaysia, the Philippines, Singapore, and Thailand signed the Bangkok Declaration expressing their desire for a good-neighborly style of cooperation. Faced with high regional tensions and many outstanding bilateral issues, ASEAN experienced a tenuous existence initially. In 1967, the Vietnam War was still raging, threatening to spill over to Thailand. Singapore had been independent for barely two years. Indonesia's *Konfrontasi* (Confrontation) against Malaysia and Singapore (1963–1965) was still fresh in the minds of their people.

Adding to this is the fact that ASEAN is also highly heterogeneous in terms of its members' economic and social development (Wong, 1979). Against all these odds, the five founding members moved ahead to set up ASEAN as a regional mechanism to help moderate inter-state relations, thereby also allowing individual ASEAN states to concentrate on their nation-building efforts and domestic economic development.

Under the circumstances, ASEAN had to start its existence with extremely modest steps. The Bangkok Declaration was a brief document, containing neither a blueprint for formal economic cooperation nor any grand design for such supranational objectives as the formation of a political bloc or a military alliance. For the first decade of its existence, ASEAN had only a simple and rudimentary organizational structure, with no formal charter and no secretariat. All this contrasted sharply with many other regional groupings in the developing world at that time, which were often accompanied by a declaration of lofty goals, along with ambitious targets, well-structured programs for economic cooperation, and a regional bureaucracy as the implementing machinery.

In retrospect, ASEAN's humble and cautious beginning actually helped the organization to survive various regional crises and to grow. It has survived the Cold War of the 1960s, the fall of Vietnam and Cambodia in the 1970s, the Asian financial crisis in the 1990s, and more recently, the global financial crisis. Over the years, ASEAN's membership has increased to ten member states. Brunei joined in 1984, Vietnam in 1995, Laos and Myanmar in 1997, and Cambodia in 1999.

At the same time, ASEAN's difficult beginning along with its underlying obstacles has created two institutional traditions. First, the survival of ASEAN as a regional organization takes precedence over all other policies, with all successive ASEAN leaders taking ASEAN's survival very seriously. Second, ASEAN's approach to all aspects of regional cooperation has been very cautious, with no member states pushing the envelope to the discomfort of the others. Every member state jealously guards its own sovereignty and independence. Understandably, such an approach ensures the survival of ASEAN, but with the trade-off of slower progress toward integration.

Today, ASEAN has been hailed not just as one of the most successful regional organizations in the developing world, but also as the longest-lasting regional grouping. Around the time of the formation of ASEAN, the developing g world had witnessed the rise of many regional arrangements or attempts to create regional cooperation schemes, particularly in Latin America and Africa: the Latin American Free Trade Association (LAFTA), the Caribbean Community, the Central African Customs Union (CACEU), the East African Community

(EAC), and the Economic Community of West African States (ECOWAS) (El-Agraa, 1982). Entering into the 1980s, however, these regional schemes had either collapsed or became defunct.

Developing countries have never experienced smooth sailing in their attempts to achieve economic cooperation. Apart from their overall economic immaturity, which gives rise to many obstacles as well as structural rigidities inimical to genuine economic integration, their economies are separately oriented toward industrially advanced countries and, thus, have a low degree of economic complementarities with each other. Their main exports are usually primary commodities or natural resource products, which are destined for the developed country markets (Robson, 1980).

Viewed in the context of the developing world's experiments of regional cooperation, ASEAN stands out as an exceptional case and the *continued existence* of ASEAN is highly significant. Not only has it stood the test of time and changing circumstances, but it has also continued to grow to become one of the few highly visible regional groupings.

ASEAN's Progress in Regional Economic Cooperation

ASEAN's *active existence* is due to one favorable condition. As already shown in Table 4.1, the ASEAN member states are among the world's rapidly growing economies. For the past few decades, the ASEAN region has chalked up an impressive growth rates of around 6 percent, which, though dwarfed by China's extraordinary growth records, has clearly out-performed many other developing economies elsewhere. Good economic performance generally increases the propensity of the region to move toward greater economic cooperation.

Accordingly, as shown in Table 4.5, total intra-ASEAN trade reached US$377 billion in 2009, with the share of intra-ASEAN trade comprising 25 percent for exports and 24 percent for imports. In the 1970s and the 1980s, the intra-ASEAN trade share was around 20 percent, mainly dominated by primary commodities. It increased to around 27 percent before the global financial crisis. The growth of intra-ASEAN trade in recent years was mainly driven by the trade in manufactured products, particularly for parts and components. This means that significant economic integration in the ASEAN region is slowly taking place. Overall, the present intra-ASEAN trade share is still relatively low, particularly compared with over the 60 percent rate for the EU. According to ASEAN Secretary-General Surin Pitsuwan, the intra-ASEAN trade share should increase to 40 percent of its total trading as it moves to becoming an ASEAN Economic Community in 2015 (Pitsuwan, 2010). But this is clearly an unrealistic expectation, because the ASEAN region is basically made up of open economies, which are also externally integrated with the more industrialized economies outside the region. ASEAN's primary exports are mainly destined for the developed country markets outside ASEAN, and its intraregional trade in manufactured products largely emanates

Table 4.5   Intra- and Extra-ASEAN Trade, 2009

Countries	Intra-ASEAN Exports		Extra-ASEAN Exports		
	Value	Share to Total Exports	Value	Share to Total Exports	Total Exports
Brunei	1,229.3	17.1	5,939.3	82.9	7,168.6
Cambodia	644.6	12.9	4,341.2	87.1	4,985.8
Indonesia	24,623.9	21.1	91,886.1	78.9	116,510.0
Laos	997.4	80.6	239.8	19.4	1,237.2
Malaysia	40,365.1	25.7	116,525.8	74.3	156,890.9
Myanmar	3,196.7	50.4	3,144.8	49.6	6,341.5
Philippines	5,838.4	15.2	32,496.2	84.8	38,334.7
Singapore	81,646.5	30.3	188,186.0	69.7	269,832.5
Thailand	32,490.6	21.3	120,006.6	78.7	152,497.2
Vietnam	8,554.8	15.1	48,136.2	84.9	56,691.0
ASEAN	199,587.3	24.6	610,901.9	75.4	810,489.2

Countries	Intra-ASEAN Imports		Extra-ASEAN Imports		
	Value	Share to Total Imports	Value	Share to Total Imports	Total Imports
Brunei	1,242.8	51.8	1,156.8	48.2	2,399.6
Cambodia	1.453.3	37.3	2,447.6	62.7	3,900.9
Indonesia	27,742.4	28.7	69,086.8	71.3	96,829.2
Laos	1,480.8	85.8	244.2	14.2	1,725.0
Malaysia	31,700.2	25.7	91,630.2	74.3	123,330.5
Myanmar	2.065.7	53.7	1,784.1	46.3	3,849.9
Philippines	11,561.1	25.4	33,972.9	74.6	45,533.9
Singapore	59,047.6	24.0	186,737.1	76.0	245,784.7
Thailand	26,759.5	20.0	107,010.1	80.0	133,769.6
Vietnam	13,566.7	19.6	55,664.2	80.4	69,230.9
ASEAN	176,620.1	24.3	549,734.0	75.7	726,354.1

Countries	Intra-ASEAN Trade		Extra-ASEAN Trade		
	Value	Share to Total Trade	Value	Share to Total Trade	Total Trade
Brunei	2,472.1	25.8	7,096.1	74.2	9,568.2
Cambodia	2,097.9	23.6	6,788.8	76.4	8,886.7
Indonesia	52,366.3	24.5	160.972.9	75.5	213,339.2
Laos	2.478.2	83.7	484.0	16.3	2,962.1
Malaysia	72,065.3	25.7	208,156.0	74.3	280,221.4
Myanmar	5,262.4	51.6	4,928.9	48.4	10,191.3
Philippines	17,399.5	20.7	66,469.1	79.3	83,868.6
Singapore	140,694.1	27.3	374,923.1	72.7	515,617.1
Thailand	59,250.1	20.7	227,016.7	79.3	286,266.8
Vietnam	22,121.5	17.6	103,800.4	82.4	125,921.9
ASEAN	376,207.3	24.5	1,160,635.9	75.5	1,536,843.3

Source: *Direction of Trade Statistics Yearbook 2009*, IMF.
Total trade is in million USD. Share is in percentage.

from the regional production networks that are dominated by industrial countries outside the region.

It will not be easy for ASEAN to raise its intra-ASEAN trade share to 30 percent or beyond in the short term. To achieve this, the ASEAN economies need to restructure and disengage themselves from their traditional economic ties with countries outside the region, and then "reintegrate" themselves by redirecting economic activities toward the region, which is an exceedingly difficult process. Some have argued that the success of the AFTA does not need to depend on the increase in intra-ASEAN trade. In fact, pushing for more intra-ASEAN trade at the expense of the more efficient producers outside the region may not necessarily benefit ASEAN (Yue and Pacini, 1997).

It can therefore be argued that, despite this relatively low intra-ASEAN trade share, ASEAN has indeed made important progress toward regional economic integration, particularly when taking into account the achievements in other areas such as the substantial reductions in tariff barriers (especially after the signing of the CEPT in 1992); simplification, harmonization, and standardization of customs processes; removal of many restrictions on trade in services, reduction, or elimination of investment restrictions; harmonization of capital-market standards; agreements on multi-modal transport and physical connectivity; and overall improvement in ASEAN competitiveness. All these directly and indirectly, albeit slowly and gradually, operate to broaden and deepen the process of ASEAN economic integration (Guangsheng, 2006; Nesadurai, 2008).

ASEAN's Wide-Ranging Extraregional Activities

From the outset, ASEAN has been very active in its "extraregional cooperation". In fact, it has achieved far more progress in the area of extraregional cooperation than its intraregional cooperation. Over the years, ASEAN has been highly successful in developing a unified perception of many regional and global political, economic, and security issues. Through the ASEAN Post Ministerial Conference (PMC), ASEAN has maintained formal dialogues with all the world's important countries: Australia, Canada, China, the EU, India, Japan, Russia, and the USA. Through its multilateral ASEAN Regional Forum (ARF), ASEAN has made significant contributions to peaceful conflict resolution in the region, as well as helping to consolidate the existing security architecture in Asia.

In the wake of the 1997 Asian financial crisis, ASEAN expanded its scope of regional cooperation by establishing another multilateral framework, known as "ASEAN plus Three" (APT), with its Northeast Asian neighbors Japan, China, and South Korea. In particular, the APT launched the Chiang Mai Initiative (CMI) in 2001, with measures for a stronger regional financial architecture as a way to prevent the recurrence of another regional financial crisis.

The multilateral frameworks have, in turn, spawned many organizations and mechanisms under Track I (intergovernmental processes), Track II (organizations and civil societies linking to the government), and Track III (mainly nongovernmental organizations, NGOs) for wide-ranging regional cooperation activities or initiatives in both formal and informal areas. They include nontraditional security cooperation related to fighting organized crime, managing pandemics and infectious diseases, climate change, energy security, and so on. These are important regional issues affecting not just individual ASEAN states but also countries outside the region. ASEAN just provides a convenient and effective platform for all the interested parties to get together to tackle those vital issues and problems.

Suffice it to say that ASEAN has actually made much more progress in a wide range of extraregional cooperation activities than intraregional economic cooperation. For some ASEAN countries, regional economic cooperation may be a desirable long-term goal, but it may not produce immediate and significant benefits for them, especially during the early stages. For the less-developed ASEAN states in particular, regional economic cooperation schemes may not even claim high priority in their domestic economic and social development. For any regional economic cooperation scheme to function, all member states have to accept some amount of adjustment costs in the initial phases. The problem of uneven distribution of potential benefits and costs is also a real one. Any regional cooperative endeavor is apt to produce varying impacts in member countries with regard to their foreign trade patterns, production structures, and employment effects. Member states will naturally extend their full cooperation only if they perceive an equitable share of the gains. Some participating states tend to perceive that other member states with a more dynamic and outward-looking economy will stand to reap greater gains. This also explains why many regional economic cooperation schemes have involved a long process of negotiation and horse-trading.

In contrast, the benefits of many extraregional cooperation schemes to the member states can be immediate, and often with little or no adjustment cost. Not surprisingly, ASEAN's extraregional cooperation in the noneconomic areas has been much more effective and smooth-going. Largely because of its involvement in those extraregional activities, over the years ASEAN has become a highly visible regional grouping in the world, with a lot of political clout.

The ASEAN Way of Organizing Regional Cooperation

It has often been argued that ASEAN has owed its survival and continuing existence to its special techniques of organizing regional cooperation, the ASEAN Way. There is no clear definition for such an abstract term as the "ASEAN Way". It has been broadly understood to be the "Southeast Asian Way" of doing things, based on the region's mainstream sociocultural norms of compromise, consensus, tolerance, and mutual respect. Translated into the business of regional cooperation and community building, the ASEAN Way is much like an implicit code of conduct rather than as a set of explicit rules and procedures. Thus, in the process of regional cooperation, it emphasizes compromise through formal and informal consultation, consensus-based decision making, and avoidance of strict reciprocity, hard legalization, and rigid implementation time-frames.

In the political context, the ASEAN Way is underpinned by the strong desire of the member states to maintain their sovereignty on the one hand and also the need to maintain peaceful intra-ASEAN relations on the other. ASEAN was first formed at the time when the member states were in the process of nation-building, with some members also having a weak statehood. Hence, all member states put a heavy premium on sovereignty and independence. Accordingly, ASEAN's first move toward concrete regional cooperation was the conclusion of the Treaty of Amity and Cooperation (TAC) in 1976. From the outset, the ASEAN Way endorsed respect for the sovereignty and territorial integrity of all member states, and the principle of equal rights and noninterference in internal political affairs of member states.

Looking back, the ASEAN Way has been a kind of behavioral norm that made it possible for ASEAN to survive as an organization in its difficult initial years, given its divergent sociopolitical and economic backgrounds, and many outstanding bilateral conflicts. The ASEAN Way might not be the most desirable way, but it was an effective means of achieving the paramount objective of keeping ASEAN going. Subsequently, as ASEAN had consolidated itself and started to grow, the ASEAN Way, emphasizing consultation and consensus, had allowed member states to discuss in an informal manner their shared interests while avoiding conflict over regional issues. In this way, ASEAN has been slowly and gradually pushing ahead with its regional cooperation activities, sometimes even in an open-ended manner.

In addition to contributing to a good relationship among the member states, the ASEAN Way has also been useful and effective for ASEAN economic integration. As noted earlier, many developing-world regional groupings had collapsed precisely because they were highly institutionalized, with their regional schemes highly structured with ambitious goals and a rigid time table for implementation. Once something had failed to perform, the whole program would collapse. This is the exact opposite of the ASEAN Way of organizing regional activities (Wong, 1985).

In its early years, ASEAN had introduced some specific regional schemes for regional cooperation such as the preferential trading arrangements, ASEAN industrial projects, and ASEAN industrial complementation scheme. They were not successful, but their failure didn't pull down ASEAN, thanks to the operation of the ASEAN Way. Some ASEAN's economic cooperation programs did have specific timeframes; but the ASEAN Way allowed flexibility in implementation. The specified time framework can be pushed back as in the case of the AFTA; but it can also be moved forward, as in the case of accelerating the implementation of the AEC from Vision 2020 to Vision 2015.

Overall, the ASEAN Way has greatly facilitated ASEAN's past cooperation efforts. But there are costs and side-effects to ASEAN for operating the ASEAN

Way. Its major negative results are slow progress toward regional cooperation. Because of the ASEAN Way, ASEAN has failed to galvanize its efforts and determination to build up a strong momentum for any significant breakthrough in regional cooperation. After more than four decades of existence, ASEAN remains a loosely integrated grouping, with little substantive internal cohesion. By and large, member states still refuse to subordinate sovereignty and independence to the common regional good.

In the longer run, it is hard to see how the ASEAN Way can continue to function without adaptation and changes. As the ASEAN economies get more developed and the ASEAN organization grows more mature, regional activities are bound to become more institutionalized and the ASEAN community as a whole to become more rules-based. The working of the ASEAN Way will get diluted.

Specifically for the coming Vision 2015, the envisaged AEC is facing enormous challenges. Many ASEAN economies have barely recovered from the global financial crisis. With rising global economic uncertainty, it is hard to see how the ASEAN economies could build up a sufficiently strong economic foundation to launch the single market within such a short time span as four yours. The ASEAN Way, with great flexibility as its operating philosophy, might come in handy to salvage the situation and provide a way out for the ASEAN leaders. One likely scenario is to push the AEC back to Vision 2020. The other could be a diluted version of an "FTA-plus" AEC, operating under the principle of "Ten Minus X" (allowing some ASEAN members to opt out). The other is a further diluted version under the principle of "Two plus X" (just a few ASEAN economies to go ahead).

That is the ASEAN Way! It is the basic mechanism that has kept ASEAN going and constantly evolving in the EA region that is economically very dynamic but politically and socially highly divergent.

Some Distinguishing Features of EA Cooperation

EA is one of the world's most heterogeneous regions in terms of culture, language, religion, ethnicity, history, and traditions. Great disparity also exists between EA countries in respect of physical area, population size, and stages of economic development. Such economic and social discrepancies among states often stand in their way of organizing regional cooperation.

Even more significant is EA's history as a turbulent region, with many historical discords and on-going political frictions between EA countries. Before the coming of international detente, EA was a region of wars and many other forms of conflicts. Before World War II, most of the region had been colonized by different colonial powers. Japan launched the Pacific War in the 1930s and invaded other EA countries. After the War, the region became the battlefield of the Cold War, which actually gave rise to two "hot" wars (the Korean War and the Vietnam War).

As legacies of their past conflicts and hostilities, some EA countries today still have lingering bilateral problems with each other, for example the continuing suspicion among Japan, China, and Korea, and that between China and Vietnam. As discussed above, Japan's rise in the region came about by riding the USA's coat tails. China's rise today is still being quietly resisted by other EA countries, particularly Japan. Mutual trust remains a scarce commodity in the region. The rise of Japan and China has brought up the issue of whether "one mountain can have two tigers". Most recently, the territorial disputes over the South China Sea among several EA claimant states have flared up as a potential hot spot.

While "politics is cold" in the region, nonetheless its "economics is hot". Economically speaking, EA has been making impressive progress toward greater integration through its open, market-driven process; that is, this is done in terms of trade and investment, and many other forms of development cooperation. Increasingly, EA is becoming the most promising regional grouping after the EU.

As already mentioned earlier, EA increasingly looks like a "natural and compact economic grouping" with strong internal dynamics for regional economic integration. This is because its different components are economically complementary with each other: Japan is highly complementary with its northeast neighbors and also with ASEAN; ASEAN as a commodity exporter is complementary with the manufacturing exporter China; and the rise of regional production networks have further strengthened regional trade and investment flow.

Geography is another positive factor for EA integration. Both Northeast Asia and Southeast Asia as regions are quite compact, with many countries contiguous with each other. By comparison, other regions such as South America are faced with serious challenges of connectivity.

Operationally speaking, several critical factors have contributed to EA's success in economic integration. First, for many decades, the region has experienced dynamic economic growth, and successful economic development has greatly facilitated the regional integration process. Second, the region is blessed with two powerful regional engines of growth, first Japan and then China. Most developing-world economies are externally integrated, which works against their regional integration. EA is fortunate enough to have Japan and China to provide the regional source of trade and investment, as evidenced by its 50 percent of intraregional trade.

Last but not least, EA has ASEAN as the formal body of regional cooperation, which serves as a base for numerous intraregional and extraregional cooperation programs. Above all, the special technique of regional cooperation in EA as embodied in the ASEAN Way has been conducive to long-term cooperation efforts by patiently building up consensus and understanding. All in all, these aspects of EA's experience of regional economic cooperation could be instructive for South America.

PART II
Economic and Social Development

Chapter 5

The Need for a New South American Economic Regionalization

Renato Baumann

Introduction

Latin American economies have presented several improvements lately, as witnessed by low inflation indexes, reasonable export performance, attraction of foreign investment, increase in social expenditure, increasing concern with the environmental impacts of economic development, and improvement of the public finance sector, among other aspects.

There remain, however, a number of challenges to economic development, such as: the reduction of poverty levels and the concentration of wealth, and the need to increase investment ratios, reduce the economic distance from industrial economies, and improve infrastructure.

According to economic theory, international trade is an important tool (though not sufficient) for those purposes, because it allows for productive factors to be employed in the most efficient way, while at the same time allowing consumers to achieve maximum satisfaction from the availability of a larger quantity of goods and services.

An intermediate step toward free trade is the concession of preferential trade conditions to specific countries. These allow the firms in those countries to have freer access to a larger market, making it possible for them to produce on a bigger scale and have an additional source of gains. There are, therefore, grounds for arguments favoring the promotion of international trade and—for the developing economies in particular—regional integration.

Any given Latin American country would find it difficult to find common ground on the objectives and concessions granted among all the member countries of integration exercises such as the MERCOSUR, the Andean Community, or the Central American Common Market. Geographical proximity is a determining factor for certain levels of integration. At the same time, Latin American economies have been experiencing fierce competition from imported items from elsewhere, and there is no joint strategy to cope with that challenge.

The departure point for this article is the argument that a new regionalism requires a pragmatic, differentiated approach to addressing the preferences of the different countries in the region, depending on their geographical proximity, while at the same time recognizing that the Asian experience with productive complementarity calls for a joint, homogeneous course of action by the Latin American countries in order to deal with the challenge imposed by low-cost Asian products. The recent example provided by the countries involved in the Asian experience is illustrative of the positive impact a high degree of complementarity can have on export performance as well as on regional output growth.

This chapter consists of five sections: The next section discusses the different expectations associated with the preferences granted to neighboring and nonneighboring countries within a region and suggests that a "variable geometry" should be taken into account in Latin America. The third and fourth sections present indicators of trade performance and output growth in Asia and Latin America in recent years, to show that productive complementarity might pay in terms of providing more homogeneous growth at the regional level. The fifth section presents some conclusions.

Neighbors and Nonneighbors

Countries that are geographically close are natural candidates for more intense economic relations than those that are geographically distant. The corollary that one should look for is a variable geometry among participants in a process of "regionalization." This refers to the several possible negotiating formats as well as to the regional mechanisms in the monetary and financial areas.

One should have clearly identified limits of what can be expected in terms of neighbors and nonneighboring countries. In both cases the benefits from a higher degree of regionalization are related to the diversification of trade flows, the stability of foreign-exchange revenue and the fostering of the technological component of production. Nevertheless, what can be obtained among neighboring countries is different from what might be explored in a relationship with nonneighboring countries.

For nonneighboring countries, indicators of comparatively low levels of regional trade signal that there is potential to be explored; it is a matter of improving the conditions for the economic agents in each country to research and explore the markets of the other countries in the region. But this should not lead to ambitious expectations of economic convergence or even complementarity of productive processes in the participating countries.

Regionalism is essentially the creation of a favorable environment for business among the countries in a given region, in comparison to third parties from elsewhere. In principle, it is expected that the potential for gains should surpass the losses, assuming that the type of agreement required for that does not comprise the adoption of common external barriers; hence the risks of trade diversion are limited.

This is different from deepening the process of regional integration, which might be comprised of various dimensions. In this case, the basic question is: Is what the participating countries want: to essentially facilitate bilateral trade? Is it a means to foster trade relations and productive complementarity? Or is it a means to reach common economic, political, and cultural objectives?

The Latin American experience, beyond purely economic objectives, has a strong component of political commitment. Even in the economic field, the negotiating agenda often goes beyond trade facilitation and in some cases even includes efforts to homogenize the incentives of industrialization and the treatment of external capital, among other dimensions. The very multiplicity of policy targets can be a consequence of the lack of precise objectives. This may be one reason for the limited success of Latin American integration efforts.

Furthermore, in Latin America, the external shocks have traditionally been dealt with on an individual basis by the different countries. One indication is the sharp accumulation of reserves of foreign currencies, as a self-insurance against shocks. As opposed to Asia, there is hardly any significant joint initiative with regard to monetary and financial cooperation in the region.

In this sense, the variable geometry proposed here should also include monetary integration, that is to say the building up of regional financial mechanisms that might help the countries in the region to cope with external shocks and to finance infrastructure projects. This is, to some extent, independent of the geographical proximity of the participating countries, and different from those projects aiming at productive complementarity.

Hence the argument presented here has three dimensions: 1. there are differences between what can be expected from the intensification of relations between neighboring and nonneighboring countries; 2. this has different impacts on the productive structure; and 3. there are benefits stemming from parallel measures promoting the convergence of the productive complementarity and monetary and/or financial cooperation.

Furthermore, there is the argument that trade liberalization reduces distortions, so that regional preferences should be considered as steps in that direction. There are at least two other arguments to be considered in favor of promoting regionalism in Latin America.

First, tariff preferences both within the region and with third parties account for a large part—two-thirds—of regional trade in Latin America. Reducing the disparities among the several preferential agreements should create more opportunities to foster regional trade.

Second, regional trade preferences tend to benefit trade in products with higher added-value. There is clearly a component of industrialized products in trade relations with other Latin American countries that is much higher than observed in trade with other regions.

The argument for a differentiated treatment to neighboring and nonneighboring countries can be clarified by a taxonomic discussion about the effects of regional trade.

Reasons for More Regionalism

The benefits associated with regional agreements can be classified into three groups: 1. those related to trade and its consequences for the productive structure; 2. the effects on external policies; and 3. the effects over the external actions of the participating countries.

The first group of effects—on trade and the productive structure—includes:

1. Direct effects related to trade
    i. Competition with products from neighboring countries leads the producers in third countries to reduce their prices in the domestic markets of the participating countries.
    ii. As a consequence, there are gains in the terms of trade for the participating countries.
2. Effects on the domestic production process
    i. The expanded regional market allows for the existence of bigger firms, while increased competition reduces prices.
    ii. Competition reduces production inefficiencies, with firms more focused on specific market segments.
    iii. Firms can shift their production activities in accordance to factor costs, hence those countries that provide better infrastructure or a more qualified labor force tend to gain more.
    iv Dividing the production process into stages located in various countries in accordance to costs can contribute to the reduction of overall costs and foster competitiveness.
3. Effects on investment
    i. Regional agreements—by signaling the access to a broader market, with improved production rationalization, hence better potential for investment returns—tend to stimulate investment by domestic and external investors.

A second group of effects include:

1. The effects on domestic policy reforms.
2. The signing of external agreements can be an important tool for governments to make viable several domestic policies that would otherwise be hard to implement. This is the case, for example, of tariff reforms, policies toward foreign investors, privatization of public firms and other policies. This assumes, of course, that there is a clear perception, by economic agents, that belonging to an association of countries provides social gains in the long-run that surpass the costs in the short term.
3. The effects of signaling the direction for economic and institutional policies
4. In some cases, the short-term costs of adhering to a regional agreement might be seen as too high by a given country. But the country might opt for participating in a given exercise if it considers that in so doing it provides

potential investors with signals that improve its capacity to attract new resources, by showing, for instance, a clear commitment to macroeconomic equilibrium.

A third group of effects—linked to the external position of the countries—include:

1. "Prophylactic" effects
   Belonging to a set of countries should allow each individual country to increase its security in relation to external shocks. Asymmetric shocks in the terms of trade, possible armed conflicts, and other threats can be avoided or monitored when there are agreements among countries.
2. External negotiating capacity
   Once the countries in a given integration exercise reach convergence in their positions about relevant issues, the very fact that they can negotiate as a group provides them with higher visibility in international forums and better negotiating capacity. A good example is the MERCOSUR experience in the negotiations for a hemispheric Free Trade Area of the Americas (FTAA).
3. Effects on security
   Belonging to a group of countries not only alters the trade and investment flows but also creates relations of interdependency among participants. This tends to reduce the risks of trade or armed conflicts, and there should exist mechanisms for cooperation.

These are some of the main effects often emphasized in the literature on regional integration. From the perspective of the argument presented in this paper, one should try to identify which effects can be expected from the association with nonneighboring countries, assuming that the agreements aim only at trade preferences and monetary cooperation, and do not include commitment clauses with regard to common economic policies or other considerations, such as security issues involved.

From the perspective of geographically distant economies in a given region, it makes more sense to think that there is a higher probability that the agreements are essentially trade preferences, with no common external tariffs for the simple reason that it is difficult dealing with "rules of origin" when there is a significant geographical distance.

One can expect therefore that the first group of effects (those on trade and the productive structure, except item 2.iv) is more likely to be obtained in preferential agreements among distant partners. The effects on investment are essentially just a possibility, depending on the structure of the agreement and the relative importance of the participating economies.

Geographically distant countries can also benefit more from the effect of regional agreements than the reform of domestic policies. Once again, this is a function of the relative importance of bilateral relations.

As opposed to geographically distant countries, neighboring countries may benefit from all the effects mentioned above. This means a varied set of potential effects that should be thoroughly explored with clear objectives by Latin American countries.

In summary, contiguous countries can expect a set of direct and indirect benefits stemming from regional integration that obviously depends on a successful and harmonious process of approximation among the participating countries. At the same time, countries that are distant in geographical terms can also have benefits, albeit more limited, associated with the impact of trade and the creation of regional mechanisms for monetary and financial cooperation.

Having stressed this differentiation, the following sections further explain the actual achievements in the region with regards to complementarity.

Some Lessons from Elsewhere

Regional trade in Latin America has seldom been based on clear economic objectives. It has been considered, instead, as synonymous with regional integration, hence dependent upon the signing of formal agreements, often with a more political motivation. The recent Asian experience (East Asia in particular) provides an example of a more practical approach, where production complementarity certainly has contributed significantly to both export performance and more homogeneous output growth.

Furthermore, in Asia the very fact that a good deal of regional trade is comprised of producer goods[1] is a determining element in providing a dynamic element to the least developed economies in the region, at the same time that it helps consolidate production links that help keep the output growth stimuli within the region.

I have named this process a "regional multiplier effect:" derived demand for producer goods within the region provides the resources for the consumption of regionally produced final goods, and both the countries that are net producers of inputs and the producers of final goods gain from regional trade. As a consequence, output growth is likely to become more homogeneous, with a higher correlation among the business cycles of the participating countries.

The relevance of emphasizing the role of producer goods for analysis stems from the two peculiar characteristics of these products:[1] the demand for producer goods is a derived demand, hence it is closely linked to the overall activity of the economy; and 2. even more important, the role of these products in the diffusion of technical progress. Technological changes are embedded in the characteristics of the productive process, so the more intense the involvement of a given economy with the production and commercialization of these products, the

---

1   These products are not only capital goods, but all those products (including raw materials, parts, and components) that are consumed in the production processes.

higher the chances that it will benefit from the opportunities of access to updated technological information.

The following analysis is based on a model with leading economies ("hubs"), that is, those economies that are big enough for their growth to affect other smaller ("spokes") economies in the region.

The presumed mechanism of a regional multiplier (using Asia as an example) would operate as follows.

An (exogenous) increase in the demand for, say, Chinese products increases imports by China of manufactured intermediate products made in a regional spoke (country A), required to support China's productive process. A's exports to China increase at higher rates than A's exports to the rest of the world (ROW). Trade with a regional hub is the dynamic component. A's export increase fosters A's industrial production and A's income. This allows for an increase, in a subsequent period, of A's imports of final goods from China. This "spillover effect" on imports from China takes place with higher intensity than on imports from ROW (due to lower relative costs, consumer preferences, and closer trade networks).

As a consequence, China's growth: (1) was made viable by the use of regional producers; (2) had a "multiplier effect" on neighboring countries; and (3) had

Table 5.1   **Asia and Latin America: Trade in Producer Goods and Other Goods, 1992–2008**

ASIA	Average 1992–1999	Average 2000–2008	LATIN AMERICA	Average 1992–1999	Average 2000–2008
Amount exported (US$ billion)					
Total goods	1.263	2.691	Total goods	217	507
Producer goods	759	1.625	Producer goods	88	201
Other goods	503	1.066	Other goods	129	305
Percentage of regional exports					
Total goods	46,5%	49,9%	Total goods	17,8%	15,4%
Producer goods	50,8%	54,8%	Producer goods	20,8%	16,7%
Other goods	40,1%	41,9%	Other goods	15,9%	14,7%
Amount imported (US$ billion)					
Total goods	1.165	2.435	Total goods	325	634
Producer goods	667	1.312	Producer goods	205	384
Other goods	498	1.123	Other goods	119	249
Percentage of imports from ROW					
Total goods	49,3%	45,4%	Total goods	61,3%	61,5%
Producer goods	44,1%	35,9%	Producer goods	65,4%	66,7%
Other goods	56,3%	57,4%	Other goods	54,0%	52,9%

Source: own processing of primary data from UN/COMTRADE Database.

positive effects on China's own trade balance and restimulates a renewed demand for A's products.

It is expected that given the production linkages among Asian countries, a similar (although eventually less intense) relationship can be found with regard to Japan, India, and South Korea. In Latin America, the natural candidates to regional hubs are Argentina, Brazil, and Mexico.

According to Table 5.1, not only is the relative importance of regional exports on total exports higher in Asia (50 percent) as compared to Latin America (15 percent in the last decade), but the percentage of regional trade in producer goods is far more important in regional trade in the former region (over half of the exports of these products are destined to the regional market) than in the latter (where this percentage fell to less than 20 percent in the last decade).

The different magnitudes of trade flows are also evident in the import side. For example, comparing the imports coming from the ROW, the ratio between the amounts actually imported by the two regions was around 3.8:1 in the last decade. When the types of products are considered, the proportion of producer goods is similar to the total (3.4:1), indicating that on the import side there is not such a marked difference as in the export side. Other products (ratio of 4.5:1) are more important for Asian imports. As is well known, these include a good deal or commodities.

The fact that regional exports as a percentage of total exports is of greater importance in Asia may reflect the simple existence of more significant business opportunities in that region, which would naturally imply more intense trade relations. A better comparison of the intensity of regional trade is to consider the actual transactions that take place in each region in comparison to what could be expected, given their relative trade flows with the ROW. This is the so-called Trade Intensity Index (ITI).[2] Figure 5.1 and 5.2 show the basic indicators.

First, in both regions the indexes are above unity, which indicates a higher intensity of regional trade than expected, based on the current place of both regions in the world market. Second, figures for Asia—both for producer goods and for other goods—have remained around 2.0 over time, indicating a relative stability in this comparative indicator. Third, and perhaps most significant, the indicators for Latin America are higher than for Asia, for both types of goods. This is in conformity with the argument presented elsewhere (Baumann, 2010a) that the achievement of regional integration in Latin America has required a great deal of effort, in view of its relatively limited (about 6 percent) participation in world GDP and world trade, hence the limited opportunities for business within

---

2   Intraregional trade intensity index (ITI) is computed as ITI $=[(X_{ii}/(X_{iw} + X_{wi})/2]/[((X_{iw} + X_{wi})/2)/X_{ww}]$ where X_{ii} is exports of region i to region i; X_{ww} is the total world exports; and X_{iw} and X_{wi} are exports of region i to the world and exports of the world to region i, respectively. The value of index above (or below) unity indicates the bilateral trade flow that is larger (or smaller) than expected, given the trading partners' importance in the world trade.

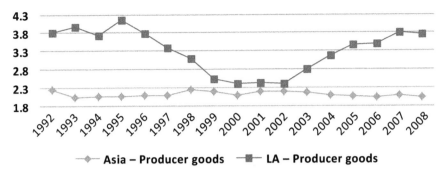

Figure 5.1   Asia and Latin America—Intraregional Trade Intensity Index—Producer Goods—1992–2008

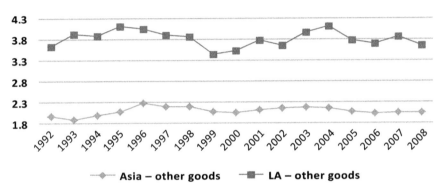

Figure 5.2   Asia and Latin America—Intraregional Trade Intensity Index—Other Goods—1992–2008

the region. It is worth noting, in any case, that the indicator for intraregional trade in producer goods in Latin America has had a very unstable trajectory over time when compared with other goods. This apparently reflects the low priority given to trade in these goods in the region.

There are obvious marked differences between the two regions, and even more so according to the type of products actually transacted. These differences also include the degree of concentration of their trade flows.

Figure 5.3 shows that the intraregional trade in "other goods" in Latin America is far more concentrated than in Asia. The remarkable thing to notice, however, is that the difference in terms of concentration between the two regions is much higher in intraregional trade: the concentration of Latin American intraregional trade is twice as much as Asia's.

As far as the regional trade in producer goods is concerned, however (Figure 5.4), the Asian countries seem to be more focused, as their intraregional trade was not only far more important in value terms, but also far less dispersed during most of the period of analysis, with the exception of the last two years.

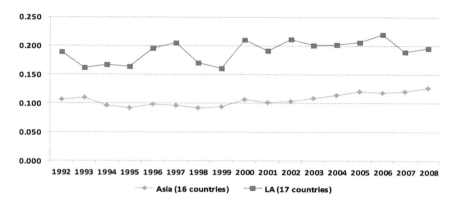

**Figure 5.3   Asia and Latin America—Export Concentration Index—
                Intraregional Trade in "Other" Goods—1992–2008**

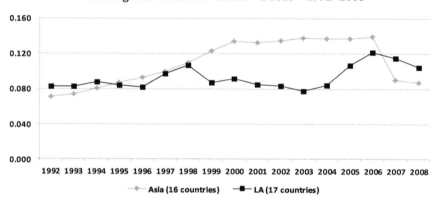

**Figure 5.4   Asia and Latin America—Export Concentration Index—
                Intraregional Trade in Producer Goods—1992–2008**

Since the present analysis stresses the role of hub and spoke countries, the next step is to evaluate these two groups of countries' trade relations with the other countries in the same region compared with the concentration of trade with the rest of the world.

As far as the trade in producer goods is concerned (Figures 5.5 and 5.6), the overall degree of concentration in Latin American exports by spoke countries to the ROW is much higher (three or more times) than in Asia. In both cases the intraregional exports by spoke countries are systematically more diversified than their exports to the ROW. This should not be surprising, since small economies tend to be less competitive in international markets, hence they have better chances of market access on the basis of preferential treatment or as an outcome of productive complementarity.

Furthermore, the Asian spoke countries have diversified their exports of producer goods to the ROW to the point that in recent years the degree of

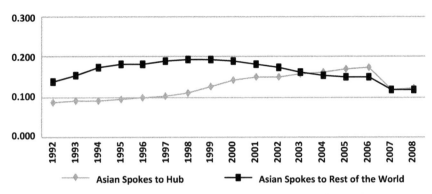

Figure 5.5   Asian Spoke Countries—Export Concentration Index— Producer Goods—1992–2008

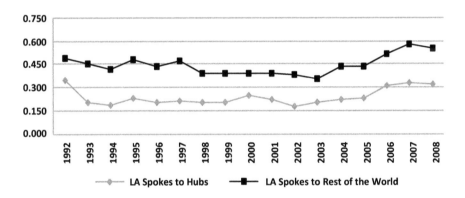

Figure 5.6   Latin American Spoke Countries—Export Concentration Index—Producer Goods—1992–2008

concentration of both trade flows is similar. In Latin America, however, the two curves show an increasing trend, indicating increasingly concentrated exports.

The evidence related to producer goods can be summarized as: 1. Asian countries export a much higher value and a much higher proportion of producer goods than Latin Americans; 2. both regions present similar degrees of concentration in their exports of producer goods to the ROW, but this is by and large explained by the similar degree of concentration of the exports of the hub countries in the two regions, whereas the differences are more pronounced among the spoke countries; 3. regional trade in producer goods is much more concentrated in Asia than in Latin America; and 4. the regional exports of producer goods by the spoke countries in Asia are more diversified than their exports to the ROW, but they have systematically increased in important proportions the degree of diversification of their exports to the ROW, suggesting a gradual gain in competitiveness, with the inclusion of new export products in the bill.

The Homogeneity of Regional Growth

These different trade patterns have various consequences for the actual degree of convergence of the yearly GDP growth rates in each region. If growth takes place in a more homogeneous way in one region than in another, this should be reflected in a reduced degree of dispersion of GDP among the countries in the former region. This hypothesis can be tested by estimating an indicator of concentration of GDPs for each region. Figure 5.7 shows the results for the estimates of the Herfindahl–Hirschman Index (HHI):[3] the lower the index the more homogeneous the set of observations.

In Latin America the (limited) degree of homogeneity among the GDPs of the several countries remained rather constant over the whole period. This means that the distance between the bigger and the smaller economies has not varied significantly over two decades. This is particularly remarkable (and worrying) for a region where there have been frequent efforts to provide preferential trade treatment coupled with common external tariffs.

As seen in Figure 5.7, during the same time period, however, there was a sharp reduction of the degree of concentration in Asia, meaning that the smaller economies have been able to grow at such a pace that the distance of their national products to the products of the bigger economies in the region has diminished at a very significant pace.

In order to check this hypothesis, we analyzed the variation over time of the GDP values in constant 2,000 US dollars of several countries in both regions. The regional total in this case is, evidently, the sum of the GDPs of the individual countries considered in this sample. Table 5.2 summarizes the main results.

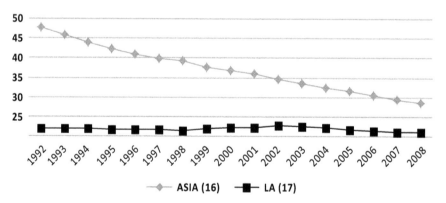

Figure 5.7   Asia and Latin America—HHI for GDP in Constant Prices—1992–2008

---

3   The Index is estimated as $Hj = \mathrm{SQRT(SUM}\ ij\ (xi/X)\text{\textasciicircum}2))$ where xi is the value of GDP of country i and X is the total value of GDP in the region j. This index (in this original, nonnormalized form) has values varying between 0 and +∞.

Table 5.2   Asia and Latin America—Indicators of Convergence of GDP Growth Rates—1992–2008

	Region	1992–2008	1992–1999	2000–2008
Standard Deviation of Individual Countries' Growth Rates in Relation to Total Regional Growth	Latin America	0.235	0.364	0.212
	Asia	0.193	0.420	0.181
Mean Correlation Index between GDP Growth Rates for "Hubs" and "Spokes" Countries	Latin America	0.625	0.267	0.871
	Asia	0.746	0.878	0.869

Source: Author's own processing based on primary data from World Bank (WDI, 2010).

According to the upper part of Table 5.2, it is clear that the degree of homogeneity of the growth process in Asia is much higher than in Latin America, as reflected by a smaller standard deviation of the growth rates of individual countries in relation to the regional total. It is worth noting that the degree of convergence in Asia surpassed the corresponding Latin American indicator in the last decade. This should be no surprise, since it is only since the late 1990s that a number of Asian countries have adopted a more open policy facilitating their production links with the regional hubs.

As already mentioned, the set of indicators presented so far are suggestive of the existence of a regional multiplier. Essentially, the idea is that where there is regional trade in producer goods in exchange for other goods between hubs and spoke countries, there is a virtuous process the exports of producer goods by a spoke might stimulate its imports of other goods from the hub, hence both countries gain and the process seems sustainable over time. There is a multiplication process.

In order to verify the existence of such mechanism the analysis has focused on 13 vectors:

- Exports of producer goods from spokes to hubs (XSpgH)
- Exports of other goods from spokes to hubs (XSogH)
- Imports of other goods by spokes from hubs (MSogH)
- Imports of other goods from hubs by hubs (MHogH)
- Imports of producer goods from hubs by hubs (MHpgH)
- Exports of producer goods from spokes to spokes (XSpgS)
- Exports of other goods from spokes to spokes (XSogS)
- Exports of producer goods by spokes to ROW (XSpgRW)
- Exports of other goods by spokes to ROW (XSogRW)
- Imports of other goods by spokes from ROW (MSogRW)
- Exports of producer goods by hubs to ROW (XHpgRW)
- Exports of other goods by hubs to ROW (XHogRW), and
- Imports of other goods by hubs from ROW (MHogRW).

Table 5.3   Asia and Latin America—Correlation between Selected Pairs of Indicators

	1992–2006				
	Asia			Latin America	
Corr (ΔXSpgH. ΔMSogH) > Corr (ΔXSpgH. ΔMSogRW)	0.954 > 0.831	OK		0.699 < 0.779	NO
Corr (ΔXSogH. ΔMSogH) > Corr (ΔXSogRW. ΔMSogRW)	0.917 > 0.826	OK		0.736 > 0.413	OK
Corr (ΔXSpgH. ΔMSogH) > Corr (ΔXHogRW. ΔMHogRW)	0.954 > 0.381	OK		0.699 > 0.515	OK
Corr (ΔXSogS. ΔXSpgS) > Corr (ΔXSpgRW. ΔMSogRW)	0.761 > 0.635	OK		0.896 > 0.614	OK
Corr (ΔMHogH. ΔMHpgH) > Corr (ΔXHpgRW. ΔMHogRW)	0.868 > 0.744	OK		0.861 > 0.501	OK

With these results in mind, we now turn to evaluate the five relationships between specific correlation indexes, as mentioned. Table 5.3 shows the basic results.

According to Table 5.3, both regions present the degree of intracohesion that characterizes regional experiments. Even with much smaller values involved, it is to some extent rather surprising—on the basis of previous reasoning—that in Latin America the variations of regional trade flows seem to be more coordinated than the trade relations with the ROW. Trade in other goods between hubs and spokes is more correlated than trade in these products with the ROW, trade among hubs is more correlated than trade of hubs in other goods with the ROW, and the same applies to trade among spokes.

The biggest difference is to be found—again as originally argued—in the actual relationship between exports of producer goods by spokes to hubs and their imports of other goods. In Asia, there is clearly a link between exports by spokes and imports from hubs that is more intense than the alternative exports by spokes and imports from the ROW. This characterizes a regional multiplier, where both types of countries gain over time. As expected, a different scenario is observed in Latin America: there is a "leakage" in the regional flow that leads part of the foreign currency earned by spokes from their exports to regional hubs to be spent in other goods from the ROW.[4]

It seems reasonable to accept, therefore, that in Asia the complementarities in the production process, coupled with the preferences for regional final products, lead to a virtuous process that is more intense than the relations with other regions. Furthermore, this result was obtained in a period of worsening of the terms of trade, yet with quite high output growth rates for the Asian hub economies.

In Latin America, however, the regional links are not sufficient to compensate for the already existing strong links with other regions, so that a given stimulus

---

4   Increasingly of Asian origin.

will sooner or later imply more imports from the ROW than stimulate regional transactions.

The Need for Differentiated Treatment Between Neighbors and Nonneighbors: The Differences Among Subregional Groupings

The indicators presented so far refer to the two regions as a whole. There are, however, some remarkable differences among subsets of countries in each region.

There are clear differences between East and South Asia, in terms of the relative weight of regional transactions. In the former, not only is the participation in regional trade significantly high—coming close to half of total trade in exports and surpassing the 50 percent mark for imports—but this share has increased further in the last decade. This is true for both producer and other goods, but it is worth emphasizing that regional suppliers provide almost two-thirds of the imports of producer goods. For South Asia, on the other hand, regional trade accounts for less than 7 percent and that share has remained rather constant since 1992 (Table 5.4).

The indication of intense trade at the subregional level reinforces the reasoning about the existence of "leading" (hubs) economies and their links with the other (spokes) economies in each group of countries. Table 5.5 illustrates this point for East and South Asia. In each line the direction of trade is identified by the origin followed by the destination of each flow.

As far as the composition of regional trade flows is concerned, the first aspect that stands out from Table 5.5 is the high share of producer goods in the indicators for East Asia: over 60 percent of the trade between the hubs and the spoke countries (as well as among the spokes) is comprised of these goods. But even more significant is the fact that this share was somewhat reduced between the 1990s and the following decade in terms of the exports by the hubs to the spoke countries, whereas the exports by the spoke countries to the hubs has increased significantly. This consolidates a productive networking at the regional level that is perhaps matched only in Western Europe, among countries of quite similar levels of development.

Table 5.4   East and South Asia—Composition of Regional Trade, 1992–2008

	Total goods Regional/total trade		Producer goods Regional/total trade		Other goods Regional/total trade	
	1992–1999	2000–2008	1992–1999	2000–2008	1992–1999	2000–2008
Exports:						
East Asia	46%	49%	50%	53%	40%	43%
South Asia	4%	4%	6%	6%	3%	3%
Imports:						
East Asia	51%	55%	56%	65%	44%	43%
South Asia	3%	3%	4%	3%	3%	2%

Source: Based on UN COMTRADE Statistics.

Table 5.5   East and South Asia—Composition of Regional and External Trade, 1992–2008

	Producer goods		Other goods	
	Mean 1992–1999	Mean 2000–2008	Mean 1992–1999	Mean 2000–2008
East Asia:				
exphubs–spokesEastAsia	69%	67%	31%	33%
expspokes–spokesEastAsia	64%	66%	36%	34%
expspokes–hubsEastAsia	58%	66%	42%	34%
expspokesEastAsia–ROW	52%	55%	48%	45%
impspokesEastAsia–ROW	59%	49%	41%	51%
exphubsEastAsia–ROW	62%	58%	38%	42%
imphubsEastAsia–ROW	43%	38%	57%	62%
South Asia:				
exphubs–spokesSouthAsia	57%	45%	43%	55%
expspokes–spokesSouthAsia	36%	51%	64%	49%
expspokes–hubsSouthAsia	22%	46%	78%	54%
expspokesSouthAsia–ROW	31%	23%	69%	77%
impspokesSouthAsia–ROW	57%	51%	43%	49%
exphubsSouthAsia–ROW	31%	35%	69%	65%
imphubsSouthtAsia–ROW	41%	38%	59%	62%

Source: Based on UN COMTRADE Statistics.

It is worth noting, furthermore, that in their trade with the ROW, the East Asian hub countries import relatively higher shares of other goods than the spoke countries, which rely heavily on the supply by the regional hubs.

These indicators are, once again, suggestive of a regional multiplier effect, where spoke countries provide producer goods to the hub countries and import other goods mostly from them.

A different scenario is found in South Asia. Over time, there has been an increase in the relative importance of exports of producer goods by spoke countries to the hub countries (as well as to other spokes). This has reduced the relative participation of these products in the regional imports from the ROW. But the figures are much lower in comparison to East Asia and the intensity of these movements has been far more limited.

For Latin America, the indications of the relative weight of regional trade are much lower than in East Asia but far higher than in South Asia (Table 5.6). Also, there are marked differences between continents. The typical figure for South America is in the neighborhood of 20 percent, whereas in Central America it does not surpass 5 percent of total trade.

The second and third columns of Table 5.6 show that the relative importance of overall regional trade in Central and South America is much lower than in Asia and has actually decreased between these two periods. This corresponds to the significant market diversification that has taken place for the exports of these economies.

Table 5.6   Latin America—Composition of Regional Trade, 1992–2008

	Total goods Regional/total trade		Producer goods Regional/total trade		Other goods Regional/total trade	
	1992–1999	2000–2008	1992–1999	2000–2008	1992–1999	2000–2008
Exports:						
Central America	3%	3%	3%	3%	4%	4%
South America	24%	20%	34%	29%	19%	16%
Andean						
Countries	11%	10%	20%	16%	8%	8%
Mercosur	21%	14%	26%	21%	18%	12%
Imports:						
Central America	3%	3%	2%	2%	5%	5%
South America	23%	26%	16%	19%	35%	36%
Andean						
Countries	11%	14%	7%	9%	17%	19%
MERCOSUR	20%	19%	14%	15%	29%	26%

Source: Based on UN COMTRADE Statistics.

This result is, of course, highly influenced by the terms of trade effects,[5] which have affected positively most economies in South America in recent years.

There are, furthermore, marked differences in trade composition among sub-regions, as shown in Table 5.7. In Central America, not only is the weight of regional trade quite limited (as already shown); there has actually been an intense reduction in the participation of producer goods in regional trade between 1992–1999 and 2000–2008. The counterpart of this movement is that the degree of dependency of both hub and spoke countries of imports of these products from the ROW has remained stable at quite high levels over time.

Conversely, in South America there was an increase in the share of producer goods among the exports of spoke countries to the hubs—indicating a movement in the right direction—and the exports of these products by the hubs to the spoke countries has remained rather constant. As an outcome, there has been a reduction in the imports of producer goods by both hubs and spoke countries from the ROW between the two periods.

In the Andean countries, the share of producer goods in the trade between hubs and spoke countries was reduced for the exports from hubs to spokes and vice versa. In the latter case (from spokes to hubs) producer goods exports decreased quite significantly, from 42 percent to only 29 percent of regional trade flows. Nevertheless—and in contrast to the Asian experience—there has also been a simultaneous fall in the share of producer goods in the trade of these countries with the ROW: there were significant reductions in the shares of producer goods

---

5   In 2000–2008 as a whole, the Asian terms of trade losses ranged from 1 percent in Hong Kong and Thailand to 3 percent in China, Thailand, Korea, and the Philippines. In Latin America, the gains ranged from 1.5 percent in Brazil to not less than 18 percent in Venezuela.

Table 5.7   Latin America—Composition of Regional and External Trade, 1992–2008

	Producer goods		Other goods	
	1992–1999	**2000–2008**	**1992–1999**	**2000–2008**
Central America:				
exphubs–spokesCAm	53%	46%	47%	54%
expspokes–spokesCAm	42%	37%	58%	63%
expspokes–hubsCAm	42%	29%	58%	71%
expspokesCAm–ROW	19%	24%	81%	76%
impspokesCAm–ROW	66%	66%	34%	34%
exphubsCAm–ROW	54%	55%	46%	45%
imphubsCAm–ROW	68%	68%	32%	32%
South America:				
exphubs–spokesSAm	50%	49%	50%	51%
expspokes–spokesSAm	37%	34%	63%	66%
expspokes–hubsSAm	31%	35%	69%	65%
expspokesSAm–ROW	20%	20%	80%	80%
impspokesSAm–ROW	66%	59%	34%	41%
exphubsSAm–ROW	35%	33%	65%	67%
imphubsSAm–ROW	70%	68%	30%	32%
Andean countries:				
exphubs–spokesAC	45%	40%	55%	60%
expspokes–spokesAC	42%	37%	58%	63%
expspokes–hubsAC	42%	29%	58%	71%
expspokesAC–ROW	19%	24%	81%	76%
impspokesAC–ROW	57%	48%	43%	52%
exphubsAC–ROW	11%	10%	89%	90%
imphubsAC–ROW	67%	61%	33%	39%
MERCOSUR				
exphubs–spokesM	64%	62%	36%	38%
expspokes–spokesM	47%	49%	53%	51%
expspokes–hubsM	31%	36%	69%	64%
expspokesM–ROW	21%	20%	79%	80%
impspokesM–ROW	69%	68%	31%	32%
exphubsM–ROW	42%	36%	58%	59%
imphubsM–ROW	67%	65%	33%	35%

Source: Based on UN COMTRADE Statistics.

both in the imports by hubs and by spoke countries. This is particularly odd, especially when one considers that the value (in constant US dollars) of the Fixed Gross Capital Formation in the Andean countries has doubled between 1992 and 2008, and its share of GDP remained rather constant (21 percent in the first period and 20 percent in the second). The explanation seems to lie in the remarkable performance of trade in other goods with developing countries.

In MERCOSUR, the trajectory has been more similar to the East Asian experience. The share of producer goods in the exports by the hub country (Brazil) to the spokes has varied slightly, but at the same time there has been a significant increase in the share of these products in the exports by the spokes to the hub. As a consequence—again, as seen in East Asia—there has been a small reduction in the share of producer goods in the imports from the ROW by both hub and spoke countries.

These indicators explain the indications of convergence among the economic potential of the countries in each group of countries. A traditional indicator of convergence and/or divergence of a set of observations—the relative entropy indexes[6] shown in Table 5.8—indicate a set of varied situations in these groups of countries. The higher the index, the more intense the movement toward an increasing degree of homogeneity of the sample, as the weight of each observation would have increased relatively.

Table 5.8   Relative Entropy Indexes of GDP, 1992–2008

	1992–1999	2000–2008
East Asia	0.139	0.161
South Asia	0.218	0.197
Central America	0.103	0.110
Andean Countries:	0.399	0.412
without Chile	0.356	0.372
MERCOSUR	0.158	0.151

Source: Computations based on World Bank WDI database.

The figures in Table 5.8 show that the most remarkable performance in reducing the differences among the GDPs of the participant countries has taken place in East Asia, where the entropy index has increased over 15 percent between the two periods. A good deal of the dynamism that provided such convergence had to do with the increasing degree of productive complementarities among the economies in this subregion.

This is not a characteristic of all Asian countries, though. In South Asia, where the regional trade in producer goods is rather limited, the dependency upon imports of other goods from developing countries is much stronger than regional trade or productive links therefore, the degree of homogeneity in GDP growth of the South Asia countries has, if anything, reduced between the 1990s and the 2000s.

These are two good examples of the importance of building up a regional multiplier mechanism. Asian countries have suffered in the 2000s quite significant losses in their terms of trade. While in East Asia this has been more than compensated for by the network of subregional production and trade relations,

---

6   The relative entropy index (IRE) is computed as IRE = $\text{sum}(Y_{ij} * LN(1/Y_{ij}) / \max(LN(1/Y_{ij}))$, where Y_{ij} is the share of GDP of country's i in total GDP of region j. Computations are based on the World Bank, World Development Indicators database.

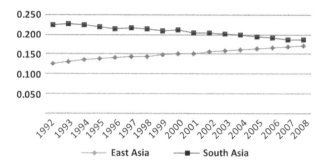

Figure 5.8   East Asia and South Asia—Relative Entropy Indexes of GDP in Constant US Dollars—1992–2008

which has allowed for an increased homogeneity of the growth process, in South Asia the dependency upon extra-regional trade has actually accentuated the differences among the economies in the subregion.

The Latin American experience is also varied. Regional trade in producer goods is quite low, even where it is most significant, such as in the MERCOSUR: in the 2000s, on average trade in producer goods within the MERCOSUR corresponded to only 1 percent of the trade in these products within East Asia.

Another difference between Latin America and Asia is that the former (especially South America) benefitted significantly from the gains in terms of trade in the 2000s. This has had, of course, a significant impact on GDP growth.

Figure 5.9 illustrates the trajectories of the entropy indexes for Central America, the Andean countries and the MERCOSUR. The first thing to notice is that since the beginning of the period of analysis, the Andean countries showed a far more homogeneous degree of GDP growth than observed in MERCOSUR and—even more—in Central America. The degree of homogeneity in the Andean countries increased up to 2003 and has reduced slightly since then. But the degree of variation is very low.

In Central America and in the MERCOSUR the variations between the two decades are also minimal, meaning that the differences among the potential of the economies in these groups of countries have essentially remained the same over two decades.

This is not to say that there has been no growth or even that growth in the second decade was worse than in the first. Table 5.9 summarizes the rates of growth in these groups of countries during the two periods. Except for Central America in the 2000s, every other grouping of countries showed more dynamism than in the 1990s.

The argument is that, out of these five groups of countries, it was only in East Asia where the existence of intense productive complementarities have been able to counter act a worsening of the terms of trade and at the same time increase the average rate of GDP growth and foster the degree of homogeneity among

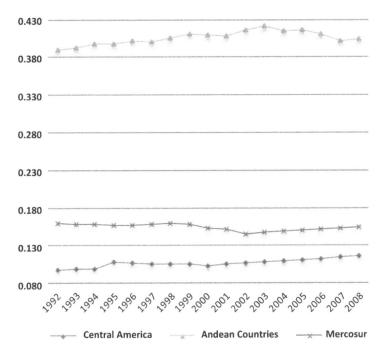

Figure 5.9 **Central America, Andean Countries and MERCOSUR— Relative Entropy Indexes of GDP in Constant US Dollars—1992–2008**

Table 5.9 **Mean (*) GDP Growth Rates (percent), 1992–2008**

	Mean 1992–1999	Mean 2000–2008
East Asia	2.9	4.0
South Asia	5.7	6.7
Central America	3.2	3.0
Andean countries	3.0	4.7
MERCOSUR	3.1	3.7

Note: (*) weighted average.
Source: World Bank, World Development Indicators, 2010.

the economies, even when the bigger economies in the region were growing at a quite fast pace. At the same time, Latin American economies have profited from favorable international conditions, but their average rate of growth was much lower than in Asia and even so the differences among the countries in the region have remained constant over two decades.

Conclusions

In this article I have argued that in Latin America a dual or multiple-track approach should be pursued to foster economic relations on a regional basis and that there is a need for promoting productive complementarity as a means to face competition of products from other regions. Additionally, it was shown that the recent example provided by East Asian countries is quite illustrative of the positive impact a higher degree of productive complementarity can have on the export performance and output growth of the countries within a region.

This requires a political decision to identify a precise direction for the regional negotiations of preferences, aiming at building up joint efforts so as to jointly explore developing markets, and avoiding the conflicts generated by the disputes in terms of the actual share each countries achieves in the neighboring market.

A more well-designed process should pay off in terms of creating a degree of complementarity and hence a regional multiplier that allows all the participating countries to automatically benefit from the upswings of the business cycle of the larger economies in the region. This should contribute to reducing the disparities in the economic potential of the countries, while at the same time it might help preserve and improve the competitiveness of their exports.

Chapter 6

Incorporation and Regionalism in Latin America

Juliana Martínez Franzoni and Diego Sánchez-Ancochea

Introduction

In recent years Latin America has experienced an unexpected improvement in income distribution along a—maybe less surprising—shift in social and economic policies. Insofar these internal shifts have influenced the characteristics of regional projects—explaining, for example, why proponents of regionalism are discussing transnational social policy for the first time—the new regionalism addressed by this book must be placed within the dynamics of country-based socioeconomic transformation.

But how should we frame and understand those changes in policy and outcomes at the national level? This chapter assess progress made along the notions of market and social incorporation. Market incorporation refers to people's participation in the cash nexus, which in turn requires the creation of a sufficient number of formal, well-paying private and public jobs. Social incorporation refers to people securing their well-being independently of the cash nexus, that is, in a noncommodified or decommodified fashion (Esping-Andersen, 1990). The political and policy challenge of securing either market or social incorporation is a complicated task. Securing both at once is even more complicated. It requires a combination of sustained economic growth, dynamic structural change, expansion of social spending, and effective relations between economic and social policies. On the one hand the former must financially sustain the latter; on the other hand, social policies must provide the economy with sound inputs such as human capital (Martinez Franzoni and Sanchez-Ancochea, 2013a).

After decades of failing to fully secure market and social incorporation (with significant exceptions like Costa Rica) (Martinez Franzoni and Sanchez-Ancochea, 2013a), in recent years the regional record has shown significant improvements. Yet to what extent has this improvement been driven by positive external conditions like high commodity prices? Does it reflects a shift in national and—as discussed in other chapters—regional policies instead? We tackle these questions by distinguishing between socioeconomic outcomes and policy change in a subset of South American countries (Bolivia, Brazil, Chile, Peru, and Uruguay) which are emblematic of diverse region.

By studying the shifts in outcomes and policies in these five countries, this chapter shows the analytical pay-off that the concepts of social and market incorporation have in depicting change and evaluating outcomes and policies in comparative fashion. We show the range of policy trajectories but also demonstrate a common concentration around social rather than economic incorporation. The chapter concludes by discussing challenges that the current positive trajectory struggles with, as well as reflections on the potential role of regionalism to overcome them.

The Double Incorporation and Latin America's Record

In many countries the informal economy accounts for half of the total gross domestic product (GDP), and low-productivity services and subsistence agriculture are still employers of last resort. The lack of incorporation to formal employment leaves many workers with low wages, vulnerable labor conditions, and limited access to skill upgrading and social rights. Expanding the number of formal jobs and increasing wages for formal unskilled workers—that is, securing market incorporation—is thus a necessary condition for a sustained reduction of inequality and requires three types of changes: (1) a rapid process of structural change toward high productivity sectors (Ocampo *et al.*, 2009; Rodrik, 2011); (2) institutional changes in labor-capital relations; and (3) a sustained increase in minimum wages. Although there is still a heated debate about what polices are needed to secure all these changes, there is growing agreement about the need to adopt active productive policies that create incentives to develop high-productivity sectors and also improve knowledge and innovation in low-productivity activities (Amsden, 2001; Paus, 2012; Perez, 2010; Rodrik, 2007).

Unfortunately, exclusive dependence on market income will leave low-income groups exposed to risks that are either unpredictable (such as accidents and sickness) or very hard to cope with on individual bases (such as aging and disability), and therefore vulnerable to sharp reductions in living standards. This is why expanding social incorporation—that is, the decommodified access to transfers and services like healthcare, education, and pensions as a matter of right, regardless of income levels—is also extremely important for people's well-being. Social incorporation usually depends on three factors: (1) periodically updating social spending policy to changes in the structure of social risks; (2) sustained increases in social spending through a wide range of means from payroll to indirect and personal and corporate direct taxes; and (3) combined criteria of targeted and nontargeted, cross-class access which makes it affordable to the poor and attractive to the middle class (whether through radical or incremental redesign of existing arrangements).

In terms of social incorporation, policies that expand the provision of social services to a majority of the population are likely to make a particularly positive contribution. This was clearly the case in the Scandinavian countries and, within Latin America, of Costa Rica between 1950 and 1980. During these three decades, higher social spending led to an increasing number of public employees, who supported a social-democratic party that favored social incorporation policies (Martinez Franzoni and Sanchez-Ancochea, 2013b). Universal policies should be complemented by other measures that try to reach the previously unprotected population such as conditional cash transfers (CCTs).

Latin American countries have historically failed to secure market and social incorporation, thus contributing to make the region the most unequal in the world for at least the duration of the last century. State-led industrialization before the 1980s did promote structural change toward manufacturing and services even in small, poor economies. Nevertheless, the amount of new urban jobs was not enough to absorb the growing supply of labor and informality increased rapidly in the service sector (French Davis, Muñoz, and Palma, 1995).

Structural heterogeneity had a negative impact on social policies and contributed to segmented social incorporation. "Bismarckian" social insurance regimes created "occupationally fragmented schemes" that pivoted around formal employment and excluded the urban and rural poor (Seekings, 2008: 25). With the exception of Costa Rica, social insurance led to high degrees of stratification under what Filgueira (2005) refers to as "stratified universalism". Stratification cut across countries with high coverage nationwide (like Argentina, Chile, and Uruguay) and high coverage among urban workers alone (like Brazil and Mexico). Most countries had minimum social policies under which few people have access to good-quality public services.

The Washington Consensus aimed to expand job opportunities through trade liberalization, the promotion of foreign direct investment, and the deregulation of the economy. Proponents argued that market-friendly reforms would increase investment levels and the use of labor-intensive production techniques. At the same time, neoliberal policies aimed to reduce segmentation in the welfare system through privatization, decentralization, and targeted social programs.

The results, however, were generally quite disappointing in terms of both market and social incorporation. Investment demand never expanded as fast as initially expected and economic growth remained sluggish (Ocampo, 2004; Taylor and Vos, 2002). Large manufacturing firms survived by reducing their employment levels and informality increased in most countries (Reinhart and Peres, 2000). Meanwhile, except in countries with exclusionary welfare regimes social incorporation shrank until the 2000s.

In the last decade, and in a quite unexpected fashion, income distribution has shown slight improvements (Cornia, 2010).[1] Figure 1 presents the evolution of the

---

1 It is too early to establish causal relations between new policies and the reduction in income inequality—although some authors have tried to do it already.

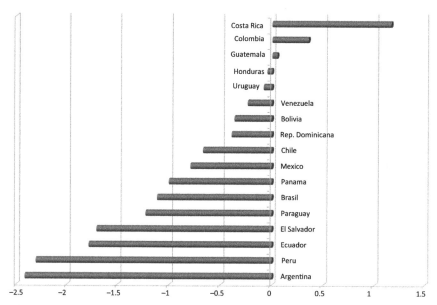

Figure 6.1   Latin America—Change in the Gini Coefficient, circa 2000–2009

Source: Data from Centro de Estudios Distributivos, Laborales y Sociales (CEDLAS).

Gini coefficient in most Latin American countries during the 2000s. Inequality decreased significantly in 12 of the 18 countries in the region and only increased in Costa Rica and Colombia. With the exception of Uruguay, all countries we discuss in the next section have experienced notable improvements in income inequality as reported by their Gini coefficients. Has this reduction in inequality been accompanied by improvements in market and social incorporation? Have there been changes in long-term policies? These are the questions we address in the rest of the paper.

Market and Social Incorporation: The Outcomes

In the last decade and after years of weak performance, Brazil, Bolivia, Chile, Peru, and Uruguay expanded market incorporation. During the period 2000–2009 the share of wage earners, a proxy measure for formal employment, increased in all countries. The percentage of wage earners among the urban working population increased by around 3 percent in Brazil and Chile, by 5 in Bolivia, and by more than 6 in Peru. Uruguay constitutes the only exception, but even there the percentage of nonprofessional self-employed and domestic workers also decreased significantly.

There is a clear contrast between the positive performance of the 2000s and the poor performance of the previous decade. Between 1995 and 2000—a year in which the region was in the midst of a recession—formal employment increased in four of the five countries considered. With a reduction of 5 percent in the share of wage-earners, Chile's performance was particularly disappointing. By 2009, Chile still had more informal workers than 14 years previously.

The growth in formal employment went hand in hand with the expansion of average real wages. In three countries (Bolivia, Peru, and Uruguay), real average income first dropped, largely due to slow economic growth, to recuperate afterwards. Growth has been particularly impressive in Uruguay between 2003 and 2009, and Bolivia between 2003 and 2006 (Table 6.1). Peru's performance, on the other hand, has been quite erratic and overall disappointing.

Table 6.1   Annual Average Rate of Growth of Real Average Earnings, 2003–2009

Countries	Percentages
Brazil	1.25
Chile	2.16
Peru	0.20
Uruguay	4.21

Source: Author's calculations with data from the International Labour Organization (ILO, 2010).

Notes: 2008 for Peru.

Social incorporation has also increased since the mid-1990s. This is clearly reflected in coverage of various programs as the most adequate proxy to social incorporation. During the 2000s increases in coverage in health and/or pensions were impressive across the region, particularly in the casual sector. Between 2000 and 2009, the percentage of non-wage earners with access to pension and/or health benefits increased from 28 percent to 47 percent, and domestic workers with access to these services went from 30 percent to 44 percent.[2] Improvements in Chile and Peru were particularly significant, while Uruguay was the only case showing no gains in coverage. This is, however, to be expected in a country where, by 2001, 96 percent of the population had already access to social insurance.

Nevertheless, there are some caveats to this overall assessment. First, improvements in Chile and Peru were just enough to recuperate the losses of the late 1990s. The case of Peru is particularly dramatic: between 1995 and 2000 overall coverage decreased from 45 percent of the working population to less than 37 percent. Second, overall levels in the casual sector are still quite low in many countries. By 2009, just 40 percent of self-employed and family workers in Latin America benefited from health and/or pensions public insurance. Third, these figures do not tell us anything about the type and quality of healthcare services

---

2   Non-wage earners in ILO statistics include firm owners and autonomous workers. Their data is based on household surveys.

and/or pension insurance that people receive and the disparities in entitlements among individuals.

Market and Social Incorporation: A Look at the Policies

Any attempt to assess changes in economic and social incorporation by looking at short-term outcomes faces two shortcomings. First, commodity-based economic growth is an intervening factor largely dependent on external factors. Second, it is really too soon to account for transformations that started unfolding just a few years ago. In order to consider how sustainable changes are in the long run, it is thus important to consider the extent to which policies to promote the double incorporation have changed. Policies rather than outcomes can shed light on whether countries may meet the requirements involved in sustainable economic and social incorporation in the future. These policies can be diverse and will necessarily reflect a combination of historical legacies and contemporary policy formation.

Below we discuss policy changes in the five countries. The analysis makes it clear that Brazil and Uruguay have experienced a more significant process of transformation than the other countries we examine. Peru and Bolivia are in the opposite situation, although, unlike Peru, Bolivia has shown some interesting innovations in social policy. Finally, Chile should be placed in between: under the governments of Lagos and Bachelet the country experienced important social policy innovations (which have led authors like Sandbrook *et al.*, (2002) to consider it an emerging social democracy) while changes in productive policies were quite timid.

Market Incorporation

Few Latin American countries have implemented the kind of policies toward structural change that may be useful to enhance employment-creating structural change or the regulatory policies that can modify labor-capital relations in a meaningful way. Even relatively successful cases like Brazil and, to a lesser extent, Chile and Uruguay have focused most of their efforts in high-productivity, capital-intensive sectors and/or have lacked clear policy direction.

Brazil has been the most active proponent of industrial policies in the region, particularly since 2002. Two policy statements signaled Brazil's new approach (Doctor, 2009): the *Política Industrial, Tecnológica e de Comércio Exterior* (Policy for Industry, Technology, and Foreign Trade, PITCE) from 2003 and the *Plano de Desenvolvimento da Produção* (Production Development Plan, PDP) from 2008. The PITCE concentrated on learning and innovation, and proposed a series of steps to create a national system of innovation. New incentives were created with particular attention to strategic sectors like semiconductors, pharmaceutical and chemical products, software, energy, and capital goods. The creation of these plans has gone hand in hand with the expansion of public resources. In just two years, the budget of the Ministry of Science and Technology increased by 34 percent from US$2.3b in 2007 to US$3.5b in 2009. According to data from Arbix and Martin (2010), the total public expenditure in science, technology, and innovation—including scientific activities and related techniques—went from US$14.3b in 2000 to US$43.4b in 2008.

Brazil's new approach to industrial policy has focused on innovation in knowledge-intensive sectors or on activities where the country has comparative advantages. Companies like Petrobras or Vale in oil and mining, for example, have received ample support and are expected to become global competitors in high-tech activities within their sectors (Massi and Singh, 2011). This is a sensible strategy but one that is unlikely to create a substantial number of well-paying jobs. Instead its impact on market incorporation is expected to be indirect: by creating linkages with other activities and generating foreign exchange, they should promote economic growth and demand in other sectors. The extent to which capital-intensive sectors lead to overall market incorporation even through these indirect means, however, should be put into question. The new approach to industrial policy has also the potential to benefit small and medium enterprises (SMEs), where a large share of formal employment concentrates. In 2005 micro and small firms accounted for 52 percent of total formal employment (Crocco and Santos, 2010) and an even larger percentage of informal employment. Nevertheless, policies toward SMEs in Brazil still have significant shortcomings: they tend to treat all SMEs in the same way; they focus on companies that already have some potential and offer little long-term support for micro-firms in traditional sectors; and they fail to adopt a systemic and coherent approach (Maco and Santos, 2010).

Probably even more important for employment growth and market incorporation was the *Programa de Aceleração do Crescimento* (Growth Acceleration Program, PAC) introduced in 2007 under the supervision of the now President Dilma Rousseff. The PAC committed the government to spending more than US$200 billion in four years for infrastructure projects like road construction, urban regeneration, and new houses for disadvantaged groups—all labor-intensive activities (ILO, 2010). In 2010 a PAC 2 was announced. It committed the government to spend US$526 billion between 2011 and 2014, with concentration on urban infrastructure, housing, sanitation and electricity, renewable energy, oil and gas, and highways and airports.

The Brazilian Development Bank (BNDES) constitutes the third pillar of Brazil's policy toward structural change and economic transformation. The BNDES participated in the design of the PITCE and committed substantial resources to new sectors. Between 2004 and 2006 alone, BNDES disbursements represented 13.3 percent of gross capital accumulation and 8.3 percent of total credit from the Brazilian financial system (Hermann, 2010). In the subsequent years, disbursements increased even faster. While most loans are allocated to promote the internationalization of large firms, the BNDES also has a number of smaller programs in support of SMEs.

Chile has paid a growing attention to industrial policy, although it is still somewhat timid and inconsistent. During the 1990s, horizontal policies that confronted market failures in all economic sectors were dominant. These measures complemented the work of Fundacion Chile, which is a nonprofit organization, created in 1976 and run jointly by the government; International Telephone and Telegraph (USA) (IT&T); and (since 2006) BHP Billiton. Fundacion Chile funds innovations in six natural resource-based sectors and also acts as a sort of venture capital firm; it succeeded in creating a salmon industry in Chile and is now involved in important projects in solar energy production and other sectors (Agosin, Larrain, and Grau, 2010).

The government stepped up its efforts to develop vertical policies that concentrated on winning sectors in the early 2000s. The Corporation for the Promotion of Production (*Corporacion de Fomento de la Produccion,* CORFO) created a new subsidy program to promote foreign investment in high-tech activities like software, semiconductors, back office, and other ICT services. During the 2000s the Chilean government has also implemented more aggressive learning and innovation policies, including new incentives for university–firm collaboration and the creation of National Council of Innovation for Competitiveness (NCIC).

Yet Chile's industrial policy still concentrates on further developing traditional comparative advantages and has little focus on employment—a primary requirement to secure market incorporation in the long run. Agosin, Larrain and Grau (2010) argue that industrial policies are still residual: there is insufficient spending, simultaneous initiatives are way too many, and there is no strong, coordinated institution. While recognizing the shift in Chile's policy approach in recent years, Perez Caldentey (2012) is even more critical based on evidence that shows an increasing turn to natural resources and inability to promote structural change. Chile lacks of strategies to promote economic upgrading beyond natural resources and to increase formal employment in nontradable sectors.

Economic policy in Bolivia and Peru has been extremely different from one another. Since 2001 under the right-of-centre Toledo and Garcia administrations, Peru maintained a neoliberal stand based on the attraction of foreign direct investment in mining and other natural resources (Tanaka and Vera, 2008). In Bolivia, on the other hand, the Morales administration increased royalties and taxes in the hydrocarbon sector significantly and tried to expand the state's production capacity (Kohl, 2010). Yet in many ways the Bolivian and Peruvian approaches to industrial policy share similar shortcomings. The combination of weak public institutions and high commodity prices against the background of a long-term dependence on natural resources have limited the ability to promote structural change and new drivers of employment. In Peru, most policies have aimed at further liberalization and creating a more "effective" business environment (Tello and Tavara, 2010). Public spending in research and development is very low: in 2009 Peru spent 0.16 percent of GDP compared with 0.54 percent in Latin America as a whole and 1.5 percent in China (Tavara, 2010). The Toledo administration did create a new institutional architecture to promote small and medium firms, including a new department in the Ministry of Labor and a new law (Villaran, 2010), but the lack of coordination and of funding remained a problem. By 2007 micro and small firms received an average of US$3.4 in various subsidies—equivalent to just 0.4 percent of total production (Tello and Tavara, 2010). In Bolivia, the government committed to add value to the gas industry and achieve economic diversification, but no policy adoption seems to have yet taken place (Kaup, 2010; Kohl, 2010; Webber, 2009).

After years of neglecting the promotion of structural change, starting in 2005 with the left-wing administrations of Vázques and Mujica, Uruguay adopted a more aggressive stand. Uruguay has begun to promote collaboration between different ministries, created new institutions to promote learning and innovation (i.e. National Agency for Research and Innovation), and implemented new tax subsidies to promote private investment, cluster development, and learning and innovation (Barrios, Gandelman, and Michelin, 2010). Investment incentives depend on meeting a series of performance requirements, including the creation of full-time employment and the signing of collective agreements which are not usually found in other countries. Nevertheless, most incentives are still channeled to agricultural products and natural resources with limited employment potential, and policies toward structural change still play a minor role in the country's overall public policy agenda. Uruguay is, on the other hand, a leader in the promotion of labor rights and collective bargaining. The Vazquez administration reestablished the Wage Councils, a tripartite forum for the negotiation of wages created in 1985 but inactive during the following two decades (Chasqueti, 2007).

Efforts to influence capital-labor relations and strengthen trade unions have been relatively absent in the other countries. Even in Brazil, where the ruling *Partido dos Trabalhadores* (Labour Party, PT) had close historical ties with trade unions, the government has done relatively little to promote collective agreements and recuperate traditional corporatist regimes. Instead, the PT's wage policy has promoted a continuous expansion of the minimum wage, which grew by an average rate of 6.7 percent between 2003 and 2009. Higher minimum wages exert an upward pressure on other wages in the formal sector and also have positive effects on pensions and other social benefits. In all other countries considered in the analysis but Uruguay, the evolution of minimum wages is rather disappointing for market incorporation.

Social Incorporation

Overall, since 2003, Latin American governments have adopted a new set of policies that are more ambitious and, in many cases, more sensitive to social incorporation. Reygadas and Filgueira (2010) echo this positive evaluation in their review of the social policies that left-wing governments have adopted in recent years. These include maintaining and expanding social assistance programs inherited from the retrenchment period, particularly CCTs, as well as creating a broad array of programs, from social-democratic measures aiming at equalizing capacities such as Uruguay's "Equity Plan" and Chile's Plan for Universal Access with Explicit Guarantees (*Plan de Acceso Universal con Garantías Explícitas*, AUGE) healthcare program, to radical measures that directly intervene in markets such as nationalizations in Venezuela and Bolivia, land reform in Brazil, and various types of subsidies and price controls in several other countries.

To address social spending, Figures 6.2 and 6.3 show levels of per capita social spending overall and in healthcare during the 2000s. Brazil's performance was particularly impressive: between 2000–2001 and 2008–2009 total spending per capita increased by 48 percent, going from real US$785 to US$ 1,165 while health spending also expanded at a similar rate. On the contrary, in Peru and, especially, Bolivia total spending per capita increased well below GDP per capita growth (8 percent versus 19 percent in the case of Bolivia, 28 percent versus 43 percent in the case of Peru). This said, increases in social spending say nothing about how regressive or progressive, exclusive or inclusive social spending is.

Increases in social spending could be reflecting a regressive allocation of resources. In other words, a few people could be getting the bulk of the new programs. As a result, we need to pay even more attention to the composition of social spending and the reform in the largest programs like pensions and healthcare. Three of the five countries studied in here, Brazil, Chile, and Uruguay, have undergone changes toward more universalism in access and benefits regarding pensions and healthcare. Healthcare but not pension reforms were introduced in Bolivia, while Peru transformed neither sector.

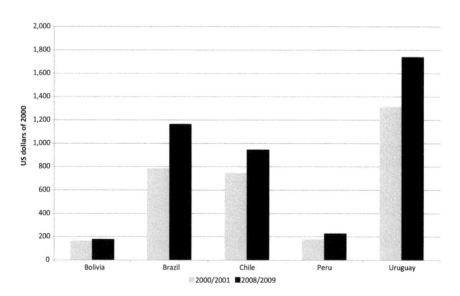

Figure 6.2   Public Social Spending (in Per Capita US Dollars of 2000), 2000–2001 and 2008–2009

Source: Author's elaboration with data from ECLAC (2010).

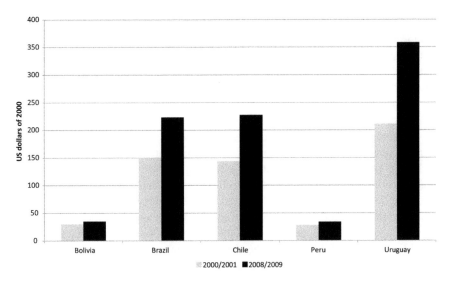

Figure 6.3   Public Spending in Health (in Per Capita US Dollars of 2000), 2000–2001 and 2008–2009

Source: Author's elaboration with data from ECLAC (2010).

Let us start this discussion with the Brazilian case. Brazil has slowly reformed its health and pension systems to incorporate new groups to social policy but without harming the interests of powerful groups (Hunter and Sugiyama, 2008). In pensions the Lula administration sought to tighten requirements (like the minimum retirement age) and redefine entitlements (like benefits for economically dependent family members) while also tax the benefits of the most affluent population. It did not change the segmented architecture of the system but intervened in the parameters defining requirements and benefits. In healthcare the reform was more fundamental and a national healthcare system was established, aimed at reaching the overall population.

In Chile the creation of the AUGE constituted a decisive move toward universalism in health. The AUGE plan created a universal mandate of services that every health insurer is obliged to provide within explicit timelines, thus stopping the practice of ISAPREs offering plans that omitted key services, such as reproductive health care for women (Dávila, 2005; Ewig, 2008). Such services are incrementally expanded and selected based upon their cost-effectiveness in preventing death and disability (Ewig and Kay, 2011).

The 2008 pension reform maintained private individual accounts as the core of the pension system while introducing a new redistributive benefit program, a Basic Solidarity Pension (*Pensión Básica Solidaria*). The basic pension can reach up to $160 per month and involves a public subsidy to households earning up to 60 percent of the income scale, and which increases as contributions lower. The reform also includes a bonus for each live birth for women, therefore acknowledging time devoted to childbirth and child-rearing (Ewig and Kay, 2011).

In January of 2008 Uruguay launched an Integrated National Healthcare System (Borgia, 2010; Pérez, 2009; Setaro, 2010). This system brings together, previously fragmented and uncoordinated public and private (mutual, collective, not-for profit) systems with unequal access and services. Before the reform the poor mostly relied on the former while the middle-class relied on the latter, either due to mandatory social insurance for workers or to voluntary affiliation among the nonactive population. With the reform, the population at large (not just private workers as before) make contributions according to their income to the National Healthcare Fund, a core aspect of the reform, rather than directly to providers. Insurance reaches the active population, retired workers, and economically dependent family members (children and spouses). In pensions, while maintaining the system of individual savings, in 2009 the Frente Amplio "expanded access to public benefits while keeping the defined contribution system of individual pension fund accounts intact" (Ewig and Kay, 2011: 36). The reform included a reduction in the minimum age for early retirement, a reduction of the minimum years of contribution, and the creation of more generous pension formulas. Women also received recognition for the period spent raising children.

In Bolivia under the Morales administration, the state took over contributory pension funds and eliminated the two private businesses previously in charge of these accounts, in addition to diminishing the retirement age and creating a reduced contributory pension for people with at least ten years of contributions. The administration also created a minimum non-contributory pension set as 70 percent of the national minimum salary (in 2010 US$66). To this purpose, the Morales administration renamed the old Bonasol universal pension program "Renta Dignidad", expanded it to reach a broader swath of Bolivians, and increased the monthly benefit by 25 percent (Müller, 2009 in Ewig and Kay, 2011).

In addition to healthcare and pension reforms, CCTs have been established in all six cases, although with very different characteristics, resources, and coverage (Reygadas and Figuera, 2010). Brazil's *Bolsa Familia* is the largest and most successful CCT program in South America. It benefits more than 12 million households, who receive a monthly check between US$20 and US$152 (based on 2010 exchange rates). In Bolivia CCTs also occupy a central role in the reorganization of social policy. The Morales administration created two different cash transfer programs: the *Bono Juancito Pinto* and the *Bono Juana Azurduy*. The former was launched in 2006 and gives a subsidy of US$28 to every student in primary school (Yañez, Rojas and Silva, 2011). It covers 17 percent of the total population and represents a total spending of 0.33 percent of GDP (ECLAC, 2010). The latter was introduced in 2009 to reduce infant mortality. It consists on small cash transfers to pregnant women and families with children under two if they attend regular health checkups. Chile and Peru, on the other hand, have devote to CCTs very little sources (0.10 percent and 0.14 percent of the GDP) and reaches 6.8 and 7.6 percent of their total population, respectively (ECLAC,

2010). However, the Chilean program is part of a larger set of social assistance programs and seeks to specifically target the extreme poor with a access to various services and a small cash transfer (US$6–20), which is not the case of the Peruvian program.

Major Challenges to Secure Sustained Improvements in Market and Social Incorporation

Are market and social incorporation likely to continue expanding in the future? Have the recent policies moved the region toward a new development path? In many countries, policies toward social incorporation have advanced more rapidly than any real effort to promote structural change. As a result, if commodity prices slow down significantly, they could face problems to further expand formal employment. Unfortunately there are additional obstacles to sustain market and social incorporation. We concentrate on three structural processes: (1) the role of China and its contribution to Latin America's primary specialization; (2) capital mobility; and (3) migration and its influence on the design of an effective social architecture.

China's steady growth has been one of the main drivers of growing demand for South America's primary goods in recent years. In 2009, for example, exports from Latin America to China grew by 5 percent at a time when all other exports decreased by 27 percent. During the first half of 2010, Chinese imports from Bolivia and Uruguay increased by 129 percent and 102 percent, respectively.

Unfortunately China's growing demand for primary goods is locking Latin America in a traditional specialization in natural resources. In 2008–2009, exports of raw materials and primary-based manufacture amounted for 59 percent of all Latin American exports, compared with 55 percent in 2005–2006 and 44 percent in 2001–2002. Four-fifths of Chinese imports from Latin America are primary goods, while a majority of Chinese exports to the region are manufacturing goods with increasing technological content. Chinese products in sectors like clothing, toys, furniture, and electronics have flooded the region, and small and medium firms have faced increasing difficulties to survive. In 2008, 22 percent of Chinese imports of Latin America were basic manufacturing goods, 25 percent were manufacturing good with medium technology, and 35 percent were high-technology products.

This trend is particularly problematic when one considers recent research on the importance of structural change for long-term growth and the expansion of formal employment (Rodrik, 2011; Rodrik and McMillan, 2011). The mining, oil, and modern agriculture sectors are not particularly labor intensive and have historically been unable to absorb the surplus labor from other sectors. Given growing deindustrialization in several Latin American countries, a slowdown in Chinese demand for commodities could lead lower economic growth, a new expansion of casual employment, and a reduction in economic-wide productivity.

The size of the domestic market and the willingness of the government to promote structural change will influence each country's responses to the Chinese challenge. Brazil is in a better position than anyone else to reduce Chinese imports and build strategic alliance in sectors like automobiles, planes, and even IT. Chile could develop new comparative advantages in primary-based manufactures with high added-value, but only if it is able to implement more coherent supporting policies. Argentina and Uruguay depend on regional integration and may suffer from further deindustrialization without it. Finally Bolivia and Peru may maintain their China-induced specialization in primary resources.

A second challenge to both market and social incorporation comes from capital mobility and the expansion of short-term financial inflows. Capital mobility has enhanced the power of the very rich and reduced governments' opportunities to increase income tax levels. This problem affects all countries in the world, but is particularly acute in Latin America, where the economic elite has always held excessive political influence and where, even before the current globalization phase, most governments have historically faced significant difficulties in increasing tax revenues. Large financial inflows can also be disruptive in both upswing and recessionary times (ECLAC, 2002; Ocampo, 2004). They enhance the procyclical nature of fiscal policy and can contribute to sharp swings in exchange rates. In the last few years, financial inflows have been particularly problematic for Brazil and Chile, which have experienced sharp appreciations of their exchange rates, with negative effects on both exporters and import substitution manufactures.

The expansion of migration in Latin America constitutes a different kind of challenge. It is one thing to incorporate people that settle down in a country different from where they were born. It is a different matter to cope with transnational workers and transnational families as part and parcel of how people commodify their labor force and provide for what then become specific and well-established types of transnational families. This is particularly challenging for welfare regimes that heavily revolve around social insurance. Emigrants make their contributions where they work, but this may not be where they retire. Workers come and go but, rather than being portable, their contributions most often stay behind them. Under noncontributory policies, public policy is also challenged by migrants and their families: for them, social rights most often precede political rights, and distinctions between legal and illegal immigration pervades the policy debate. Acknowledging the pervasive and permanent presence of migrants, whether emigrants or immigrants, not just workers but their families as well, seems to be one of the next frontiers for successful social incorporation.

How can Regionalism Contribute to Enhance Positive Change?

We can place the study of regionalism within these processes of national-based market and social incorporation. South–South regional integration projects will only be successful if they enhance an individual country's opportunities to develop more equitable models. They will only be supported by all participants if they respond to the specific challenges that each country—and key actors within them—face.

Let us conclude with a brief discussion of two ways through which regional integration can expand development opportunities in Latin America. Following traditional arguments in economics and political economy, regionalism could result in the creation of regional value chains in the manufacturing sector. The automobile sector in MERCOSUR, where Argentina and Brazil have developed some complementary capabilities, constitutes a good example. Regionalism in this context should involve some level of protection from China and other major global producers together with state-induced arrangements that facilitate collaboration between firms across borders. There has also been some talk about creating new monetary unions, although the recent experience of the European Union illustrates the huge potential downside involved in adopting the same monetary policy among countries with different economic structures and levels of development and in eliminating the possibility of competitive devaluation.

A process of regional integration oriented toward the promotion of regional manufacturing activities—including those based on natural resources—would require Brazil's commitment and leadership (see Baumann's chapter in this volume). Brazil is not only the largest economy in the region, but also the only one able to develop a significant domestic market and promote new comparative advantages in high-tech. Yet Brazil would have to commit to play an enabling role, including support to promote structural change in smaller countries like Bolivia. Unfortunately, as several decades of MERCOSUR have demonstrated, there are reasons to be skeptical about Brazil's willingness to be a regional leader (and the desire of others to follow).

South American regionalization could also contribute to established shared social-protection systems or at least some components of such systems. First steps that have already been taken have involved more effective exchanges between social ministries in the various countries. A primary aim would be to map similarities and differences in coverage rates, level of benefits, and so on. Participating countries should then commit to establish basic floors for social services (particularly health and pensions) that benefit all citizens within the region—irrespective of nationality or current place of residence. Further steps would probably require the creation of either regional institutions or regional mechanisms that promote shared standards concerning the access and benefits involved.

At the end, we argue, regional integration should be primarily evaluated by its contribution to market and social incorporation in all South American countries. This should be the measuring stick to determine whether MERCOSUR, Alba, and all other initiatives are contributing to socioeconomic development and whether efforts to strengthen them should continue in the future.

Chapter 7

Rescaling Responsibilities and Rights: The Case of UNASUR Health

Pía Riggirozzi

Regionalism can be defined as an instance of policy making of cross-border formation advanced through institutional arrangements, bureaucracies, political motivations, and social mobilization. State and non-state actors engage in political projects to relocate the governance of a particular issue or policy domain beyond the scope of national politics. This is a process by which regional projects move from one level of policy deliberation, negotiation, and implementation to another in what Hameiri identified as region-building (Hameiri, 2012). In the vast research field of regionalism that has flourished since 1993, expectations of what regional governance can deliver, however, have been evaluated primarily in terms of economic and security governance (Mansfield and Solingen, 2010). While much has been written about economic integration, regional institutions, and security communities, a discussion of how significant other policy domains have been in the process of regionalism has lagged behind. Specifically, a rather neglected issue in the account of contemporary forms of regionalism has been the extent to which regional integration can promote social development. This has been particularly the case in the study of regionalism in the Americas, where regional motivations have often been defined by an unrelenting path of political economic projects, often marked by the reach of the US as a regional hegemon (Fawcett in Fawcett and Serrano, 2009; Tussie, 2009). This has not been simply a matter of academic neglect, but a consequence of a political decoupling of economic integration and social policies in regional governance. As in Europe, advancing a "social agenda" has often been undermined by the task of removing barriers to trade. However, while Europe saw efforts to build practices of social inclusion become institutionalized in the open method of coordination (OMC) in the 1990s (Scharpf, 2007), Latin America is now experiencing a "social turn" where regional cooperation is reconnecting with social policy-making beyond a rhetorical aspect (Grugel, 2005). This chapter analyses the place of social policy as a driver of current dynamics (re)defining region-building in South America.

Since the early 2000s, a process of political renewal underway in Latin America, and mostly in South America, meant that regionalism may be "catching up" with social concerns embraced by a new tide of Left/Left of Centre governments championing ideas to improve redistribution of income and social services (Panizza, 2009; Grugel and Riggirozzi, 2012). At the heart of this process is a reconnection between the regional space and the transformations in the political economy of many countries in the South. Loosening the harness of the neoliberal myth as an organizing principle of national and regional political economy turned into a process of transformation and recomposition of regional politics. In this context, social rights are emerging in the debate about regionalism in Latin America, validating new practices and a research agenda that concentrates on the place of regional social policy and social development goals in regional integration. This emerging agenda is pioneered here by the case of health, where governing arrangements and regional practices led by UNASUR are carving South America as a distinctive region.

The chapter argues that, as regionalism unfolds "on the edges" of its most usual approach to market-led integration, Latin America offers new grounds to evaluate symbolic, material, and institutional foundations defining a regional project, and at the same time the region's ability to interact autonomously as an international actor. By looking at the institutional structure, programs, resources, and policy action of the newly established regional Health Council within the Union of South American Nations (UNASUR), this chapter explores two interrelated yet largely unexplored issues: the linkages between regional integration and social development beyond the historical hub of regionalism and beyond Europe—can we genuinely talk about a "social turn" in regional politics, where regionalism is somehow "catching up" with efforts to advance Right-based models of governance (Grugel and Piper, 2009: 79–98; Grugel and Riggirozzi, 2012; Yeates, 2002)? Second, what regionalism through social policy means for how we theorize regionalism as a process and region as an actor. In answering these questions, the chapter hopes to contribute toward a more nuanced understanding of region as a space for collective action advancing regionalism as a project for the region and of the region.

The analysis proceeds in three parts. The first part evaluates the conceptual contributions to the discussion of what region and region-building means in international relations. The second part looks at the neglected place of social policy in the process of regionalism in Latin America. The third part evaluates the factors that allowed for a reconnection between regionalism and social policy in Latin America, and how new institutions, resources, and practices in UNASUR Health manifest as new modes of regionalism and regional diplomacy. The final part offers some concluding thoughts about the social purpose of regionalism, and the extent to which we can genuinely talk about regional responsibilities and rights defining current regional governance.

Recasting Region as Space for Policy and Action

Region, in many ways like the state, should be seen as a place for deliberation and collective action over certain policy domains. It could be defined as either or both a conventional field of institutions and regulations (a sphere of territorial representation) or a more informal domain of sociability (a space for action). Regions are thus formed and operate in very different ways, and are advanced by different actors through dynamics of transnational and transsocial cooperation and competition. Regions are, in short, expression of that action, as the space where politics happens (Fawn, 2009: 5–34). Regions include many forms of political and social interaction led by actors that share motivations, concerns, ideological stands, goals, and perceptions of what the region *is for*. From this perspective, the terms of regionalism can be defined not simply by visions of how collective action in a specific geographic area can respond to challenges and needs from external actors (or other regions), but also by perceptions, motivations and norms based on social interactions. This notion was captured by constructivist approaches which claim that regions are social constructions (Adler and Barnett in Adler and Barnett, 1998: 29–65; Katzenstein, 2005; Hurrell, in Fawcett and Hurrell, 1995: 37–73). From this perspective, regionalism can take a variety of paths and paces, and overlapping and even competing projects may manifest within one region as specific practices and different narratives in different domains (Riggirozzi, 2012). For Scharpf, regions may be bounded by more or less institutionalized forms of interactions within the continuum *intergovernmental cooperation–supranational integration* (Scharpf, 2010). For scholars in the so-called New Regionalism Approach the space of non-state actors advancing this process must be seen as important force in the making of regionalism, or regionalization (Hettne and Söderbaum, 2000: 457–74).

Furthermore, the institutionalization of cooperation and coordination among actors within a given region can further define the region's sense of "regionness". The term regionness, as advanced by Hettne, and Hettne and Söderbaum, has become critical in our understanding of a region as an institutionalized polity that operates over a policy domain while reproducing common understandings, values, and, in coherent settings, a regional identity (Hettne and Söderbaum, 2000: 461; Hettne, 1993: 211–32, 2008). Regionness denotes two sets of fundamental dynamics defining the contours of region-building: first, a sense of identity and belonging of state and non-state actors to a particular region based on shared values, norms, and institutions that govern their interaction and the ways they perceive themselves within a common polity (self-recognition). Second, regionness denotes cohesive action based on a manifested sense of belonging, common goals and values (symbolic foundations), and institutions and regulations that enhance the region's ability to interact autonomously in the international arena (external recognition as an actor).

There is something of a paradox in how the field evolved despite this well expanded framework. Accounting for the dynamics outlined by New Regionalist Approaches, most contributions explained the role of the EU as an actor in the international arena, often falling in the a-critical trap of taking the EU as starting point to analyze other regions and their regionness (Hettne, 2005: 543–71; Warleigh-Lack and Rosamond, 2010: 993–1013). Little has been explored as to what determines region-building, identity, sense of mission and belonging in other geographical areas. For instance, theorizing about regionalism in the Americas has been subsumed to binary notions of "old"/"close" versus "new"/open" regionalism based on the characterization of regional cooperation agreements associated with post-war economic protectionism, and those taking place since the 1990s within a fundamental and ongoing neoliberal consensus and expansion of the EU (Tussie, 2003: 217–34). In the Americas, regionalism became defined as either the "regional laboratory" for US-led policies on trade, investment, and services, or as a defensive reaction to it(Serrano in Fawcett and Serrano, 2005: 1–24, 13). In this context, academic debate was marginally concerned with the regional space as one of policy formulation and collective actions in areas of social policy. Region-building was part and parcel of commercial and productive concerns, that is how to position the region in a stronger position vis à vis external influences, or how to capitalize on external flows of trade and finance making the region synonym of extended markets. Other considerations related to sociopolitical definitions were marginal. At best, it was assumed that issues of social development would be tight to the logic of healthy markets and hence the focus on regional trade-led growth. Furthermore, when the economistic view met politics, regionalist projects were seen as outcomes of hierarchical arrangements in reflection of specific forms of (hemispheric) power relations and leadership (Lemke, 2002; Lake, 2009: 35–58; Nel and Nolte, 2010: 877–9; Malamud, 2011: 1–24).

In this context, it could be argued that the practice of regionalism conditioned the study of it. As a consequence, some analytical gaps were left unexplored in the way regionalism and models of regional governance were addressed by the studies of regional integration, especially in the Americas. First, the emphasis on regionalism as trade and finance-led attributes tautological significant to *what* regionalism is and what region *is for*; namely a project modeled by *neoliberal* economics, defined to enhance the position of its members within the global economy, and often led by a regional hegemon (Gamble and Payne, 1996; Breslin and Hook in Breslin and Hook, 2002: 1–22). If a notion of resistance, or "regionalism with a human face", was to be expected, this was attributed to an overstated role of social actors with the capacity to contest state-led neoliberal regionalism (Hettne in Hettne, Inotai and Sunkel, 1999: 1–24). According to Mittelman, regionalization "from below" defines processes of contestation led by civil society organizations in their attempts to achieve "transformative regionalism" (Mittelman, 2000: 225). But these arguments not only define a false divide between state and society in terms of political motivation and action, but also conceive civil society as the only agent capable of bringing about a sense of social regionalism. This is even more problematic in the Americas where the place of social actors advancing practices and social agendas has been rather ambiguous. During the 1990s, social activism targeting regional integration was led by what was perceived as US-led "hyperliberal" projects of continental reach; first against the North American Free Trade Agreement (NAFTA), that includes Mexico, the US, and Canada, and later against the negotiations for the Free Trade

Agreement of the Americas (FTAA). Despite these campaigns, networks of civil society organizations were not always politically influential or able to articulate "alternative" proposals beyond carrying genuine social demands. Social activism was often limited by a tradition of "hyper-presidentialism" in the construction and negotiation of regionalism in the Americas that affected the capacity of civil society to engage with governments, unless spaces for dialogue were coordinated under state initiatives or by business actors through lobbying (Marchand, Bøås, and Shaw, 2005; Phillips, and Prieto Corredor in Warleigh-Lack, Robinson and Rosamond, 2011: 129; Grugel, 2004: 603–26, 605). This is a distinctive political and institutional feature that, as much as the neoliberal political economic project, explains Latin American "open" regionalism in the 1990s. In this context, it could hardly be expected that the region become a space for transformative regionalism.

This tendency, started to be reverted by profound changes in the political economic orientation in many countries in the region since the early 2000s. New forms of regionalism and transnational solidarism, although still highly led by state initiatives, reflected more radical models of political inclusion and citizenship adopted by the so-called New Left across the region (Panizza, 2009; Tockman, 2010). The New Left has been explained as a reaction against what came to be seen as excessive marketization and the elitist and technocratic democracies that accompanied market reforms at the end of the 20th century (Grugel and Riggirozzi, 2012). As a project, it is understood as a call for a "new form of social contract between the state and people" (Wylde, 2011: 436–45, 436), and the construction of a new consensus about state responsibilities and a vision of a more equal distribution of national income. This project sits alongside an attempt to "reclaim the region", not simply as a way of resisting US power and neoliberal dogmatism but more significantly as a new understanding of what Latin American as a region should do and should look like. In this context, it makes sense to revaluate what region is and is for, and depart from the dominant assumption that (domestic or transnational) economic coalitions committed to economic liberalization shape regionalism. The dynamics that support regionalism are not taking place within or modeled by neoliberal economics, nor are responding to the pressures and constraints of a globalized economy, they are the result of a more complex way by which domestic politics and regional regimes accommodate (Hameiri, 2012: 17). The debate over how to best serve participatory, redistributive, and greater autonomy in both national and the regional agenda in Latin America opens new questions about forms of regional governance, shifting the attention toward new policy domains and new ways of organizing regional politics. In this context, region-building in the Americas demands a closer look at alternative models of development and accumulation across the region that underpin new principles of regional solidarity and complementarities expressed in regional projects for sharing resources, decentralizing power, and reconnecting social development and rights in regional practices. While regionalism is expression of the social practices and mechanisms that sustain these regional projects, cohesive regional projects can, at the same time, (re)position the region vis-à-vis the external environment.

This takes us to the second part of our understanding of region building; namely how regionalism projects politics, or how regions engage as an actor in external interactions to foster the internal regional program or programs. The institutionalization of political, social economic, and cultural relations formalizes the regional space as a cohesive unit. In other words, region is not only the place where agents act, but an actor in itself that projects the regional program through internal coherence and external interactions. Region as actor refers to the region's ability to interact autonomously with its external environment, and its formal and symbolic manifestations as a unit within its internal environment (Schmitt-Egner, 2002: 179–200, 191). This perspective focuses not only on which relationships, networks practices, and institutions are created, but also on the regional institutional and legal status, that is, the formal and informal foundations by which regional arrangements hold competence to stand independently vis à vis national member states and external actors, states or regions, and to project a sense of identity, mission, or what Hettne and Söderbaum called regionness.

The regional question in the context of these arguments is thus about rescaling social relations in a regional space; reclaiming the region as a space for political deliberation and policy delivery, where the region becomes a space for the provision of regional goods beyond trade and market competitiveness—redefining and perhaps reinventing principles of solidarism and responsibility; and rebuilding the institutional pillars that sustain new projects within the region and vis à vis external actors. Understood this way, region as space for action and as an actor are two dimensions that open new questions for research particularly in the current regional political economic changes.

Recasting the Social in South American Regionalism

There is something of a paradox in the way regionalism unfolded in South America; although the appeal to social norms and human development has been in the regional imaginary and even manifested in institutional forms, regional integration was crafted on the understandings that trade and financial investment were the main catalyzers of growth and social development. This indirect connection, or rather disconnection, between regionalism and social policy, meant that integration initiatives in South America subsumed issues of poverty and inclusion to the promise of trade-led growth in the definition of regional policies. This has been particularly the case since the 1980s when developing countries were facing the collapse of their economies in the wake of the debt crisis. Nationally and regionally, it was expected that by loosening the restrictions on finance and trade new market projects could enhance the capacity of states to manage the pressures of the global order (Hettne, 2005; Hurrell, 1995; Marchand, Bøås, and Shaw, 2005). The establishment of the Southern Common Market (MERCOSUR) in 1991 grouping Brazil, Argentina, Uruguay, and Paraguay, and the North American Free Trade Agreement (NAFTA) signed by the US, Canada, and Mexico in 1994, as well as other resilient projects from the past, like the Community of Andean Nations (CAN) created in 1969, were established in this understanding and aimed at locking-in market reforms and embedding capitalism through regionalization (Phillips, 2003a: 327–49).

Despite the emphasis on market-led regionalism some "social clauses" were introduced in regional agreements, specifically in the Andean Community and MERCOSUR, where the legacy of developmental welfare states steering development projects since the 1940s has been significant for the formulation of commitments in the areas of labor rights, health, and education (Riesco in Deacon *et al.*, 2009: 108–39). In this sense, social policy through regionalism is hardly "new" as some cross-border projects on health, education, and labor regulations were supported since the creation of both Andean Community and MERCOSUR. In the case of Andean Community, for instance, two managing bodies were created to manage common challenges in the areas of health and education. The Hipólitio Unanúe agreement and the Andres Bello Convention established the foundations for the coordination of health and education policies respectively since the early 1970s. In the area of health, active policies in relation to the prevention and control of diseases affecting border areas were implemented, whereas in education, policies toward the harmonization of curricula, mobility of students and professionals, and quality assurance programs were set up for the Andean region (UNDP, 2011). In MERCOSUR a Health Minister Assembly was established in the mid-1990s as a ministerial forum for the discussion of health policy and strategies as part of the regional agenda (MERCOSUR Decision CMC No 03/1995). Similar advances were also seen in the area of education, which together with health pushed social policy into the agenda for activities and surveillance with some degree of impact in these fields (see UNDP 2011). Yet, further commitments and institutionalization of cooperation and implementation of social policies have been erratic and with mixed consequences for human development in both regional integration schemes during the 1990s (UNDP, 2011; Riesco in Deacon *et al.*, 2009). In practice these embryonic regional social agendas were working on the edges of financial constraints and cross-national asymmetries, and thus could not overcome difficulties related to lack of action plans and fundamentally funding constrains (Deacon *et al.*, 2009). In this context some commitments over a range of social policy areas were made but low levels of institutionalization for implementation, coordination, and compliance affected the depth and pace of regional social policies. Politically, rudimentary institutional structures in both Andean Community and MERCOSUR often delegated decisions over regional policies and politics to intergovernmental negotiation processes. Intergovernmentalism, or rather interpresidentialism, left social policy subject to the discretion of policy makers, ministers, and private providers—and to their struggle for distributional benefits (Malamud, 2005: 421–36; Sanchez, 2007). Consequently, the capacity of social actors to penetrate the regional policy debate and negotiation of policies has been severely curtailed by a regional political culture that sealed off from society while responding to market pressures.

Despite this difficult relationship between regional politics, social actors, and social agendas, some initiatives in the direction of social participation were created, actively creating opportunities for social activism. This has been the case in MERCOSUR where the establishment of the MERCOSUR Social Institute (Instituto Social MERCOSUR) supported by the Ministries of Development of its members in 1999, represented a hub for research on social policy and policy recommendation. Likewise, a think tank, Somos MERCOSUR, created in 2005, opened a new space for civil society and governments to engage in discussions and deliberation of policy priorities and agendas. While these events and institutional initiatives helped promoting and reinforcing a sense of need for a genuine social agenda, policy action, and regional norms remained plagued by procedural ambiguities and fundamentally held back by economic and financial hardship (Di Pietro, 2003; Grugel, 2005: 1061–76). This was even more the case as, during the 1990s, spending in social sectors was bundled with macroeconomic reforms, privatization, and deregulation, advanced by Washington Consensus, supporters which reduced state investment in social policies (Birdsall and Lodono, in Birdsall, Graham and Sabot, 1998: 111–45; Gwynne and Kay, 2000: 141–56).

The mix results of regional integration agreements in tackling and coordinating social issues meant that regionalism was mainly practices and thus measured by growth in trade volumes both intraregion and externally; alignment of macroeconomic policies; policies that support disadvantaged regional economies or sectors, and the role of political will in achieving integration (Schiff and Winters, in Velde, 2006). In other words, as the region was defined in terms market opportunities, so were social policies and the understanding of regional public goods. The regional space, in this context, can hardly be associated with a space for collective action but rather as a collection of economic policies in a multiscalar way. Not surprising studies of regional social policy have been restricted to normative analyses of what regional organizations should be doing to develop regional policy for poverty reduction and/or mapping what regional organizations are formally saying about social policy (Ortiz, 2007; Deacon *et al.*, 2010).

One of the striking characteristics defining current dynamics of political economy in Latin America, however, is the attempt to redefine new boundaries (geographical and ideological) for what constitutes regional political economy. One manifestation of this has seen the election of a series of Leftist governments in much of Latin America. At odds with neoliberal policies, these governments embarked on a search for alternative models of development and governance. The change in the political orientation in many countries in the region since the early 2000s was not simply rhetorical. This opens a new opportunity to recreate formal and informal "rules of the game" that shape behavior in economic, social, and political life, at national and regional levels of collective action. In general new Latin American governments adopted more radical models of political inclusion and citizenship, implementing highly interventionist policies, redistribution and, in cases of nationalization, in support of a new attitude to state building and representation. This, combined with a greater emphasis on the inclusion of previously excluded groups and the significance of ethnic politics, supports the notion of "postneoliberalism" as a combination of Keynesian welfare politics and socialism (Tockman, 2010; Grugel and Riggirozzi, 2012). In this context, reclaiming the region by state and non-state actors became not only a way of resisting neoliberal politics but a genuine reflection of what Latin American should do and should look like. The changes in political economy, in other words, led to the rediscovery of the region as a common space for pulling together resources in support of alternative practices and in rejection of the idea of neoliberal-led regionalism. What "region" means in this context can be re-signified as motivations, interests, ideas, narrative, and political economic policies undergo changes. "Region" is, paraphrasing Wendt (1999), what actors make of it.

How far can we genuinely discern new regional governance at a time when trade has ceased to be the mechanism for the transmission of neoliberal principles? In a context where the very pillars of neoliberalism—as a political and economic paradigm, as a model of market democracy, as a sustainable and inclusive model of development—are critically questioned by academics, politicians, social actors, and practitioners and many other stakeholders, there is in Latin America an effort to reassert fresh rules of regional engagement and cooperation based on the reconfiguration of alliances and new motivations that are redefining the contours of regional governance. This process has not been empty of contradictions. Serbín and Saguier, for instance, argued that social demands were absorbed by a new surge of intergovernmental politics (Serbin, in Riggirozzi and Tussie 2012: 147–65; Saguier, 2007: 251–65). While this discussion is genuine and on-going, what can also be suggested is that new practices defining regionalism should be seen as led by governments but also as opportunities for social actors to engage in networks that can advance a broader sense of regional social policies.

Regional Health Governance: New Forms of Collective Action by the Region and for the Region

As an alternative model of regional governance, UNASUR crystallized in 2008, building from, and capitalizing on, preexisting trade-led agreements, specifically MERCOSUR and the Andean Community. Unlike previous regional formations, UNASUR's strength and emphasis is on areas of regional cooperation beyond trade and finance. in many ways, UNASUR must be seen as a project that rebuilds the regional space capitalizing on resilient arrangements of the "open" regionalism of the 1990s but redefining the complexity of transborder practices and cooperation. As a system of governance, UNASUR is heading toward a deep intergovernmental institutionalized project based on the agreement that South America has the authority and capacity to autonomously manage natural resources, infrastructure, and security, and the responsibility to reconnect economic growth and social development through regional practices. New institutions and permanent structures of decision-making have thus been established in these areas deepening intraregional relations, and seeking new interregional (South–South) cooperation.

Although UNASUR was established in 2008, its origins must be traced back to the beginning of the decade, when Brazilian president Fernando Henrique Cardoso called in the 1st Summit of South American Presidents, in 2000. This Summit created the foundations in which South American integration settled and contested US continental ambitions (Briceño-Ruiz, 2010: 208–29). From this perspective, although embryonic, this emerging model of regional governance needs no trivialization. The renewed commitments on social principles, development, and rights, together with its institution-building, gave new impetus to ambitious projects that, since the early 2000s, attempted to boost infrastructural and energy integration throughout the continent, and the autonomous management of security and regional affairs restricting US power and US-led institutions' influence, and redefining the inter-American system (UNASUR, 2012; Tussie and Riggirozzi, 2011).

Certainly, region building in South America reflects complex dilemmas of politics, where national interests may be pursued in a multiscalar way, and so the role of Brazil is explained—and perhaps, although more controversial, that of Venezuela—advancing new goals of regional social and political economy (Schirm, 2010: 197–221; Malamud, 2011: 1–24). But region-building involves more than a balance of power between leaders and followers. It is also a reflection of new choices of policies and political assertiveness that, in the case of South America, is expressed through numerous efforts to build regional projects echoing a generalized spirit of political change with important implications for inter- and intra-American relations.

Beyond national interest calculations and symbolic politics, what current regional politics in South America represents is a clearer commitment to address relegated and deeply rooted unsolved dilemmas of development, inclusion, and social rights by reclaiming the regional space for the crafting of policies and policy-making mechanisms. In this context, the governance of health in UNASUR is a key policy area based on policy commitments and institutionalized practices that not only embrace a new sense of regional collective action, but fundamentally a new mode of regionalism that enables both new responsibilities and a new policy instance advancing social development.

In the creation of UNASUR, social policy was presented as a critical aspect reconciling in many ways the lack of progress in the social agenda and the region as a space where social politics happen and rights are enforced. UNASUR official documents speak of a new morality of integration linked to a rights-based approach to health, as it is considered a transformative element for societies, a vehicle for inclusion and citizenship; and an active aspect in the process of South American integration (UNASUR, 2011; UNASUR, Declaración Presidencial, 2009). Health from this perspective became "locus for integration", incorporating efforts and achievements from previous regional integration mechanisms but creating a new framework for formal integration with regard to health. The way UNASUR embraced new commitments of social development was visible in the health area. This unfolded as a three levels of policy practice: (i) institutional, as a regulatory actor; (ii) diplomatic, engaged in extraregional relations; and (iii) project-led, engaged in intraregional activities. These levels are interconnected in novel forms of exchange of human and economic resources, and institutionalization of regulatory frameworks and best practices. In many ways, UNASUR health responds to social needs in the region while strengthening the autonomy of South America vis-à-vis external actors.

Institutionally, the South American Health Council or UNASUR Health was created in December 2008 to provide an opportunity for integration with regard to health. The UNASUR Health Council was one of the first Councils to be approved in UNASUR with the aim of reducing social and health inequities in the region. The UNASUR Health Council works at the ministerial level to consolidate South American integration in the health field by means of the establishment of policies based on mutual agreements, coordinated activities, and cooperation efforts between countries (UNASUR, *Declaración Presidencial*, 2009). The UNASUR Health Council establishes policies and the agenda for regional provisions on health. The agenda is implemented by Technical Groups formed by members' representatives to tackle five issues that defined the South American health agenda, or the Five Year Plan (Plan Quinquenal) approved in 1999 (UNASUR, 2009). The Five Year Action Plan outlines actions, coordinated financial resources, capacity building activities, and regulatory frameworks through the establishments of new institutional arrangements coordinated by specific Working Groups. The Working Groups coordinate the following specific goals: creation of the South American "epidemiological shield" for the coordination and surveillance through networks implementing international health regulations. The priorities in this area are early detection and response to outbreaks, and elimination of communicable diseases such as malaria, dengue fever, and tuberculosis. Within this framework, new regulatory procedures have been established to enhance surveillance capacity through committees that monitor prevention and control of communicable diseases, intoxications due to pesticides and the quality of water, and coordination among countries for these and similar risks, as well as to enhance the delivery in terms of regulations and health systems for the most vulnerable groups (UNASUR, 2009). A second area of priority relates to the development of universal health systems in response to peoples' universal right to health. Likewise, the promotion of universal access to medicines has been prioritized by establishing new drug policies and the development of a South American health-production complex. Relatedly, new measures are established through the South American Commission on Determinants of Health. Finally, new mechanisms of assessment and evaluation, as well as research and development have been critical to enhance provisions, resource management and governance in relation to access to medicine. To achieve this goal two mechanisms have been created: the UNASUR Health

Scholarship Program, and the South American Institute of Health Governance (Instituto Sudamericano de Governancia en Salud, ISAGS).[1]

The South American Institute of Health Governance is made up by its member countries' Ministers of Health with the goal of supporting and strengthening national and subregional capacities in formulating, implementing, and evaluating long-term policies and plans, and respond to the needs of training human resources in response to the other goals of UNASUR health agenda. ISAGS leads a network of similar country-based institutions dedicated to the production of knowledge and preparation of key professionals for the management of national health systems (UNASUR Plan Quinquenal, 2009). The establishment of ISAGS is a pioneering step that creates an institutional pillar to tackle issues of management and redistribution of resources in the form of human capacity for better governing of health as a regional goal as well as professionally for enhancing research and development. ISAGS activities range from the organization of seminars, courses, internship programs, and other initiatives to improve leadership at the level of health systems, to the coordination of research programs in support of a more autonomous pharmaceutical industry. In this respect, ISAGS seeks to identify existing industrial capacities in the region to coordinate common policies for production of medicines and other goods, advancing the industry, and creating competitive advantages in global negotiation and provision for regional health.

The implications for this new institutional force is particularly significant for the regionalization of human capacity and knowledge as tools that can give leverage in negotiations vis-à-vis private and multilateral organizations. UNASUR Health institutions, the Council, and ISAGS, are crucial mechanisms for establishing rules and regulations for the managing of health regionally. While the Health Council essentially organizes the rules and procedures fostering relationships between actors; the ISAGS represents an important mechanism, a type of knowledge bank, in support of policy making and policy action, while establishing new boundaries between public and private actors.

The significance of these developments has to be seen in the process of region-building and modes of "regulatory regionalism", as expressed by Hameiri and Jayasuriya, in response to social and redistributive needs (Hameiri, 2012; Jayasuriya, 2009: 335–47). But the institutionalization of new discourse and practices is not only opening a new space for action in regional social development but also new practices that are projected externally, mainly in terms of "regional health diplomacy" and South–South cooperation, defining the region as an actor (Buss, 2011: 1722–23). Regional action is hugely supported by the more confident presence of Brazil in the international arena, which in the case of global health has taken an increasingly active role and new protagonism over the past decade (Buss and do Carmo Leal 2009; Gomez, 2009; Soares de Lima and Hirst, 2009:

---

1 For information about ISAGS, see website of the Instituto Suramericano de Gobierno en Salud. Available at http://ISAGSs-unasul.org/site/sobre/?lang=es (2 April 2012).

21–40). Nunn *et al.* explored the various efforts of Brazilian diplomats and health officials to change global norms regarding access to medicines as a human right in various United Nations bodies, World Trade Organization negotiations, and campaigns involving South–South cooperation (Nunn, Da Fonseca, and Gruskin, 2009). But while Brazil has been instrumental in promoting discussions over policies in important areas concerning the impact of intellectual property rights on access to medicines or the monopolist position of pharmaceuticals on price setting and generics, it has also acted in tune with a region that is redefining the terms of redistributional politics, managing common resources, and harmonizing policies and capacities, while using the region as a platform for contestation in international negotiations. From this perspective, UNASUR has increasingly emerged as a legitimate and proactive actor in pursuit of controversial aspects within the global health governance agenda, in particular issues of intellectual property rights and access to medicine (Kickbusch, Silberschmidt, and Buss, 2010; Buss, 2011). For the first time, joint actions are being promoted at the Pan-American Health Organization and the World Health Organization to change policies regarding representation of developing countries in the executive boards of these bodies. Likewise, UNASUR governments have settled a strategy of joint negotiation, through the revolving fund of the Pan-American Health Organization (PAHO) to guarantee equitable access to medicines. In another manifestation of collective action, UNASUR countries have committed not to buy medicines above the prices settled by the PAHO's fund, attempting to prevent commercial interests taking advantage of panic and uncertainty caused by epidemics. Patents and access to medicine have demanded a more nuanced assessment of how regional arrangements can maximize and enhanced the reach and outcomes of public policy, emphasizing that economic interests in the global health industry and intellectual property laws should not impede efforts to protect public health (UNASUR Salud, 2011).

The presence of UNASUR in this type of global health diplomacy, and its coordinated efforts to redefine rules of participation and representation in the governing of global and regional health, is pointing at a new rationale in regional integration in Latin America that in many ways resembles the region becoming an international "actor". The notion of region as actor denotes a space for new policy coordination and collective action through regional institutions and responsibilities for the delivery of common policies in issue areas. In the case of health, this is an important development with tangible results for national governments in terms of how to deliver better and more inclusive policies, and for local populations in terms of improving their well-being.

Finally, at the level of policy implementation, UNASUR is coordinating new transnational-risks projects and effective funding for health and food security programs in specific countries. One of the most salient interventions has been the reconstruction and health cooperation with Haiti after the earthquake in January 2010. The 12 members of UNASUR disbursed US$ 70 million, out a total of US$ 100 million committed to the reconstruction of Haiti. These funds are allocated for the implementation of 144 projects identified, coordinated, and funded by UNASUR (APS, 2011). UNASUR provided relief supplies to assist counter-cholera efforts targeting Haiti's dire sanitation crisis after the earthquake. Within the coordination of UNASUR, Venezuela sent medicine supplies to help combat the outbreak of cholera in the island. Likewise, a UNASUR mission has also undertaken an extensive vaccination against H1N1 influenza and dengue (Pan-American Health Organisation, 2011). Additional bilateral aid from Ecuador and the Dominican Republic provided support in the form of funds, logistics, sanitation, and personnel, reinforcing the regional response. UNASUR's cooperation with Haiti has also complemented health assistance with food sovereignty and improvement of infrastructure, housing, and institutional strengthening.[2] The Secretary General of the UNASUR, María Emma Mejía, made clear that the regional cooperation with Haiti not only focuses on "circumstantial support to deal with emergencies arising from the earthquake [i.e. immediate needs related to budget support, maintenance, shelters], but also interventions to help the country move forward" (Agencia Latinoamericana de Informacion, 2011). In view of this, an important food program has been implemented, the so-called Pro Huerta project, which provides technology and training to farmers for the implementation of technology in agroecological self-production of food. The project is based on an investment of USD$3 million and capacity building from an Argentine agronomist, involved in the Pro-Huerta program in Argentina, a program that has been running since the mid 1990s in that country. Another important project supported by UNASUR in Haiti is the so-called roof for my country, in collaboration with the Chilean Foundation of the same name, which aims to build just under a thousand houses, surgeries, and schools (UNSC, 2011; UNASUR, 2010). UNASUR Health Council also played a key role in the support for reconstruction after the earthquake in Chile in 2010. What these institutional arrangements, projects, and practices suggest is that health is becoming a salient element redefining the terms of region building as a space for new political and social manifestations away from the trade-led and financial rationale, and as an actor that faces and negotiates more confidently the challenges of the global political economy. In this context UNASUR is moving toward the consolidation of a regional complex on which transborder practices and cooperation are deepening intergovernmental relations and their commitments toward social inclusion, development, and autonomy.

The Social Purpose of Regionalism: New Coordination, New Rights?

While the extent to which regional institutions can close the gap of unequal development in South America is still to be seen, UNASUR offers a new institutional architecture, policies, and action plans that opened a new space for action in a field of high social sensibility and practices for integration that can have

---

2   Página 12/Argentina, 1st September 2010, 'La UNASUR ya tiene Oficina en Haiti'.

enormous consequences on social development. But UNASUR also speaks of a social policy as a transformative element in terms of delivery of policies, a vehicle for inclusion and rights. The implications of these developments are twofold. In the first place, it confirms the importance of understanding the connection between national politics and regional politics, something that far from being obvious has been largely overlooked in the analysis of regional governance. Regionalism has been defined as and by a regionalism–neoliberal globalization relationship, and therefore little attention has been paid to how states respond to their own national commitments and to region-building projects. This is a pressing research question as the relationship between neoliberal globalization and regionalism does not hold firmly any longer. Regional politics not only contest the established architecture but go beyond it to align national institutions and socioeconomic goals with new forms of regional regulation and policy delivery in a combination of national level statecraft and regional political economy. From this perspective, a research agenda on current regionalism beyond Europe needs to further explore the ways and extent to which regional politics can narrow inequality and asymmetries in the region. How can regionalism support national policies? Can we talk about regionalism as an alternative way of delivering social rights and strengthening rights-based domestic policies? At the same time new questions are opened for further investigation on how regional arrangements sit against global negotiations. Can we genuinely talk about a new regional diplomacy in global health? In this view, UNASUR Health and its Five-Year Plan could be seen as both the outcome and context of a developing regional political community that is transiting toward a deeper *institutionalized polity* with a permanent structure of decision-making, capacity-building institutions, and supportive nationally based projects. In practice, these elements define new responsibilities within the region, as well as an enhanced, or more confident, capacity to be a global actor. Theoretically, this gives substance to arguments about region-building and *regionness* that has been productively applied to explain social cohesion and social governance in EU but largely overlooked in the study of Latin American regionalism (Riggirozzi, 2012).

Second, the analysis of the UNASUR Health system gives new substance to what Jayasuriya termed the "domestic political mainsprings of regional governance", by which regionalism is not only expression of intergovernmental arrangements but also a driver of change of national practices (Jayasuriya, 2003: 199–215, 199). From this perspective, regional regulations, institutions, and procedures engender distinctive forms of "regulatory systems" that affect national practices. In other words, regional policies may be originally driven by national interests but have the potential to develop formal and informal forms of coordination that create a sphere of authority independently from national interests and intergovernmental politics. In the case of UNASUR, this is seen in the way new institutions regulate a range of policy domains, from external relations to the sharing of material and epistemic resources through the coordination of research and development. These institutions have the capacity to act in reflection of regional interests and to establish at the same time new benchmarks, targets, and goals of policy that can affect practices or redistribute resources at national levels of implementation. In addition, regional epistemic communities and professional associations, such as the Working Groups or ISAGS, open new opportunities for the participation of non-state actors in the definition of regional policies and practices, with the potential to downplay the excessive intergovernmentalism that underpins current regional developments. If so, the reconfiguration of the role of region in South America will transcend new forms of bureaucratization and institutionalization of regional goals toward a more fundamental place where state and society can reenact their social contract reinforcing different levels of policy.

Conclusion

This chapter conceptualizes the relationship between regional governance, social policy, and the political space that this relationship generates. There are elements to sustain that the governing of regional health in UNASUR represents a new form of regionalism anchored in the institutionalization and practice of goals that are at odds with traditional goals of trade and finance, while creating new capacities for a more confident South American regional actor to negotiate goals vis à vis external actors. Regulatory aspects and practices of UNASUR Health reconnect national motivations, models of political economy, and regional integration, breaking with deterministic assumptions of external determinants of region building and the regionalism–globalization relationship. From this perspective, we are able to move beyond arguments about the relative importance of globalization as a structure of constraints for developing countries and developing regions that have often considered regionalism as a defensive reaction to external pressures and influence. As the analysis in this article suggests, regional cooperation in health, although allegedly embryonic, has the capacity to drive a transformative process, creating new spaces for action in which to reembed socially responsive models of development and citizenship rights.

Of course this process is not free from contradictions. All politics engender struggles that in the case of region building in South America can be defined by the lack of participation of civil society organizations in the definition of UNASUR social policies, agendas, and institutions. In fact, the creation of UNASUR has not seen yet new mechanisms for the incorporation of social actors in the definition of social agendas. This creates a contradiction in spaces that embraced real commitments with regional provisions for social policy—despite social actors' demands having been brought in under the auspices of the state into new dynamics of regional cooperation and integration. Nonetheless, a lack of an institutionalized broader dialogue may inhibit the transformative capacity of UNASUR as a new instance of social policy delivery. These challenges will define the prospects of social policy through regional integration and the extent to which we can identify a new route to public policy at a cross border level of governance. As such, while health is a thriving case in terms of new regional practices and policies, the politics that may affect furthering this social turn in regionalism are still an open agenda of investigation.

At the moment, Latin America is a continent of contradiction where diversity in motives, ideologies, and leadership aspirations are driving alternative (postneoliberal) models of integration. Despite the much longer route to walk in terms of social policy and regionalism, undeniably the region recovered a novel capacity to reassert new modes of regional organization with an enormous potential for social development. Those interested in regionalism and development cannot afford to ignore this issue. The lesson we can draw from the case of UNASUR Health in particular is that, unlike the past experiments in regional governance, we can now talk about a new start, analytically and politically, on the bases of concrete explorations of institutions, practices, new opportunities for collective action, and projects on the ground. New forms, and domains, of regional governance allow us to speculate about the complexities and contradictions of social-based regionalism, as well as a new sense of the value of the region as another policy-making instance enacting social goals.

Chapter 8

Global Contexts and Challenges of Building a Regional Governance of Social Policy and Its Implications for South America

Nicola Yeates

Introduction

Regionalism has taken hold as a major focal point of ideational, and political struggle to define how social, political, and economic relations among peoples and territories are to be organized in an increasingly integrated world. Social policy, broadly defined here as "collective interventions directly affecting transformation in social welfare, social institutions, and social relations" (Mkandawire, 2001: 1), is a vital part of these struggles, because it defines who is a full member of the political community with all the rights and responsibilities that membership bestows—and who is not. Across all continents, a wide range of political actors from within and outside individual regions are contesting what social model is to underpin prospective regional public policies in relation to economy, finance, industry, energy, and trade, as well as the extent to which regionally defined and coordinated policies in relation to broad goals of social equality, inclusion, participation, and cohesion and in relation to specific sectors such as health, education, labor, social protection, and food security are to be adopted. The kinds of regional social policies emerging reveal much about the nature of regionalist visions and strategies, as well as the character of the regional formation itself.

Cross-cutting these ideational struggles over what kinds of social policy for what kind of regional integration, are a range of "practical policy" issues to do with whether social policy is to remain a sovereign matter (that is, essentially confined within political borders of the different member countries) or whether it is to evolve over larger integrative scales and become a matter for supranational governance. If social policy is to become a matter of supranational governance, questions arise as to what sorts of political cooperation and institutions are most conducive to promoting regional social policy and regional social convergence forged upon common interests and under conditions of economic asymmetries and political disparateness; whether the strategic ambition of regional social policy should be confined to minimal interstate coordination necessary to promote labor mobility and address cross-border harms, or whether it should be founded upon principles of social inclusivity, democracy, and developmentalism.

Analytically and politically, then, regional social policy is of central importance for understanding plans for organizing the region and its relation to other parts of the world. Just as the formulation of strategies and policy goals supportive of the right to the means of social participation reveal much about the nature of welfare settlements and social citizenship in any given country context, so too they illuminate the nature of regionalism (as political strategy), regionalization (as social process), and regional formations (as institutional arrangements). The forms and goals of regional social policy can be regarded as a defining element of the character of regional integration—indeed, of "regionness" (Hettne and Söderbaum, 2000) itself. Questions about the extent to which regional integration processes are accompanied by regional social policies, and the nature of the social model and forms of social action these policies promote, "speak" to issues of the transformative potential of political agency and of transnational action to shape globalizing processes in the interests of equitable social welfare.

This chapter discusses some challenges of building a regional governance of social policy and relates them to the contemporary South American context. After briefly reviewing why regional social policy has taken hold on global and subglobal agendas, the discussion proceeds to review the outcomes of efforts to "socialize regionalism" and "regionalize social policy" in recent years. Here, the discussion focuses on the extent to which social policies in relation to health, social protection, labor, and education are manifest features of regionalist projects/ formations. It also delineates key axes of political struggle over the orientation and goals of social policy that are played out through these policy arenas. Examples from a range of territories around the world are brought into the discussion to situate and contextualize South American experiences and to consider what might be possible for those wishing to socialize regionalism in the continent.

The significance of such an overview is of particular import at this current juncture with the rise of leftist and populist governments in South America in recent years, the advancement of a social investment approach to social policy and the raising of social welfare issues on political and policy mandates of governments, and the reinvigoration of regionalism as an ideal and as a set of institutionalized practices. It is also clear that contemporary developments in regional social policy in South America are unfolding against the backdrop of a strong historical legacy in which the idea of regional integration is as old as South American independence, and the developmental welfare state has been integral to the twentieth-century history of South American regionalism (Riesco, 2010). Such legacy brings markedly diverse experiences of political practices among governments and non-state actors around regionalism and the coexistence of multiple scales and forms of regional integration. The establishment of UNASUR, with its nascent social developmentalism, and its alter-model, the quasi-socialist ALBA, in particular have thrown into relief the starkly different models of regional social policy that may be instituted and the possibility of more radical visions of regional social policy than was previously thought possible. As the chapter discusses, the key axes of debate and contestation are not around whether regional social policy is possible or not, but what kind of regional social policy for what kind of regional community is to be instituted.

Contexts of Regional Social Policy

The idea of regional social policy has grown in salience at the current juncture in the development of the global system as scholars, policy-makers, and activists debate how to develop transnational social (and wider public) policies based on social equity and justice (Yeates, 2001, 2005; Yeates and Deacon, 2006, 2010). In part this has been a response to threats to national public social provision, arising from the advance of political projects to organize social relations along neoliberal lines. The widespread and multiple effects of informalization, commercialization, and privatization of welfare services, combined with liberalized social regulation of distributive systems, created new and widespread social risks, exacerbated social inequality, increased displacement, and intensified social conflict. These effects (actual and anticipated) have been an integrating force for contemporary social movements and civil society organizations which have organized on national and transnational scales, whether part of the alter-globalization movement or not. Multiform citizen movements and organizations have been regionalist in their own organizing strategies alongside taking their concerns to regional fora to press for an alternative social model for regional governance and policy that eschews the spread of "free" trade-based regional policy and promotes a policy based on social solidarity and social justice (Brennan and Olivet, 2010). Calling for the establishment of regional mechanisms for coordinating and implementing policies that protect public services, promote citizens equitable access to decent work, adequate income, livelihoods, public health, water, and food sovereignty (Brennan and Olivet, 2010), they have been instrumental in laying the foundations for an inclusive, democratic, and developmental social policy and governance.

The growing appeal of regional social policy on the policy agendas of global actors is also to be traced to those in the reformist wings of the alter-globalization movement who have argued in favor of creating new countervailing and pluralistic sources of power and policy spaces attuned to the developmental and self-determination interests of the Global South. As Bello, for example, argued: "[W]hat developing countries and international civil society should aim at is not to reform the TNC-driven WTO and Bretton Woods institutions, but ... [a strategy that] would include strengthening diverse actors and institutions such as UNCTAD, multilateral environmental agreements, the International Labor Organization, and *regional economic blocs* (Bello, 2004: 116–17, my emphasis; see also Keet and Bello, 2004). Devolved global economic governance, by this account, would not be restricted to the development of (more) regional commercial trade blocs, but would institute strengthened regional political institutions to foster and govern more sustainable and socially just forms of production and consumption. Such alternative visions of regional integration have also resonated with the historic ambitions of some Independence movements, especially in Africa and South America, as well as with on-going practical efforts on the part of (some) governments—sometimes in response to agitation by social movement and nongovernmental organizations—to build regional political capacities that amplify their voices in global fora.

The impasse in global multilateral pro-"free" trade negotiations and the difficulties of agreeing universally acceptable global social policy have shifted International Governmental Organizations' attention to the potential contributions of strengthened regional blocs. The World Commission on the Social Dimension of Globalization argued that regional integration can contribute to a more equitable pattern of globalization, but only if regional integration has a strong social dimension that helps build the capabilities needed to take advantage of global opportunities and improves conditions of integration into the global economy (WCSDG, 2004: 71). Since then, regional integration has received increasing attention within the ILO and UNESCO, and within the UN system (UN, 2005, 2006; Deacon, Ortiz, and Zelenev, 2007) as an alternative to neoliberal globalization. However, the overwhelming focus of these organizations remains on the national policies of member countries, in which regional social policy (as distinct from the national social policies of individual members of a regional group) occupies a minor place in their policy focus and activities and policy advice to regional associations often neglects issues of social policy (Deacon and Macovei, 2010). This also holds true for the UN regional economic commissions (though there are some notable exceptions, e.g. ESCAP on ASEAN capacity-building in migration management; ECA's work in terms of the importance it attributes to subregional communities; ECLAC on cross-border social security in the Caribbean; and ESCWA on lesson learning and policy dialogue across borders in social policy in the countries of the Arab region) and regional development banks (Deacon and Macovei, 2010). Finally, the World Bank has also begun to acknowledge the merits of a coordinated *regional* approach to social policy, recently arguing in favor of scaling up individual country initiatives in the Caribbean to incorporate health-worker training into a CARICOM regional strategy (Yeates, 2010). However, like the UN, its operations in relation to social policy are overwhelmingly directed at individual member states rather than regional associations.

Principles of Regional Social Policy

There are several principled advantages in building a social policy dimension to regional groupings of nations. First, since regional formations often entail groups of countries with similar cultural, legal, and political characteristics they can (compared with multilateral negotiations) offer countries access to a broader menu of social policy alternatives and greater ease and pace of agreeing on the scope and nature of social policy, including greater possibilities for advancing their own social standards. For smaller and developing countries in particular regional formations offer enhanced access to and influence over policy developments. These influences are not necessarily negative: more developed countries can force social standards upwards in the poorer members, while smaller countries can have a strong blocking effect on the liberalizing ambitions of larger ones. Also, individual countries acting through regional associations can have a louder voice in policy discourses in global fora than by acting alone. And regionally coordinated responses can overcome the limitations of small-scale (bilateral) initiatives which may not sustain the interest of all the countries involved. Second, regional economic and trade strategies can protect, promote, and reshape a regional division of labor, trade and production in ways that promote cooperation and generate fiscal resources for national and regional social policy purposes. Too often global trade comes with tax exemptions for local and global companies that erode fiscal resources. Third, regional social policy enables economies of scale and the pooling of risks and resources. For example, there is a strong argument for uniting forces and resources to create regional provision in advanced specialist education, training or health facilities. Limitations of small-scale social insurance schemes can be addressed by pooling and spreading risks regionally. For example, one reason why agricultural insurance experiments have failed across the world is their size; that is, they collapse when a major catastrophe occurs (e.g. drought, plant pest, or cattle disease affecting a whole country), and insurance funds are unable to cover all losses. However, by pooling risks internationally, with adequate reinsurance, schemes can work (Ortiz, 2001). In similar vein, a regional policy offers the possibility of more effective preparedness and response to natural disasters, including the provision of humanitarian and economic aid (Yeates, 2005; Yeates and Deacon, 2006).

UNDESA similarly argued the case for a focus on cross-border regional social policies as a contribution to poverty alleviation (Deacon, Ortiz, and Zelenev, 2007). It argued that, in principle, regionalism would make possible the development of regional social policy mechanisms of cross-border redistribution, regulation, rights, investment, and lesson-learning, using a range of methods such as exhortation, standard-setting, policy coordination, legislation, and identity mobilization. In terms of regional social *redistribution* mechanisms, regionally financed funds can take several forms, ranging from targeting depressed localities, to tackling significant health or food shortage issues, to stimulating cross-border cooperation. If such mechanisms are in place, then North–South transfers funded either by ODA or by global taxes, or funds raised or contributed by the member states of the region, could be transmitted to specific localities or address social issues via the regional structure according to regional priorities. Regional social, health, and labor *regulations* can include standardized regulations to combat an intraregional "race to the bottom." Regional social security and health agreements setting out portability rights can help manage cross-border migration more effectively and with greater justice. Such regulations are commonly thought of as relating to health and safety, labor and social protection, and agreements on the equal treatment of men and women, and majority and minority (including indigenous) groups; but they can also extend to other areas such as food production and handling standards and utilities. Regional formations may also be in a stronger position in relation to private suppliers to set, monitor, and enforce cross-border rules regarding, for example, access rights to commercial services.

Regional social rights mechanisms give citizens a legal means of challenging their governments over breaches of law in relation to labor and access to social protection, medicines and health, and education. Principles of social policy and levels of social provision can be articulated and used as benchmarks for countries to aspire to. A regional court can be a useful mechanism for citizens to challenge perceived failures to fulfill social and human rights. Regional *intergovernmental social policy cooperation* in terms of regional health specialization, regional education cooperation, regional food and livelihood cooperation, and regional recognition of social security entitlements can take different forms. Cross-border social sector investments, for example, can address various common social policy priorities, for instance the production of cheaper generic pharmaceuticals to benefit from economies of scale, common programs to avoid cross-border transmission of diseases, or the sharing of health specialisms or higher education facilities within a region; while cross-border lesson-learning mechanisms provide an opportunity to learn from good practices and develop solutions that are amenable to scaling up.

Expressions of Regional Social Policy Worldwide

We now proceed to examine the extent to which different regional formations around the world have adopted regional social policy and the nature of the policies adopted. The discussion also considers key axes of strategic difference among those seeking to develop stronger regional social policies. This discussion draws on a recent major survey of regional social policy across four continents (Deacon *et al.*, 2010), a summary overview of findings is presented in Figure 8.1.

Many regional formations have adopted a "social" agenda and enjoy wider political legitimacy within the region and support from outside of it (e.g. in certain global fora) for doing so. However, initiatives vary in terms of the methods they use, ranging from exhortation to standard-setting to legislation to policy coordination to practices of cross-border information exchange and lesson-learning. Crucially, most regional formations limit collaboration in social policy to little more than facilitating cross-border labor mobility. Notable among such measures are: the partial or full removal of work visa requirements (e.g. Southern African Development Community (SADC); Caribbean Community and Common Market (CARICOM); Economic Community of West African States (ECOWAS); South Asian Association for Regional Cooperation (SAARC)); mutual recognition of professional and educational qualifications and educational institutions (e.g. MERCOSUR; CAN; ASEAN; Australia and New Zealand Closer Economic

Regional association	Redistribution	Social regulation	Social rights	Cooperation in social sectors	Cross-border lesson learning
EUROPE					
EU	Yes	Yes	Yes	Yes	Yes
Council of Europe	No	No	Yes but not force of law	No	Yes
LATIN AMERICA					
MERCOSUR	Yes	Soft law*	Yes but not force of law	Yes	Yes
Andean Community	Yes	Soft law	Yes but not force of law	Yes	Yes
CARICOM	No?	Soft law	Yes but not force of law	Yes	Yes
ALBA	Yes	No	No	Yes	Yes
ASIA					
ASEAN	Yes	Soft law	Yes but not force of law	Yes	Yes
SAARC	Yes	No except trafficking of women and children	Yes but not force of law	Yes	Yes
AFRICA					
AU	No	Soft law	Yes but not force of law	Yes via sub-regions	Yes
ECOWAS	No?	Soft law	Yes	Yes	Yes
UEMOA	Yes	Covered by ECOWAS	As ECOWAS	As ECOWAS	As ECOWAS
SADC	No	Soft law	Yes but not force of law	Yes	Yes
SACU	Yes	Covered by ECOWAS	As SADC	As SADC	As SADC

Figure 8.1   Regional Social Policies in Practice on Four Continents

Source: Deacon, Macovei, van Langenhove and Yeates, 2010, Figure 10.1.

Note: Soft law means that regional declarations/agreements on standards etc. are left up to countries to implement with exhortation from the region.

Relations Trade Agreement (ANZCERTA); and SAARC; and transborder social security portability entitlements (MERCOSUR, CARICOM, ANZCERTA, SADC).

Contrary to the general initiating policies on the labor market and labor mobility, regional social policy cooperation goes beyond the strict requirements of action for the creation of regional commercial markets. For example, SADC has developed an infrastructure and capacity for the implementation of trans-border social policy that includes cooperation on issues of child labor, communicable diseases, and the referral of patients between member states. CARICOM is active in issues of health policy as regards institutional and human resource capacity, and communicable diseases in particular. ECOWAS has a regional court of justice adjudicating on national labor rights. ASEAN has instituted a regional human rights body. MERCOSUR has instituted regional harmonization of pharmaceutical legislation and regulations to facilitate economies of scale in the production of generic drugs. SAARC has a Social Charter that enshrines access to basic services and a set of development goals in poverty alleviation, education, health, and environment. The Andean Community has a Social Humanitarian Fund and Integral Plan for Social Development to unite efforts to fight poverty, exclusion, and inequality. ALBA is financing anti-poverty activity in neighboring countries and operates trade relations and schemes rooted in the solidarity economy. SAARC and ASEAN have instituted regional food security schemes which in effect function as redistribution mechanisms (Deacon *et al.*, 2010, part 2).

Although many of these regional social policies have progressed faster as exhortative declarations of aims and principle rather than as binding regulatory or redistributive mechanisms, it is also important to note the symbolic and practice uses of exhortative policy (such as Social Charters) in creating greater awareness of a range of common issues and a world of possibilities on a wide front and in contributing to the forging of transnational political alliances and political dynamics that may in turn stimulate more substantial regional cooperation. Exhortative declarations are important because they can be important precursors to the development of more substantial social policies. Indeed, it is this sustained, incrementalist, long-term project involving the participation of labor, development, and civil society groups alongside governments and business interests that in the Western European context at least gave rise to the transformation of a customs union with limited labor mobility rights into a full-blown economic and political union with (by contemporary world standards) a relatively substantial regional social dimension with regional mechanisms of social provision, redistribution, regulations, and legally enforceable rights of citizenship. This is not to offer regional social policy as practiced in the EU as *the* model to be aspired to or emulated; rather, it is to point to the fact that multiform, sustained civil society participation in processes of policy formation within the bureaus and boardrooms of regional institutions, alongside social action outside of them, have in the EU context been crucial to the development of a substantial regional social policy forged upon common interests, oriented to convergence and alignment, cognizant of sovereignty sensitivity, in conditions of economic asymmetry and political disparateness.

That said, and on experience to date, we need to be somewhat cautious about the potential of regional formations to develop a regional social policy embedded in an inclusive, democratic, and developmental social policy rather than one emanating from elite projects to create larger economic scales and spaces. Regional formations originate in discussions and negotiations within policy elites and, historically, there has been little popular demand for such projects. This does not deny subsequent involvement and support by labor and development organizations, or that regional processes and commitments can be levered to demand "more" social policy, or a "stronger" social policy, or a different kind of social policy. However, it does mean that regional formations have mostly operated for and as commercial trade agreements and political agreements of various kinds and their purpose is not primarily for the development of comprehensive social policy and development based on social equity. Even where it would seem that regional formations have gone beyond minimal measures to regulate cross-border labor movements and adopted a substantial regional social policy, the extent to which this presents a fundamental challenge to extant social models of regional integration is unclear. Returning to the EU, EU social policy has developed a set of regional social rights, regional social and labor standards, regional mechanisms of redistribution, and the right to legal redress from its original remit of facilitating cross-border labor mobility (work visas, social security portability) and some anti-discrimination measures (to prevent sex discrimination in waged labor from distorting international economic competition) to accompany its creation of a common market. However, it remains a matter of debate as to how far EU social policy has ever managed to fully break from its market origins, and recent proposals to extend the liberalization of trade in services has encroached further into the realm of public welfare provision in recent years.

The issue is not simply a matter of *whether* there should be a regional social policy accompanying regional integration. There are, to various degrees, already such policies accompanying such integration. There are versions of regional social policy that are entirely consistent with neoliberalism and with open regionalism, and there are versions of regional social policy characterized by stronger tendencies toward socially protectionist and developmentalist agendas. Competing visions and agendas for what kind of regional social policy should be developed are often present in the same region. In the Caribbean, where increases in intraregional migration following the implementation of the Caribbean Community Single Market and Economy (CSME) have raised the need for regionally coordinated policy on education, training and labor, such conflicts are evident. CARICOM's Managed Migration Program (MMP) addresses nurse recruitment, retention, deployment and succession planning throughout the Caribbean and instituted a range of projects comprising a range of policy approaches: training for export; the establishment of an "offshore" global nursing school in partnership with foreign investors; temporary nurse migration program with the possibility of frequent rotation between Jamaica and the USA; intraregional sharing of nurse-training resources (between Grenada and Antigua); measures to encourage emigrant Caribbean nurses to return to nurse on a voluntary basis and share their nursing expertise; recruitment of nurses from destination countries to work in the Caribbean for a limited period; and incentives for emigrant nurses to return to the Caribbean alongside disincentives to stay in the destination country (Yeates, 2010). Within the MMP no single project had greater significance than others, but during its implementation has become a site of contestation among competing visions about the prospective nature and orientation of CARICOM social policy. On the one hand, we see WHO-inspired visions of a self-sufficiency policy that would reduce the attractions of emigration and improve intraregional health worker migration and regional health worker resource management mechanisms competing with the World Bank's vision of a regional migration policy oriented toward an export-oriented model of health labor production in which the Caribbean becomes a major global provider of health care labor worldwide. This latter is increasingly taking hold in the regional secretariat and among CARICOM governments. What started out as visions to forge a regional self-sufficiency program may be transmutating into a regionalized, industrial nurse-export production model resourced by governments, private organizations, and recruitment agencies within and outside of the region (Yeates, 2010). As this example reveals, markedly different approaches and resources are brought to efforts to develop regional social policy, and the working out of regional social policy is entwined with struggles over the model of regional integration itself. The essence of this struggle as it has been played out to date lies between a socially protectionist model of economic integration founded on "deep" intraregional political relations and a model of open regionalism in which issues of social regulation and provision are treated as a matter of trade relations.

Such "games" are being played out across South America, where social regionalism is a key part of "post-neoliberal," "third wave" initiatives aimed at transcending the model of open integration characteristic of the 1990s. The establishment of UNASUR and ALBA in the mid to late 2000s was born from the struggle against the FTAA and from alternative proposals about the role of international integration in rights-based, equitable, and sustainable development; but they have otherwise developed markedly distinct purposes and objectives, and offer different degrees of alternative and challenge to US-led integration and to neoliberalism more generally (Kellogg, 2007; Riggirozzi, 2010; Tussie, 2009). Grugel and Riggirozzi (2007: 9) summarize the contrasting orientations thus:

> UNASUR is fundamentally a project that ranks from free trade areas to security alliance. It represents a regional construction that capitalizes on pre-existing trade-led agreements, as part of the "open regionalism" of the 1990s, such as MERCOSUR (Argentina, Brazil, Uruguay and Paraguay plus Venezuela, Chile and Bolivia as associates) and the Andean Community (Bolivia, Chile, Colombia, Ecuador, and Peru). UNASUR is aimed to strengthen its institutional

structure while seeking open markets abroad and autonomous position vis-à-vis external influences such as the USA or the EU. ALBA, on the contrary, represents a radical, ideologically transformative project that extends Chávez's twenty-first century socialism into a regional integration scheme pursuing, in direct opposition to neoliberalism. A type of transnationalized welfare based on intraregional cooperation in areas of health, education and housing. The contrasts with other regionalist projects such as NAFTA, MERCOSUR, and UNASUR are seen not only in its social dimension but, paradoxically, in its construction of a regional space whose members (Venezuela, Honduras, Cuba, Nicaragua, Bolivia, Ecuador, Dominica, Antigua and Barbuda, and Saint Vincent) do not share any contiguous borders. Resource endowment here is also critical. Oil revenues have been key to move ALBA's social agenda forward.

If the social development agenda is critical in understanding differences between the two models of regional governance (Riggirozzi, 2010), then we can summarize these as UNASUR approximating a version of social liberalism "under construction," whereas ALBA is based on welfare solidarism. The trajectories of the two models take them toward regionalized social democratic relations of welfare and regionalized socialist relations of welfare, respectively. It is in this regard that the contemporary Latin American social regionalism constitutes such a vitally important and interesting "experiment" in the contemporary global social politics and practices of regionalism. Whereas the significance of UNASUR—in social policy terms—is that it compares relatively favorably with the more progressive versions of social regionalism worldwide, the significance of ALBA is its emphasis on and version of transnational redistribution and solidarity which redefine the boundaries (and, crucially expand the scope of) what was previously thought possible, let alone practiced.

Conclusions

On-going attempts to move to define a more coherent transnational social policy to govern border-spanning social issues and harms have, in the context of stalled global multilateral social and economic policy negotiations and a rising tide of critique against neoliberal globalization, reinforced trends to build more robust regional formations with a pronounced social agenda. The content of this social agenda has become the focus of political struggle. Such struggles to define the nature of regionally coordinated responses on issues of poverty, economic security, and social inequality and across welfare, health, and education are not just key "markers" of the character of the political community but are actively formative of the community being constituted. The struggles involved are not only about narrow "welfare" issues: they "speak" more broadly to issues to do with competing visions about the desired social models of integration, the prospective nature of the regional community being created, and the governance of development itself.

Regional formations, as we have seen, are engaged with practical policy questions such as: how to forge an appropriately balanced relationship between trade and social (labor, welfare, health) standards; how to maintain levels of taxation and progressive tax structures in the face of international competition to attract and maintain inward capital investment; how to balance national risk- and resource-pooling systems and mechanisms with regional ones; how to fund regional mechanisms of redistribution; and: What is the balance between intraregional and international contributions? A major strategic issue in the regional governance of social policy is the extent to which relatively "closed" regions that currently have, or might develop, a social policy dimension are cut across by relative open regions that function essentially as global trading blocs, and by bilateral and interregional trade and investment agreements that downplay social equity considerations. Regional social policies that have been instituted have been, with some notable exceptions, mainly confined to minimal social (labor) regulations and provision to facilitate economic regionalization and alleviate the worst of social disruption and inequality. Regional social policy has been recognized by the international political community and "development industry" as a matter of strategic importance. Here, the role of development banks and allied groups in promoting a regional social policy that builds on "free" trade agreements and socially conservative conceptions of welfare was critically noted. These visions coexist with visions of regional social policy that attempt to socially regulate economic regionalization processes and harness the potential of regional integration in the interests of social welfare and regional social development.

The playing out of these competing agendas was examined in this chapter in the USA, the Caribbean, and Latin America. In the former, attempts by the international development industry to link intensive labor production, inward investment and services trade was examined. There, the recent crisis of neoliberal global governance has cut across, but—crucially—not led to the abandonment, of regional social policy as an object, or target, of political action by elite groups pressing for open regionalism. Whereas older versions used the language of "free" trade, current discourses harness the language of social investment and regional development. This represents to a degree an acknowledgement of the need to improve "returns" and benefits to the region, but to the extent that the underlying social model of regional integration (and of integration into the global economy) is based on export-oriented commercial trade one might reasonably question how far this represents a radical departure from older models. In South America, the struggle to surpass neoliberalist open regionalism has involved the definition of prominent social agendas, and to embed principles of human welfare and social protectionism in the new institutions set up. Much of the debate on the "new" Latin American regionalism has rightly gravitated around the significance of UNASUR and ALBA, where we see markedly different expressions of regional social policy taking hold. Though UNASUR is often held up as a more acceptable geopolitical model and prospective "global actorness," ALBA undoubtedly offers the more radical vision and set of institutional practices of regionalized social welfare and policy. The future of these different models of regionalized social policy will be in part be an ideological struggle between (regional) social liberalism and (regional) socialist welfare; but it will also be tied to wider developments in the political economy of international integration in the region and more globally.

With international agencies of many persuasions starting to consider regional formations (rather than individual countries in a region) as interlocutors, one issue arising is whether regional formations are in a position and have the capacity to set their own social policy and development agendas or whether they are to be confined to "conduits" that channel and translate multilateral (Northern) economic and social policy into "local" contexts. One major question to be confronted is, therefore, the extent to which Southern regional integration initiatives have the resources to lead the definition and institutionalization of an inclusive, democratic, and developmentalist regional social policy within the context of robust institutions of regional governance. Though the institutions and policy mandates of regional governance are still in the making, the "new" politics of South American regionalism may inspire some confidence that regional institutions are to be so resourced and mandated as to become a robust political actors within the continental context and within wider arenas of global governance. With the renegotiation of the Millennium Development Goals in 2015, the time has never been better to flex what capacities as exist to spearhead a more robust and ambitious vision of regional social policy on the world stage.

PART III
Broadening Regionalism: Crime, Intelligence, and Defense

Chapter 9

Drug Trafficking and Organized Crime: UNASUR Perspectives

Daniel Pontón

Introduction

Drug trafficking is one of the illegal activities that has created the most condemnation and intolerance by world governments in the past 40 years. While this situation was brought about by the enormous physical and mental damage caused to the population by the consumption of psychoactive substances, combat, and global war against drugs, it has been maintained principally by the need for geostrategic control of an illegal activity that produces substantial and uncommon economic figures and that is capable of activating a criminal mechanism with an enormous power for infiltrating all spheres of the State and society. This connection has transformed drug trafficking into one of the proprietary themes of internal and external security for countries, and, as such, significance in international relations in the current world.

In light of this, the connections between drug trafficking and organized crime is not a statistical nor unidirectional matter; rather, it is a dynamic and complex relationship that affects, moves, and adapts to diverse economic, social, political, and geographic contexts. For this reason, this chapter seeks to analyze the problem of drug trafficking and organized crime in the South American region during the past 11 years and the challenges this issue presents for the security of countries in the context of the new framework of South American integration.

The issue is based on the hypothesis that the changes of the economy of drug trafficking during the past 11 years create a new dynamic of organized crime with broad powers of territorial infiltration. This creates the need to strategically revive a cooperative new vision, articulated within the new framework of South American regional integration, that confronts important challenges such as the institutional weakness of the police and justice systems, corruption, the excessive militarization of this issue, and the emergence of sovereign political movements that do little to foster genuine integration on this problem.

The following article will be divided into four parts. The first part will present an analytical framework that allows us to understand the relationship between the political economy, drug trafficking, and organized crime. The second will seek to describe the hegemonic model of antidrug policies in the region and will analyze their results. We will then provide another analytic description of the new problematic situation of drug trafficking and organized crime in the South American region over the past 10 years, which revives the need for a new cooperative view and strategy toward the issue. Lastly, we will look at the political context of the perspectives and challenges of UNASUR with regard to this problem.

The Political Economy of Drug Trafficking and Organized Crime

The concept of organized crime was introduced for the first time in the 1930s when police in the USA began using it to describe a type of criminality characteristic of the Italian-American mafia's commercialization, monitoring, and trafficking of highly profitable illegal activities. Since that time, this type of criminal activity has been characterized by its capabilities for organization and infiltration of the social and political spheres of countries, its flexibility and adaptation to new social, economic, and political scenarios, and especially its transnational significance.

The economic revenue of organized crime may come from activities other than drug trafficking such as human trafficking, arms trafficking, trafficking in cultural property and natural species, trafficking of organs, and many other extremely lucrative illegal activities. However, drug trafficking is by far the most important current financial engine of the main criminal organizations in the world and without a doubt in the Latin American region. In the past 40 years, there has not been an organized criminal structure which has not used the control and commercialization of illicit drugs as a fundamental pillar from which it bases its enormous economic power and influence in the political economic structure of the countries affected by these criminal organizations.

An example of this is global cocaine trafficking. It is estimated that this market moves around 100 billion dollars annually worldwide; however, the capacity of reproduction of this economy only needs 30 percent for their maintenance (operating costs), the remaining 70 percent, if we take into account that each dollar invested produces 6 dollars of return, moves about 400 billion dollars, which constitutes the annual GDP of any country in the developed world with average income.

Precisely in the understanding of drug trafficking within the economy of organized crime lies its strategic importance. According to the recommendations of crime control authorities around the world and the famous antimafia judge Giovanni Falcone, who started a campaign of research, capture, and dismantling of mafia criminal structures in the 1980s and early 1990s in Italy, by targeting or weakening the financial engine of a large criminal organization traditionally anchored to a type of highly lucrative activity such as drug trafficking and subsequent laundering of money, you can strike and dismantle organized criminal structures. This proposal has been utilized methodologically by authors such as

Albanese (2008, 2010), who proposes focusing on criminal economic activities rather than groups as a measure to control and prevent organized crime, taking into account that these activities are businesses that are driven by objectives that stem from the maximization of profits and economic gains as a product of their illicit transactions (Bustelos Gómez, 2003).

To understand the financial importance of drug trafficking in the criminal industry, it is necessary to understand this activity as an illegal economy in which a market of supply and demand of services meets the operation and articulation of criminal rationalities that affect, flow, and adapt to new scenarios while looking to get the most benefit from these activities (Pontón and Rivera, 2011). Any change in the economy of drug trafficking, therefore, implies changes in the articulation of the criminal actors and dynamics of control and prosecution of this offence.

Now, when looking at global changes in criminal activities rooted in the economic variable, we are necessarily speaking of the field of the Political Economy of International Relations to the extent that it conceives of economic factors as a cause or consequence of an important fact in society and the world (Frieden and Martin, 2001, in Bustelos, 2003). This discipline has naturally been used by International Studies as a result of a relational or interactive approach to economics and politics, to analyze various global topics such as: globalization, international trade, international finance, multinational enterprises, economic integration, the environment, gender, the inclusion of regional groups of countries in the world economy and other national and sub-national aspects in their relationship with global issues (Bustelos, 2003: 157).

For this reason, as Vivares (2013) says in the Introduction of this book, we extend the concept of development to the analysis of security and conflict, understanding these latter issues as key threats affecting governance, development, well-being, and the economic growth of countries.

Looking at the theme of security and conflict, it is important to emphasize that international relations has traditionally focused on issues of defense and State sovereignty. Thus, the main focus of attention has been on the states themselves, the same that are conceived of as rigid sovereign units and key actors in the balance of power of the international system.

According to this logic, the analysis of drug trafficking and organized crime is based on the structural and institutional vulnerability of states as a determining (not to mention causal) variable in the processes of deployment and infiltration of organized crime and its economies. From this point of view, the geopolitical vision of "Failed States" is derived from and currently widely used for the classification of countries according to their degree of danger to the international community for being considered sites of operation of organized crime and international terrorism (Santos, 2009; Rotberg, 2003). However, this approach distorts political and methodological elements that do not allow for a real understanding of the complex and dynamic relationship of this problem at the global level.

As a result, this article is based on two meanings for understanding organized crime from the view of political economy:

1. The first derives from conceiving of a diffuse authority of State power; i.e., no longer centered on the State as the center of political and economic structure, but also as the decentralized power resulting from other non-State actors (markets, companies, international organizations, NGOs, lobbyists, criminal groups) (Bustelos, 2003: 19, 21). For the purposes of this research, this could be considered the articulated decentralized power of organized crime and its capacity for infiltration into the State, and the economic and social spheres of a country.

2. The second meaning makes the rationalities of the legal and illegal economies analogous. This despite the fact that the criminal agents are periodically accused of not operating within a realm of rationality due to their low risk aversion, their propensity to resolve conflicts through violent means and the weak stability of agreements and transactions; that is to say, short-sighted behavior which is far from the ideal of a modern rational economic agent. However, far from deepening the long debate, addressing the non-rationality of criminal actors is nothing more than considering the attributes or moral characterizations a posteriori without taking into account that the criminal markets are a consequence of a type of political economy based on illegality. In other words, these are markets with their own characteristics, dynamics, and rationalities where agents or actors converge with internalized rules that somehow ensure their sustainability over time through the optimization of profits and protection to minimize risks (Pontón and Rivera, 2011).

This combination of a vision of political economy not centered in the State, but rather in the power of non-State actors (which include criminal groups), with a vision of market economic rationales, methodologically gives a different view to the analysis of drug trafficking and organized crime. In this sense, the dynamics of illegal economies and the configuration of organized actors are factors that either favor or work against the infiltration of organized crime in a territory.

From this point of view, the phenomena mentioned are essentially distinguished by their high capacity to evade or absorb the State and institutional power, and above all, to cross borders and expand beyond the control of the Westphalian nation-state. The territorial expansion of illegal as well as legal economies is, as a result, a product of the dominating power of globalization, world economic integration, and the liberalization of capital. The State and its structural institutional strength or weakness, therefore, are not regarded as leading forces of organized crime, but conditions or supportive environments that encourage or facilitate its operation (Pontón and Rivera, 2011).

The growth of criminal markets may be on the temporal level (new forms of business launched by criminal organizations) or in terms of space (control of territories for illegal activities). What is certain is that the high dynamism and mutability of the criminal markets constantly necessitates new forms of criminal operation that ensure the production of the business and generate mechanisms of infiltration into legal and illegal activities for the purposes of protection of illicit money. That is to say, a force proactively and dynamically linking the local with the global and vice versa; infringing, adapting, and coexisting with the states' processes of monitoring and restriction.

In conclusion, this approach to political economy assumes three characteristics of illegal economies: 1) a structural necessity for economic production, 2) a high criminal proactivity that ensures and adapts to new social and political scenarios but at the same time ensures illegal economic production and, 3) conducive environments that translate into State vulnerabilities that facilitate the development of these activities.

The focus of public policy on this problem should therefore understand the multiple interrelations between these levels and build strategies that respond dynamically to the constant changes in the criminal markets. Therefore, if it accepts a high level of interdependence between criminal economies and their organizations in the current context, a view of integration and cooperation is necessary for states to combat and neutralize their effects on societies.

The Hegemonic Drug Policy Model

The changes in the current political economy of drug trafficking in South America cannot be analyzed without looking at the legacy of the "hegemonic model" upon which the global drug policy was built for more than forty years, driven mainly by the USA.

This assertion does not pretend to say that political concern about drugs has appeared recently in the four decades of debate in the international context. The world market for drugs grew increasingly global during the previous century, which brought international attention. According to Thoumi (2009), international regulations on drugs have their origin in the Shanghai Opium Commission in 1909 and were the prelude to multilateral treaties at the global level such as the International Opium Convention signed in The Hague in 1912, 1915, and 1925. Similarly, in 1961, the Single Convention on Narcotic Drugs reflected the concern of the United Nations, incorporating the coca leaf and marijuana as dangerous vegetables (Paladins, 2011).

Despite this, it was not until the 1970s when consumption reached exponential levels. This situation led to President Richard Nixon declaring the first frontal war against drugs, which was initially associated with the consumption of marijuana, LSD, and heroin on the streets of the USA. However, this initial concern was quickly replaced by a rise of cocaine use at the end of the 1970s, staging it as a political priority in the early 1980s. That is how the head of the American state, Ronald Reagan, in 1982 was able to introduce an "all-out war" against drugs with the aims of overcoming past mistakes and responding to the growing epidemic of addiction to cocaine affecting his country and to accomplish the goal of "national security" that had been discussed for many years (Bagley, 1990; Bonilla, 1993).

Even though this policy had a configuration process that took several years to adapt to different times and local contexts during the decades of the 1980s, 1990s, and 2000s, it made its mark on the dynamics of global geopolitics and therefore the supremacy of the "hegemonic view" with respect to the type of strategy to be followed by countries, with a huge impact on interstate relations (especially in Latin America and the Andean region) and therefore in the current behavior of the illegal economy of drug trafficking.

Much has been written about the characteristics of this policy; however, far from wanting to establish an "ideal model," it can be summarized in the following points:

1. Cocaine as the primary objective of the intervention due to its high power of addiction and the enormous profits generated by the criminal groups that produce and market the drug;
2. The geopolitical world classification of consumer countries, characterized by their high purchasing power (developed countries) and producing countries (developing or underdeveloped);
3. Focus on production rather than consumption;
4. Control of the supply in situ through a strategy of interdiction in the territories of production or the drug supply routes worldwide, the eradication of crops, dismantling of drug organizations, the destruction of laboratories, and blocking the delivery of chemical inputs, among other actions;
5. Bilateral cooperation and interventionism in the producer and transit countries through treaties, conventions, and mechanisms for transfer of economic, technological, and technical assistance (the Colombia Plan and the Merida Plan are the two most representative cases), which resulted in:
   a. Militarization of the strategy of interdiction, crop monitoring, and dismantling of drug trafficking cartels. This includes support for the struggle of armed groups which were related to drug trafficking through logistical and technical support to selected military and police units and training human talent in military doctrines.
   b. Intervention in the passing of special laws with respect to the criminalization, through severe penalties, of all forms of cultivation, production, marketing (trafficking and microtrafficking), and consumption of illicit drugs, as well as the trafficking of precursors and inputs for the manufacture of drugs, as with the 108 law in Ecuador and 1008 in Bolivia. Political pressure is also exerted to implement extradition practices of major traffickers to be tried under US laws.
   c. Control and direct influence on police intelligence and regional domination of intelligence agencies.

6. High degrees of intervention in global and regional multilateral spaces for the enactment of legislation, treaties, and mechanisms of regulation of drug trafficking: all this through the control of these agencies, a strong ability to lobby or negotiate in the decision-making processes of these agencies, and the management of communities of academic experts and of opinions published.

In short, this is a strategy based on the assumptions, premises, and logic of pragmatic realism. In other words, a policy based on asymmetrical power relations, based on negotiation, conviction or imposition of postures and homogeneous strategies by force, which does not take into account different countries' economic and social realities, which explains why the USA continues using the same principles and strategies in its war against drugs after 30 years (Bagley, 2001; Bagley, Bonilla, and Paez, 1991).

So, this policy has had wide repercussions in the Latin America region, which has been material for criticism for the international expert community. Among the main criticisms are: A) the debate over the results of the policy of a worldwide war against drugs in terms of declining production, drug trafficking, capture, and dismantling of large drug trafficking syndicates (Corporación Nuevo Arco Iris, 2009; Isacson, 2009; Youngers and Rosin, 2005); B) the social impacts and those on human rights, such as a crisis of overpopulation in prisons as a result of the primacy of the repressive approach, humanitarian crises due to displacement and the impact on the health of populations affected by the eradication of crops and sprayings, reports of abuses by the forces in the antinarcotics struggle, among other debates (Núñez, 2006; Corporación Nuevo Arco Iris, 2009; Ramírez, Staton, and Walsh, 2005; Rivera, 2005); C) the effects, and political and institutional impacts, of the mechanisms of cooperation, and military and police assistance to the war on drugs (Neild, 2005; Tokatlian, 2010); D) the geopolitical impacts in the Andean region and tensions between countries (Fardid, 2008; Bonilla and Paez, 2006), among other criticisms. Nevertheless, the effect of the American drug policy has not yet been analyzed from the perspective of the South American integration mechanism and the challenges that this view presents to the region.

For this reason, we can say that there are four effects that the hegemonic antidrug policy has left in the South American region:

1. Differentiated geopolitical vision of the region regarding drugs. While the Andean region was viewed as the place of production and therefore the central site of the conflict and intervention, the Southern Cone conceived the drugs problem as a problem of consumption.
2. Fragmentation and disputes between countries with regard to the advantages, costs, and results of the antidrug policies. While countries such as Colombia and Peru are highly favorable of the American policy on the war against drugs, other countries (Venezuela, Ecuador and Bolivia)

with governments that have progressive trends showed reluctance and are highly critical.

3. Lack of a comprehensive view of the public policy toward the problem of the illegal drug economy. On the one hand, the effects of American cooperation have privileged the areas of the military and the police and, to a lesser extent, the judiciary but from a limited point of view. A result of this is the formation of groups of elites in these institutions who respond to the problem from a repressive posture that has generated a high level of professional differentiation in these units, but at the same time creates a break in the chain of institutional command and violations of national sovereignty creating these units' high level of dependence on American cooperation. Similarly, while this model of intervention favored them, these elite units remained in institutional environments marked by problems of corruption, a lack of social legitimacy, and little of no modernization of processes and administrative reforms. On the other hand, the primacy of the repressive approach was to leave aside other areas of intervention linked to social and economic issues.

4. Absence of a strategic vision on the current problem of organized crime, criminal market transformations, their origins and consequences for the social, economic, and political structure of the region.

These four points are the political context circumscribing the current problematic scenario of drug trafficking and organized crime in the region, which we will detail below.

A New Problematic Scenario

The political economy of drug trafficking has presented significant variations that have shaped a new problematic criminal scenario in South America. These changes in the region can be classified into: transformations in the illegal drug market, the antidrug policies' balloon effect, the emergence and configuration of new criminal actors with more power and territorial deployment, and new rational actors and modalities of illegal markets.

The Transformation of the Illegal Drug Market and its Impact on the Region

For decades, cocaine has been recognized as the second-most harmful drug (after heroin) in terms of public health worldwide and probably the most problematic in terms of traffic related to violence according to the 2011 World Drug Report. Similarly, cocaine has been the principal and most profitable product of illegal export from South America and the main engine behind the power of the criminal economy in the region. While one can't disregard the importance of marijuana and poppy (opium and heroin) in this illegal economy in decades past, the appearance of new producer countries and the eradication of these crops during the campaigns of the 2000s, have decreased the economic importance of these markets in the region. In this context, the Andean region remains the leading producer of cocaine worldwide with more than 95 percent of world production today, which makes it a highly disputed territory and in the "eye of the hurricane" of the international community.

However, in the last decade there have been important changes in this illegal economy in terms of the reduction of the world consumption of this substance due to the appearance of new consumer markets, the emergence of new forms of commercialization of cocaine and the onslaught of the synthetic drug market.

While the USA is still the main consumer country of drugs at the global level to this day, and therefore a highly profitable market for any criminal faction, consumption of this drug has decreased drastically since the late 1990s. According to the World Drug Report (UN Office on Drugs and Crime, 2011), in 1998 the annual general cocaine consumption of the USA was 267 metric tons. Ten years later, in 2008, the consumption was reduced by approximately 165 tons, which means a decrease of almost 40 percent.

This constant decrease is having significant effects on the trend of annual world consumption, given that, for the year 2009, the USA occupied 40 percent of the total annual consumption while in the decade of the 1990s this consumption reached approximately 70 percent. For this reason, a fall in consumption in the USA undoubtedly plays a role in the decrease in annual consumption.

However, the decrease in consumption in the USA goes hand in hand with a substantial increase in the levels of demand in Western and Central Europe. Between 1998 and 2008, Europe increased demand for cocaine from 63 to approximately 124 tons per year, i.e. an increase of almost 100 percent in total (World Drug Report, 2011). Added to this issue is the fact that in Europe, a gram of cocaine is worth two to three times more than in the USA, which serves to compensate for the loss of profitability of the world cocaine market. It is estimated that the market for cocaine in Europe soared from $14 billion at the end of the 1990s, to $33 billion in 2009 (33 percent of the total market) (World Drug Report, 2011).

But not only Europe appears as a growing market in recent years. According to Bruce Bagley, there are other markets that began to grow significantly, such as South America. This reaches a point that, if one does a summation of the potential of consumption of all South American countries, they would occupy the third place in the world; Brazil leads with 33 percent of the total market, followed by Argentina with 25 percent (World Drug Report, 2011).

There have been several interpretations of this shift in demand. Among them are the prioritization of the "War against Drugs of the United States" in the monitoring of drug trafficking routes and the policies against consumption that could have influenced the decline in demand for cocaine in that country. The truth is that this change brought about a shift in demand, opening the door to the "globalization" of consumption.

This shift resulted in new and desirable drug trafficking routes to meet the growing demand for cocaine into the lucrative European market through the use of Central and Southern African countries. Hence, there are new routes to serve the growing markets in the countries of the Southern Cone, and one also notes a growing level of consumption in certain Asian and African countries.

Despite this, the general trend in the world drugs market is decreasing if compared to previous decades. According to the 2011 Report, it is estimated that in 1995 the world cocaine market exceeded \$160 billion (at 2009 dollar values), while in the year 2009, it exceeds \$80 billion. For this reason, an important issue to be addressed in the drug market is new forms of marketing cocaine and the potential economic effects that a market like this represents to a criminal economy. If we follow the hegemonic model of supply and demand for cocaine worldwide, the supposed interest of drug trafficking cartels is exporting large quantities of drugs abroad to achieve colossal fortunes. The form of marketing in the destination countries is done through local intermediaries who managed networks of micro-traffickers in the cities, giving a certain discretion to those vendors regarding the mixture of cocaine for sale.

Despite this, it is often argued that currently a huge source of economic production of the drug lies in controlling micro-trafficking networks, to the point of saying that the future of the profitability of the cocaine market is in street level drug-dealing rather than in drug trafficking on a large scale. The essence of this market consists in the ability to control the lowering of the purity of the material of the drug to obtain better profits at the micro-scale. For every gram of cocaine in its purest form, you can get up to 3 g of drugs mixed in the streets (López, 2010).

In this way, the so-called drug-dealing has begun to gain strength in major drug organizations, since this form of marketing has the potential effect of regulating in the short- and medium-term its huge income regardless of the global supply and demand for cocaine in the world. To do this, it is necessary to control the streets and territory of several cities in the world (including in South America). In addition to increasing territorial influence, it also increases the exercise of violence resulting from disputes.

Finally, another important issue in South America is the increase in demand for synthetic drugs. Despite the fact that the World Drug Report (2011) doesn't put South America among the main consumers—much less producers—of such drugs on the global scale, the potential conditions for this market are huge. That's due to the difficulty in controlling the precursors for production (production of the basic molecule of this drug can be made in various ways and even with legal precursors), because of its difficulty in the detection of laboratories (usually home laboratories), and because its profitability justifies small-scale production. While we still can't estimate the market for synthetic drugs in the region, there have already have been exchange of natural drugs (cocaine) and synthetic drugs between drug cartels or drug trafficking groups, which forebodes an increase in the market.

The Global Effect

According to the World Drug Report (2011), coca crops have reduced in the Andean region to a significant degree since the beginning of the last decade. From approximately 221,000 hectares cultivated in 2000, it has declined to 141,000 hectares in 2010. Currently, it is estimated that total production of pure cocaine hydrochloride in the region reaches more than 900 metric tons. However, this reduction does not imply that the phenomenon of drug trafficking there remained especially stable. For this reason, if American policy was characterized by in situ control of the supply of cocaine, bilateral cooperation with producer and transit countries, and the repression of drug groups, then one of the major effects of the legacy of counter-narcotics policies is, without a doubt, the effect of the displacement of the problem of drug trafficking and criminality with a high power of de-concentration and territorial economic influence in the region.

On the one hand, there is the matter of the displacement of crops. In this sense, the partial success of the war on drugs of the Colombia Plan generated a reduction in illicit crop cultivation in that country, but at the same time, it created a shift of coca crops to countries such as Peru and Bolivia. This meant that by the year 2010, Peru and Bolivia had more than 60 percent of the global extent of cocaine cultivation at the regional level, unlike Colombia which reduced their participation from 72.57 percent in 2000 to 38 percent in 2010 (World Drug Report, 2011).

However, Colombia was by far the main producer of cocaine during the past 40 years given the high processing capacity in the territory. Despite this, for the past decade, there has been a demonstrated shift in this Colombian prominence in processing to countries such as Bolivia, Peru, and even Ecuador and Venezuela.

Similarly, there have been shifts in the geography of routes or ports of departure for cocaine in the region. According to the Report (2011) in the year 2009, 60 percent of global cocaine seizures were made in South America, where the country with greatest participation in this activity was Colombia with 253 tons seized in 2009. However, the rising levels of drug seizures in countries such as Ecuador, Venezuela, Bolivia, Peru, and Brazil in recent years are striking. Only in the year 2009, Ecuador reported more than 60 tons of cocaine seized, making it a record year. This situation more than proves police successes in the seizure of cocaine in certain countries, while it also shows that there is a diversification of the ports of departure in South America for drugs to be distributed to the major world markets.

This situation, in economic terms, means a remarkable growth of the importance of the power of drug trafficking in those countries, if we take into account that the true power of economic production of drug trafficking is in the processing and marketing. Thus, on the issue of the supply of cocaine you could say that the important legacy of the past decade, is that this illicitly trafficked product has brought the capacity of illegal economic de-concentration in the region through two factors: 1) on the empowerment of local drug networks which over time are becoming more powerful; 2) in the capacity of economic production that this type of market has on the legal and illegal economy in different countries.

But this balloon effect is also reflected in the displacement of criminal organizations and their respective leaders to other territories due to the loss of conditions resulting from police and judicial persecution. This allowed known drug traffickers to establish their operations headquarters in other countries of the region to increase their economic and criminal influence and their power in other territories.

New Criminal Rationalities

One of the objectives of all criminal economy is undoubtedly the quest for protection. This has led authors such as Gambetta (2007), to say that the real goods of the mafia—not as an organized group, but as a criminal entity—are the sale of protection. This protection could be provided to people through physical means, through private armies, mafia infiltration in the State and corruption, legitimacy among the population or by the use of electronic security devices, etc. Despite this, criminal economies such as the drug trade have found other forms of economic protection of their illicit trade through money-laundering. Therefore, the objective of any criminal activity for the protection of its economy is to make lawful money from illicit activities through this system, which can be understood as a primary capacity of risk diversification of criminal economies.

Traditionally, the goal of money-laundering is not investing the money in lawful activities that are considered profitable. Generally speaking, the resources from major drug trafficking organizations were characterized by investments often in high value luxury goods and economic activities that work at a loss from the financial point of view. For this reason, one of the objectives of the institutions against the laundering of assets has been to identify abnormal economic behaviors in certain sectors or persons that do not justify the origin of their funds nor profits.

However, due to the stagnation in the growth of the business of drug trafficking at the global level, one of the increasingly common strategies lately is risk diversification (very similar to the legal economy) into both legal and illegal portfolios with high profitability. It is, without a doubt, sophistication in the practices of risk diversification of the global criminal economy.

All this is thanks to the use of complex financial transactions through tax havens, allowing them to bypass controls established by the international and local community. However, an argument against this hypothesis that can be applied to the region is that, because of their size, the economies of certain South American countries lack the capacity to receive an injection of financial flows as aggressive as those from drug trafficking because they would be quickly identified and clearly evident. There are even studies that show that much of the financial flows of illegal economies end up in high income countries rather than developing countries.

Despite this, one of the most common strategies currently used by criminal drug trafficking organizations in the region is the use of micro-laundering practices in the territories too complicated to monitor by the supervisory authorities.

Among these practices are: small-time loans to the population, control of illegal casinos, investment in real estate, control of public procurement, investment in other illegal activities with high economic production such as piracy of movies and illegal mining, among many others. Finally, criminal markets in the current context go beyond growing in their real capabilities, they also grow in their potential capabilities, meaning the range of opportunities and spaces for the highly lucrative illegal economy are potentially enormous.

New Criminal Actors

One of the most notable effects of the changes of the political economy of drug trafficking, is the presence of new forms of criminal organization in the region.

In the 1980s and primarily the 1990s, the hegemonic model of the "war on drugs" created enormous efforts to dismantle large drug cartels. However, far from achieving the expected results, this kind of policy has made possible the appearance of new criminal actors linked to the trafficking of cocaine with greater economic power, organization, territorial influence, and infiltration into the social, political, and economic area of countries. For this reason, we can say that we have gone from the decade of great local drug organizations, to the decade of the influence of transnational organized crime in the region.

First of all, we have the rise of prominence of the Mexican cartels that have slowly replaced the large Colombian cartels. Although the phenomenon of Mexican organized crime is not new, because they were already present in the 1980s and 1990s controlling certain marijuana and cocaine traffic routes bound to the USA and they controlled the dispensing of drugs on the streets of many cities in that country, their economic power and notoriety has reached significant levels since the beginning of the previous decade, to the point that some say Mexico is a state co-opted by organized crime. Indeed, the growth of these organizations is such that the leader of the Sinaloa Cartel was included in the list of the 40 most powerful people in the world. Similarly, more than 50,000 deaths are attributed to the war between drug cartels during the past 5 years.

There have been several organizations that emerged during this time and in recent years, the Sinaloa Cartel, Los Zetas, and the Gulf Cartel have violently disputed over control of drug trafficking routes and drug sales in various regions of the continent. Also, one can't dismiss the influence of the Tijuana cartels, the Carillo Fuentes Organization, the Organization of the Michoacana Family and emerging Cartel of the South Pacific, where they have launched into new illegal business such as kidnapping and extortion, trafficking in persons, and the commercialization of synthetic drugs, among others.

A central point of difference between the Mexican cartels and the Colombian drug trafficking cartels of the 1990s model lies in the fact that the latter had a close and often local control of the harvest, production, and distribution points of the drug to the world. In the case of the Mexican cartels, given they're in a country that doesn't produce cocaine; they need greater logistics to maintain a strategic control of the production, ports of departure, routes, and distribution in consumer countries. This type of control is carried out by the physical presence of these cartels in the countries, or through partnership with local drug trafficking networks in the service of these cartels. For this reason, South America has become a strategic site to expand the wake of influence of these cartels and expand its machinery of violence and infiltration in various areas of these countries.

Another important issue in the emergence of new criminal actors in the region is attributed to the criminal transformation associated with drug trafficking in Colombia. At the end of the 1990s, the fall of the large drug cartels sparked an explosion in the number of criminal actors who have taken control of the drug trafficking business, often in connection with Mexican cartels. Although this dismantling resulted for the first time in the appearance of new drug trafficking organizations, no less violent or powerful, such as the Norte del Valle Cartel and other minor groups, the main legacy of the past decade was the deepening of the immersion of dissident armed groups like the FARC (Pécaut, 2008) and paramilitary groups (Duncan, 2005) into the drug business.

This situation was the prelude to the resulting process of demobilization of the so-called Self Defense Forces that was promoted by President Uribe in the middle of the previous decade, and it is from this time that we begin to witness in Colombia a different criminal phenomenon with extensive reach in the regional area. This situation has to do with the growth of armed criminal groups (called *Bacrims* by the same Uribe) coming mostly from paramilitary groups but also from dissident groups in control of drug trafficking in that country.

These groups have been characterized for being mercenary armed groups in the service of drug traffickers, offering the control and protection of exit routes of the drugs going abroad; all this through the control of large territories and populations through extortion, the use of violence, corruption, and mafia style infiltration into the State. Likewise, they participate in the laundering of illicit money at the micro- and macro-scale through investment of other types of legal and illegal activities, and control of the budgets and public procurement in decentralized governments, which certainly helps the economic production of drug trafficking and its respective protection (López Hernández 2010; Romero, 2011). Among the main groups are the Rastrojos, the Urabeños, the Paisas, the Black Eagles, the ERPAC, and other organizations.

In the South American region, there has not yet been a real consciousness and evaluation about the actual risks of the infiltration of such organizations. There still doesn't exist a clear policy of confrontation and neutralizing these groups by the Colombian government, which is the most focused on the fight against subversion. However, if we look at these groups' potential by focusing on the economic power of drug trafficking, their power and knowledge of strategies and military tactics, their power of infiltration in the State, knowledge of local (especially rural) populations, and their extensive ability to diversify and reproduce the criminal economy through legal as well as illicit businesses, we can say that this constitutes a real emerging criminal actor and therefore a threat to the region.

Currently, there are already traces of the presence of these actors in territories contiguous to Colombia such as Ecuador, Venezuela, Peru, and even Panama. For this reason, it seems that the real regional threat to the security of countries has not been so closely tied to the impact of the FARC or ELN subversive groups, but rather to these neoparamilitary groups.

On the other hand, the presence of networks of transnational criminal groups such as the Ndrangheta, the Russian mafia, and African mafias, among others, is also important. The interest of these transcontinental organizations lies in the economic potential of drug trafficking in the region to ensure strategic routes for drugs, and in offering money laundering services and protection of illicit money in other parts of the world (Bagley, Bonilla, and Paez, 2003).

Finally, the relevance in this emergence of new illegal actors of local criminal groups has grown as a result of the influence of the economy of drug trafficking in the region. While the power of these groups is important in each of the countries without having an important regional effect, their importance has come about due to the association with more powerful transnational criminal networks such as Mexican and Colombian, Russian and Italian cartels. For this reason, the presence of drug trafficking by criminal gangs that dominate the drugs in the slums of Brazil, local gangs, and the current significant growth of criminal groups in Venezuela such as the Cartel de los Soles that has flourished precisely because of the strategic importance of that country on the global cocaine route.

Perspectives On and Challenges for South American Regional Cooperation

Changes in the economy of drug trafficking associated with the proactive activity of new criminal actors in the region creates a situation in which the scope of multilateral integration is, without a doubt, the main challenge of public policy for South American countries. Despite this, the task doesn't seem easy given that on the issue of drug trafficking, this region has shown more disagreements and divisions than commonalities and joint regional proposals. While they may declare that organized crime is a new threat to the states in almost all forums and conventions in the region, it is necessary to understand the dynamics and economic rationalities to strategically understand its potential and real impact. Therefore, the first challenge to addressing this problem for the respective countries doesn't lie in a technical approach or signs of good will, but rather in commitment and political maturity with a broad strategic vision.

A space that seems to have reached these dimensions is the current Union of South American Nations (UNASUR). As a result, on August 10, 2009, the heads of the South American states approved the decision to create the South American Council for the Fight against Drug Trafficking, which was ratified in May, 2010 with the approval of the states of UNASUR's South American Council on the Global Drug Problem.

For this reason, UNASUR has become a promising space that includes a new look of integration in the region, despite the fact that many of the objectives and their corresponding Action Plans have been only intentions and without any concrete actions taken so far. Thus, the question that is obvious at this point is, "Why UNASUR and not another cooperation agency with sub-regional, regional or hemispheric scope?" taking into account that the phenomenon of drug trafficking has worldwide repercussions and that countries such as Mexico and those of Central America have common agendas with direct involvement in the South American region.

The answer to the question has to do with the very strength and political will that has been given to UNASUR lately. In recent years, UNASUR is the body of regional integration with the greatest initiative, willingness, acceptance, and political legitimacy given by the South American states for the treatment of economic, social, commercial, and cultural problems as well as security and drug trafficking issues. This political will from the beginning will enable countries to overcome or harmonize old tensions, have a better capacity for collective action and promote synergies and interstate efforts. These are key elements for the development of a strategic vision to the problem.

At the same time there has been a move away from the influence of other multilateral organizations such as the Organization of American States (OAS) and sub-regional bodies such as the Andean Community of Nations (CAN) and the Common Market of the Southern Cone (MERCOSUR). Therefore, UNASUR has become the only promising and legitimate multilateral integration forum regarding drugs in the region.

Another point to highlight in this political context is that for the first time in decades, there is a loss of the hegemonic influence of US cooperation in the region due to the position of some countries (i.e., Venezuela, Bolivia, and Ecuador) regarding the damage as well as the social and political distortions of the impact of this model. This does not eliminate the still-important influence of the USA, particularly in countries such as Colombia and Peru. However, in the past two years, President Santos of Colombia has based his policy on a pragmatic opening with other countries—namely Venezuela and Ecuador—that the previous administration had branded as threats to the security of that country. Similarly, they have placed a special emphasis on UNASUR, to the point that they selected a close collaborator of the government as president of this body. If to this issue we add the entry of President Humala into the political scene, and Brazil's leadership on the issue of drugs in the region with extensive interests in the issues of consumption, internal traffic, and new drug routes, it creates a good scenario to neutralize the influence and distortion of American cooperation in South America. This will allow for a common and autonomous strategic agenda that will strengthen the region's interests in multinational discussion and negotiation forums and have a better position in the process of bilateral or interregional cooperation.

Finally, the strategic issue should also be seen as a point in favor of UNASUR in the fight against drug trafficking and organized crime.

The effect of this situation is that they have gone from having a geopolitical vision differentiated between producer countries and consumer countries, to having a vision of a region that is highly involved in, related to and affected by their own current dynamics of supply and demand for drugs and the corresponding criminal sphere which it promotes. In other words, they recognize a common criminal market and problems with the current situation, with huge growth potential and with its own particularities and vicissitudes. Therefore, there is a need to rethink a new vision of pubic well-being not focused on the particularities of each country, but on the regional strategic interests.

An additional subject that is obvious in this systemic and integral vision is the situation of Mexico and Central America. For many, an exertion of regional integration on the subject of drug trafficking wouldn't be reasonable if it didn't also look at these territories. In the last decade, Mexico and Central America have been the places in the world most heavily impacted by the presence of drug trafficking and organized crime, which does not exempt South America from its wake of influence and a relationship to the problem. Consequently, the absence of these countries would cause a deficiency in the strategic vision of the region.

Thinking about current South American integration on the issue of drugs and drug trafficking does not mean in any way failing to recognize the strategic importance of Mexico and Central America on this subject. Multilateral cooperation with these countries would largely neutralize the extensive influence that the American drug policy has in this region of the continent.

A first element is that UNASUR's challenge will undoubtedly be constantly weighing two spaces (local and regional), which could be in many cases antagonistic but does not mean that they are not complementary.

A more timely issue has to do with overcoming the model of American cooperation through targeted assistance to selected units of the police, armed forces, and justice systems for the antidrug and antiterrorist fight. In this sense, despite having gained highly specialized professionals, it is impossible to maintain an adequate institutional response model unless the problem is looked at integrally. The police and judicial systems in the region have serious problems with modernization and democratic reforms that contribute little to establish efficient police forces. This is mainly in the field of criminal investigation. Therefore, improving the capacity of criminal investigation in the region is certainly an important challenge for this new mechanism along with regional integration through technical assistance mechanisms.

Another important issue is institutional corruption in all areas and worst still, political corruption. One of the major problems of the institutions of law in South America, mainly in the police and judicial systems, is the high impact of corruption in these institutions that ends up undermining the trust of society and thus aggravating the problem. Similarly, corruption at the highest political level and in the decentralized system is becoming common in each of the countries. For this reason, establishing regional cooperation mechanisms to improve the processes of internal and external monitoring of these institutions could be a good step in this area. It does not preclude this, as a good idea, to generate coordination mechanisms to improve the political intelligence that allows them to decipher the complex relationship between politics and crime in the region.

Recovering the anticrime strategic intelligence community is another important challenge to South American integration. Generally, the domain of these communities of intelligence has been exercised by the USA through the presence of intelligence agencies in the respective countries of the region and their direct relationship with and influence on national intelligence units. This situation generated harsh criticism from various countries by breaking the chain of institutional command and violating the sovereignty of the countries regarding the management and access to sensitive information. However, despite the problems raised, interagency and interstate information sharing and intelligence communities are a strategic element in the fight against drug trafficking and organized crime. For this reason, a way out of this problem is to build a community of independent regional intelligence organizations based on principles of mutual trust that neutralize, compensate for, and improve in light of the loss of influence of the US agencies in the region.

A momentous issue for the region is also money-laundering, especially in large economies such as Brazil and Argentina where it becomes more complex to identify because of their size. Thus, a major challenge in the region is to create, from the beginning, a categorization that allows countries to separate the subject of terrorism from a real agenda in the fight against organized crime, taking into account that they are phenomena with distinct characteristics and different political interests and therefore with different methodologies and strategies.

However, one of the most threatening issues facing the entire region is small-scale money laundering that is very difficult to identify through traditional financial mechanisms. Usually these issues of small-scale criminal financial infiltration are found in environments in territories characterized by a social economy based on: underemployment and informal finances; lack of coverage of services of the State, creating high rates of social vulnerability and exclusion; and, the presence of a permanent culture of lawlessness that permeates the idiosyncrasies of society in many countries. For this reason, beyond the institutional efforts to monitor large-scale assets, a challenge for the countries of the region is to broaden their horizon and vision of intervention, and incorporate measures aimed at involving comprehensive prevention strategies through these same policies of development, cooperation, and technical assistance.

Finally, another important challenge of UNASUR is its own institutional development. There is the adage in public policy that the "institutional development of an organism is closely linked to the type of information that it produces for decision-making." In this sense, South America does not have standardized measurement mechanisms of its potential for drug use and trends, as do Europe and the USA. It is therefore an important challenge to identify mechanisms of articulation of methodologies and production of information strategies aimed at having a better input for monitoring this issue in South America.

Conclusion

One of the issues which no doubt stands out for readers of this article is that the key to controlling criminal activities in the region is found precisely in the criminal economy itself. This situation could well lead us to maintain radical ideas about ending illegal economies through abolition, and banning the supply and demand for drugs globally. However, while there is some degree of reason and innovation in this proposal, it also assumes a skeptical and realistic stance towards the real political viability of this project in the short-, medium-, and long-term. That is why the objective of this research is medium-range in so far as it proposes to control and neutralize the criminal economy by understanding its dynamics and thereby design public policy strategies.

Integration, interstate synergies, and the strength and independence of the South American bloc in international negotiations to combat drug trafficking and organized crime are other main objectives of this work. This situation was not designed in axiology nor regulatory integrationist principles that govern the current political debate, but rather in a strategic relevance based on the complexities of a new problematic criminal scenario that will undoubtedly appeal to the reconfiguration of a new notion of regional public good. For this reason, a review of the basic features of the American drug policy in South America was presented, to look at their affects on the processes of regional integration.

Another of the issues raised is the illegal cocaine trade as the main source of financing of the economic power of the criminal organizations of the region and as one of the main sources of funding of criminal organizations in the world for more than forty years. Despite this, changes in the economy of drug trafficking are observed in the last decade, characterized by: (1) the appearance of new lucrative consumer markets of consumption which include Brazil and the Southern Cone as an emerging market, the appearance of new forms of marketing and the emergence of another type (synthetic) of drugs; (2) the displacement of cultivation and the appearance of new routes of exit for conventional and emerging markets that involves a de-concentration of the criminal economy of drug trafficking in the region; (3) the risk diversification of the drug trafficking economy in other types of highly lucrative legal and illegal activities; (4) the emergence of new criminal actors with greater power, use of technology, and territorial influence in the region. This is a new South American problem that creates a situation in which criminal markets in the current context, beyond growing in their current possibilities, also grow in their potential capacities.

The challenges of the UNASUR facing this new crime scenario rest mainly on the need for joint intergovernmental efforts without losing sight of the specificity and priority of each territory and locale in this theme. Against this, there are deficiencies of analyses and studies that should be included within a pragmatic agenda that has to do with the same institutional situation of its monitoring organs (lack of modernization), problems with institutional and political corruption, a rethinking of their development policies based on territories highly exposed to and conditioned by the emergence of illegal economies, and the technical strengthening of the very authorities of UNASUR to address other agencies or bodies and multilateral organizations.

Chapter 10

Defense and the New South American Regionalism: Exploring New Conditions and Perspectives on Defense in South America

Germán Montenegro

The Construction of the Political Government of Defense and the Emergence of New Forms of Defense Institutionalism

During the course of the past 25–30 years, we have witnessed an increasing complexity of the issues associated with defense and international security in global terms. Some of the circumstances that have contextualized these processes are centered on the de-activation of the conflict between East and West that acted as a driving force behind conflict in global terms. The increasing complexity can also be attributed to the acceleration of globalization and the deepening of global interdependence, as well as a relative erosion of the role of the national state as the predominant motivator of social life, although in recent years, in light of the financial and debt crisis, a notable revival of a more active attitude is seen in nation states. The emergence and the growing role of non-state—including nationless—actors should also be noted in the international panorama, as well as the increase in conflicts that do not fit into conventional terms and a renewed perspective about the issue of natural resources, their access, exploration, exploitation, extraction, preservation, and protection as they are beginning to be seen from a more strategic perspective and related to security.

In the global military arena, we are witnessing an unprecedented situation of military asymmetry between nations, related to the predominance of the United States. In strict military terms, it should be pointed out that this State holds a position of undisputed supremacy characterized by, among other elements: the equivalent of half the world's defense spending, an unquestionable leadership in what has been called "the revolution of military affairs", a military presence without precedence on the global scale, and the maintenance of the criteria of unilateral intervention in cases that affect the interests of national security (PEN Decree Number 1714/2009).

Indeed, the international system combines military unipolarity centered around the USA, with a relative and growing political–economic multipolarity in which the USA also holds an important position, although increasingly shared, according to the situation, with the key nations of Western Europe and especially with the so-called emerging powers such as China, Russia, and India, among others. It is necessary to point out that a far-reaching process seems to be taking shape, in which a redistribution of resources and power is happening on the global scale, namely from the central powers of the East toward the principle emerging powers of the West. The financial debacle of 2007–2008 and the continuation of the current debt crisis have contributed significantly to generate the perception that, at least in the political–economic aspects of international life, the latter, particularly China, have strengthened their relative position which starts to raise expectations—of little possibility in my opinion—about an eventual competition in the military arena with the USA.

The use of power politics witnessed in recent years, the reproduction of behavior of a unilateral character, as well as the renewal or establishment of doctrines of "preemptive attacks" by some states, has operated in recent years to undermine international rights, international institutions, and multilateral interstate practices in the dimension of international security and defense. This confluence of circumstances certainly creates a risky scenario for nations that are relatively weaker in terms of material power within the international system, as is the case with the countries of the South American region. Thus, it should be pointed out that there exist regions of the planet clearly differentiated in terms of international security and defense. For example, in some regions—such as in the Middle East, Southwest Asia, and Southeast Asia—the factors and variables that configure and characterize the realities of security and defense include: rivalries and (developing or highly likely) interstate conflicts; offensive military mindsets; the high probability of military resolutions to differences; efforts to maintain or procure arms of mass destruction; and clear interventionism, power politics, and direct action used for extraregional powers.

In this dynamic and interdependent global context, affected by a profound and sustained economic and financial crisis in the Western powers, the weakening of global multilateral schemes, and the existence of unilateral actions, the states of the South American region are developing a much more assertive and active role than in the 1990s, in search of new development schemes, and new forms and methods of autopreservation and of insertion in the world.

In this sense, and on the basis of a critical vision of the very methods of the "Washington Consensus" years and the traditional inter-American institutionalism that came to light during the Second World War and was consolidated during the Cold War, we can observe a combination of actions and diversified, unilateral, and extraregional implications, beginning with the development of articulation schemes of regional interests, in which (in general) the state has once again taken an active central role that had been weakened in the recent past.

In that respect, the conformation of the Union of South American Nations (Unión de Naciones Suramericanas, UNASUR) in 2008 is a manifestation of this type of insertion method on behalf of the countries of the region in the current world. It reflects the clear political roots at South American countries' attempts to generate agendas regarding their problems and common themes, and seek joint solutions to address these issues, in an institutional scheme that is based on mutual respect for the political sovereignty of each of the States—a traditional Latin American feature. It is interesting to also note that the most significant issues that have been developed in the agenda of the UNASUR are closely linked to "strategic" or "hard" aspects of national power and the social order, for example: the question of physical integration, energy infrastructure, the preservation of natural resources, and the development of defense.

From the point of view of international security and in this context, it should be pointed out that the South American region is a zone of relative calm, now and in historical terms. The regions has been historically marked by local conflict that gave rise to a regional balance of power, numerous unresolved border conflicts, strategic competition for regional influence among some of the states with greatest influence, the existence of structured military mechanisms within these situations, numerous diplomatic-military incidents, and the prolongation of the rhetoric of the Cold War in regional terms. Nevertheless, the region has been the scene of very few international military confrontations and, in general, when interstate war has manifested, it has acquired rather blurred edges. It should be pointed out that in general terms the democratic restoration, the development of initiatives of dialogue and political harmonization, and the development of growing social and economic links that have become more evident with shifts since the 1980s have contributed to the creation of a type of mindset less inclined toward political–military conflicts and more aimed at trust building in these matters.

Throughout the past three decades, the region was influenced by a notable number of measures and initiatives aimed at building trust and at accompanying in some way the change of scenery traditionally developed in terms of balances and equilibriums of power. Beyond the political push that these initiatives received, in general they were implemented from and among the armed forces of the region, taking advantage of the previous existence of historical ties between the military powers and of a notable organizational similarity. In this regard, it should be noted that they preserved in general terms the national criteria of equipping, organization, function, and traditional military deployment in synch with this process of rapprochement, cooperation, and trust building. Only more recently does one observe a consistent attempt on the part of the South American political leadership authorities to lead and more closely direct these processes, including controlling these dimensions. In fact, this was exactly one of the central arguments that the Brazilian Minister of Defense made in 2008, when his country proposed the idea of the South American Defense Council.

Certainly in this sense the constitution of the South American Defense Council in the framework of UNASUR has allowed for the first time the creation of a natural political setting institutionalized through the Ministries of Defense for the elaboration and management of a South American defense agenda with the intent of generating perspectives and foci, actions, and regional initiatives regarding these issues. Written in the framework of the South American Defense Council is the formation of the Center for Strategic Studies, the first authority dedicated to trying to produce their own studies and regional concepts about defense issues. Both initiatives are indications of the need to return to thinking from a more authentic and collective regional perspective with regards to the methods, doctrines, organizations, and concepts in which the defense of this region is based.

It is important to note that since the 1990s there have existed some initiatives aimed at establishing a political direction for military and defense issues. The Summit of the Ministers of the Defense of the Americas, initiated toward the middle of the 1990s, is an example in this sense. However, the consequence of the continental reach of this initiative was the inclusion of numerous states with very distinct perspectives, problems, institutional organizations, and legal frameworks, including many countries that participate in the Summit but do not even have Ministries of Defense or Armed Forces. While it continues to develop—the last two summits took place in Canada in 2008 and Bolivia in 2010—what is certain is that the dynamism and the impact of the participant countries on the agenda and defense activities continue to be weak, at the very least (Montenegro, 2011).

South America, from the lens of international security and defense, has two more or less delimited regions with their own characteristics: the Andean region and the Southern Cone. The first finds itself impacted by more active conflicts in conventional terms, due to the recent development of situations of instability and political confrontation, the existence of conflict situations tied to the development of organized crime and the necessity to attend to and incorporate social sectors and territorial zones into the development of the nations. What is more, regarding the latter challenges, in this region there exists an important and sustained participation of the military institutions in matters of public security and civil support in the community while at the same time there are certain weaknesses in the police institutions and of the state apparatuses dedicated to the strengthening and supporting development.

Likewise, this zone is the object of a specific intervention strategy of the USA centered on the problem of drug trafficking, which has lead to a massive commitment of armed forces in the efforts against drugs while some of the countries in the region—particularly Venezuela, Bolivia, and Ecuador—maintain a tense relationship with the hemispheric power, although with subtleties from a political–ideological perspective.

The so-called Southern Cone is itself a zone of relative calm in terms of interstate conflicts, where the predominant and traditional causes of conflict have practically been overcome among the principal actors, basically Argentina, Brazil, and Chile. This has allowed for the development of activities of cooperation on the military and defense issues that has give rise to different auspicious circumstances for the maintenance of peace and stability in the zone. For example, the formation of a combined military force for peace operations between Argentina and Chile ("Southern Cross" Binational Peace Force) or the development of agreements of cooperation for the manufacturing of military planes between Argentine and

Brazilian factories. In general terms, they maintain a clear political, normative, and political separation between the spheres of public security and defense, which is very clear in Argentina, Chile, and Uruguay, and is a little bit more diffuse in the case of Brazil. In addition, in general the zone is considered fortunate to have a situation of relative political stability and at the same time maintains a certain distance from the majority of the security issues relevant to the USA (Rojas Aravena, 2003; Fuentes, 2008).

The South American reality in matters of international security and defense finds itself characterized by the limited possibility of interstate armed conflicts on a large scale and by the extended commitment to international security regimes. It is also a region free of arms of mass destruction and, in general, is relatively respectful of international rights and of the principles of peaceful conflict resolution. That is to say, it is a relatively peaceful region in the general context of the world. In fact, there is a South American agreement to define itself as a "Peace Zone".

Despite this generally optimistic perspective, it is important to mention that during recent years, there have been situations of diplomatic disputes and political conflicts that included relatively intense military activities, a limited use of armed forces and the projection of a military presence in the region by extraregional state actors. Also—re-addressing the issue of natural resources in light of security—the South American region certainly appears to have significant and diverse resources and a promising potential their exploitation. The union of these circumstances has contributed to feeding certain turbulences and conflict perspectives. They do not get to the point of arguing against the reclaimed condition of the Zone of Peace but, at the very least, they impose the need to start thinking a little more about the existence and persistence of a certain level of conflict with some military derivation, although relatively minor when compared with the rest of the world. Certainly the emergence of the South American Defense Council is in part associated with the necessity to generate a political defense authority in a context of international security that has tended to become complex in recent years.

In this sense, and as an example, one can point to, among other events: the development of the conflict situation between Ecuador and Columbia, rooted in the Columbian air strike on a Revolutionary Armed Forces of Colombia (FARC) base in Ecuadorian territory; the political–military tension between Columbia and Venezuela, which even included the mobilization of military forces, as was later confirmed; the presence of the US Fourth Fleet and the installation of North American bases and facilities in Columbia; the rapprochement between Iran and some of the countries of the region, particularly Venezuela and Bolivia; the internal turbulence spurred by separatist factions and the political confrontations they produced in the north of Bolivia (Pando Department) which implied a military mobilization on a grand scale; and the renewed and persistent diplomatic conflict situation between Argentina and the UK, due to the unilateral attempt to explore for and extract hydrocarbons in the basin of the Maldives Islands by British companies.

With reference to the last point, the issue of natural resources and the most strategic perspective with regards to those who are developing them impacts the region in a relevant way, as a function of the actual possession and of the encouraging expectations that exist regarding the reserve of diverse and varied resources. In this sense, and from a critical perspective, the ties that are being attributed to resources and defense is still very lineal. I would say almost primitive in some cases; for example, when it is proposed that there is a need to form a naval force to protect an oil well or a military unit to protect a lithium deposit. In this regard, it is necessary to reflect on what type of political conflict can eventually be generated, starting with a conflict of interest regarding natural resources and in this framework what sort of military conflict can result from that situation or from the effects of raising the issue of defense regarding this problem.

While one cannot point to the existence of a shift toward a highly conflictive or apocalyptic scenario in terms of international security and defense for the region, one cannot fail to notice those events that produce situations of tension and generate expectations of conflicts and disputes, in which the use of political coercion and the threat of the use (or the actual use) of force, although it may be limited, has again become an ever-more recurring behavior in the recent past in the global framework, where it appears to be in fashion again.

It is also pertinent to point out that, as has been mentioned, the South American region includes two areas with agendas, concepts, problems, and international defense and security actors that are very different, thereby creating circumstances that could clearly challenge the viability of an institution with regional scope such as the South American Defense Council. But on the other hand, it is important to shed light on some aspects—which are not minor—that they can work on to shore up validity of this initiative.

In general, the States of the region are committed to a concept of national defense that aims to strengthen the political government over defense and armed forces. Despite their "back and forths" and differences in their levels of institutional development and political commitment, what is certain is that the majority of the South American States are moving in that direction. The progressive development of ministerial authorities with legal attributes for the exercise and the formulation of explicit policies on the issue are facts that shore up this process of construction of the political democratic capacity on such matters.

Additionally, and in the military dimension, one can also observe in the region a tendency in general (although still in its earliest stages) toward the development and strengthening of joint authorities of military organization and function to the detriment of the traditional fragmented operations of armed forces. That is to say that beyond the existence of differences on one side of the military agendas and even at times the military roles, there is also a convergence of other substantial aspects, such as political leadership and military organization, that contribute to construct an identity or at least disseminate common aspects in the realm of the organization and the regional political–military doctrine that can help to establish the base of the common concept in some central aspects of defense and military issues in South America.

Consideration of Defense and the Armed Forces in South America: Conceptual and Political Aspects

Defense is an activity of an essentially political nature that is referred to as the protection of the national State in the face of an aggression initiated by an armed social actor that threatens the political sovereignty, the territorial integrity, and/or the well-being and liberty of those that make up the population of a state. That is to say, it deals with one of the concrete manifestations of a distinct attribute of the modern State—the exercise of a legitimate monopoly on violence and, as such, the implied existence of a specific bureaucratic/governmental apparatus prepared to complete the task. In the case of South America, that is the armed forces and an authority of political direction of the same, the ministries of defense.

The historic development of defense as a state action and as a specific governmental and bureaucratic mechanism has been intimately associated with the construction and consolidation of the national State, of a national identity, and of the concept of interests in terms of material power, and it has a strong territorial connotation. Beyond the contemporary existence of threats or situations that could be seen as falling into the realm of defense but that do not necessarily have a territorial basis, the disposition of the apparatus committed to attend to the defense and the concepts that have taken priority in its development have been and are strongly influenced by the ideas and suppositions grounded in these national, realist, and territorial concepts. In the same way, in South America, a good part of the development of defense has implied and has also been influenced by the emergence, development, and consolidation of the highly corporatized State structures such as the armed forces, which have been able to develop and exercise extremely high levels of political and functional autonomy throughout their historic development, thereby becoming central political actors of the political regime.

Defense is a natural policy, that is to say it is integral and considered to be the general action of the State directed at planning, coordinating, and exercising the protection of the nation in the context of conflict and war, to guarantee its survival in the face of perceived risks and threats (Battaglino, 2011). Thus, it deals with the ample, interjurisdictional activity that is referred to as the general force of leadership of the nation (that is, of the State and the society together) on behalf of the maximum political authority in such situations. In this framework of activity, under circumstances of crisis, conflict, war, conclusion of hostilities, and consolidation of peace, the armed forces obviously occupy an instrumental central position, although they form part of a more general and larger mobilized institutional and social mechanism that includes them.

Therefore, defense includes a policy—the military policy—referred to as the political leadership of the armed forces, which is dealt with as a dimension that is fundamental although not unique. As indicated by a renowned scholar of civil–military issues, civil control refers to "the capacity of a democratically elected civil government to implement a general policy without interference from the military, define goals and the general organization of the national defense, formulate and carry out a defense policy and supervise the application of military policy" (Agüero, 1995).

In times of peace, this refers to the preparation—enlistment, training, and support—of the military resources for their eventual use in situations of conflict and/or war, or for their use at the disposition of the government in a wide and diverse range of nonmilitary uses. And, in times of conflict and war, this refers to the political leadership of the same. Certainly, in the South American environment and given the relative scarcity of international military conflicts, the first meaning is that which materializes more often, given the relatively low conflict and war situations and (limited) characteristics of the experiences of conflict and war that have generally been the case in the region.

Indeed, it must be pointed out that there could be faculties and responsibilities also assigned to a Ministry of Defense and to the very armed forces that may not have a direct relationship with the principal mission of the military institutes.[1] That is to say, a Ministry of Defense of the armed forces themselves can exist and develop their activities—including for example industrial, business, and scientific–technical competencies, as well as those specifically needed for the direction and control of the armed forces and the preparation for war—and not stop being a ministry of defense or military force. However, for those matters that have to do with the preparation and leadership of the armed forces, making up the central and distinctive nucleus of activity of defense policy, these authorities cannot separate themselves from the latter and dedicate themselves to the former, as in that case they would cease to be a ministry of defense/armed forces and they would have to invent another name for themselves.

Now, in general terms, all competent forms of the exercise of the political government of defense suppose certain basic conditions for their application, such as (1) the manifestation of a clear and firm will of the exercise of governmental leadership in favor of formulating and implementing policies aimed at dealing

---

1   For example, in the case of the Argentine Ministry of Defense, there are several entities that depend on it: the Naval Hydrographic Service, an organization dedicated to maintaining nautical information updated for civil navigation; the National Meteorological Service, a body charged with disseminating official meteorological information; and the National Geographic Institute, a state department created for the elaboration of official maps of the Argentine Republic. Also, some industrial departments such as the Argentine Naval Industry Complex (CINAR), a shipyard dedicated to the manufacture and maintenance of civil and military vessels, which includes a factory and a large-scale workshop for submarines; and the Argentine Airplane Factory (FADEA), a state company dedicated to the manufacture of airplanes and airplane parts and the maintenance of civil as well as military aircraft.

with the problems in question; (2) support of the necessary technical–professional knowledge of the problems to resolve and situations to administer to or transform, and of the mechanisms to apply, the resources available and the social–political conditions and their implementation; and (3) putting into practice certain operative–instrumental capacities in the development of the imperatives of the corresponding implementation of the agreed-upon initiatives of policies. It should be said, will of leadership, technical–professional knowledge, and operative–instrumental capacities constitute the necessary requisites for an effective governmental practice to reach the proposed objective (Sain, 2003).

Likewise, there is a group of activities that are utilized in three overarching planes: (1) a plane that we could define as the most creative and intellectual, the design and formulation of the policies themselves, that is to say the concept of these and their characteristics and general guidelines; (2) the effective management aimed at implementation of the defined policy; and (3) the treatment and daily management of the administrative affairs and institutional policy that fall into the orbit of the action of the determined political authority.

In a complementary manner, it can be affirmed that the concrete activity of the exercise of the political government of defense is moved forward through groups of instrumental political and technical bureaucratic authorities, such as: (a) organic-functional structures, (b) the faculties and competencies that these structures have assigned, (c) the employees, advisors, and functionaries, both those permanent within the public administration as well as the managing political authorities, (d) the laws, regulating norms, political directives, regulations, procedural decisions, and actions; that is to say all those initiatives and formal and/or implicit activities through which there materializes an effective manner to exercise the state management.

As has been pointed out in the case of defense, the political government is essential although not exclusively referred to in the exercise of the management and superior administration of the Armed Forces, whose central mission in times of peace is the preparation of the material and human means that make them up for the exercise of war in defense of the nation and in times of conflict is, among other things, the political management of military operations. In this sense, it is worth the effort to try to provide a characterization—although it may be superficial and brief—of the armed forces and the professional activities in which they are involved.

In general in South America, the armed forces are complex, bureaucratic, and technical state organizations composed of a relatively large quantity of men and women organized in numerous specialties, as well as entities that carry out different functions, which essentially commit themselves to the task of preparing for combat and that also take part in a group of secondary nonmilitary activities of a very diverse nature. The operations themselves and even peace-time training imply in many cases functioning under situations and conditions of technical and physical demands that carry personal risk. This task requires levels of preparedness of materials, equipment, and weapons systems, whose management requires significant standards of technical and professional preparation, such as the demand for a sustained level of preparation that should be permanent in order to be able to complete the assigned tasks with efficiency and security for the preservation of the means and the protection of personal. All of this implies a broad vision for the preparation, organization, equipment, administration, and planning, and also demands increasing levels of training and professional specialization.

Therefore, the task of politically managing the armed forces refers to the creation and definition of political criteria of the organization and functioning, and to the supervision and control of completion of these objectives on behalf of those same armed forces. It has to do with making decisions, developing initiatives, daily activities, and strategies related to a group of basic and central spheres of military function; for instance: (1) the missions and specific functions of said organizations in different state organisms; (2) the structure and organic, as well as functional and doctrinal administration, meaning the themes having to do with the deployment, organic-functional structure, preparation, operations, planning, doctrinal development, education, administration of personal, logistics, equipment, and so on; (3) the organisms, mechanisms, and institutional channels through which the state government is linked to the Armed Forces; meaning the ministerial structure and organisms of political management and of the superior military command; and (4) the issues and activities derived from the political institutional functioning of the Armed Forces or that have ties or institutional intervention with them, in those aspects that do not have a direct relation with the specific role of the armed forces (Sain, 2002).

Therefore, it is regarding this group of activities of the armed forces that the possibility of effectively constructing and exercising a capacity for management and political conduct should be considered and contemplated. In this way, the political government of defense is executed in reference to the command of the armed forces, from and through a political and administrative authority (the Ministry of Defense) and is concreted through and over the group of technical–bureaucratic dependents (the Armed Forces). Thus, the political leadership of the armed forces is an activity that is done in an intermediate manner through a network of relations, political and bureaucratic, as well as civil and military organisms associated with: (a) the establishment of the political criteria for the leadership of diverse spheres and a "professional military" dimension; and (b) the exercise of the supervision and control of the effective completion of the group of associated political criteria. To be relatively effective and efficient, the specified role demands a specific organization, political criteria, and technical human resources as well as politicians with knowledge on the issues.

In general, in South America, the armed forces are relatively old entities. In fact, during the processes of establishment and consolidation of the national states during the nineteenth century, the armed forces played a central and important role. To a large extent, the success of these processes was associated with the capacity of the national states to structure relatively professional and modern armed forces that allowed them to, among other things: a) execute the penetration and consolidation of territorial political control of the space they sought to regulate; b) destroy the more or less formal armed entities, that responded to political projects that challenged the organizing purposes of the national state; c) establish, ensure, and sustain the borders with neighboring states, who were in similar processes, and d) exercise internal and external armed protection of the economic and social structures that were articulated in the framework and those effects that materially sustain those national projects (Montenegro, 2006).

They were at that time—along with those departments charged with collecting taxes and those in charge of imparting public learning—one of the few areas of the administration of the new nation states structured on the basis of relatively modern parameters of organization and function. In particular, the armed forces were the object of political professionalization, of importation and development of doctrines and modes of organization and complex function for that time, and the acquisition of technically advanced equipment, as opposed to the relative backwardness that the rest of the national administrations experienced.

Throughout the following century, the armed forces of the region followed a relatively homogeneous development. On one hand, they maintained a relatively advanced and increasingly complex organizational development—lead by the incorporation of military technology and of development of a corresponding organization—with respect to the administration, and this led to a growing functional autonomy with respect to the civil political leadership. In general terms, they structured themselves around a group of threats and conflicts derived from three environments: a) the regional sphere of the border/territorial disputes derived from the processes of national consolidation; b) the global sphere of the antagonisms and competition derived from the confrontation between East and West, in which the South American states constitute a type of tactical-peripheral reserve of the USA; and c) the internal sphere, the resulting conflicts of the confrontation with armed political groups. In this way, they form a type of structure with two fronts: one with authorities dedicated to the management of conventional military conflicts, and another dedicated to the tasks related to internal political control.

At the same time, due to the very circumstances of the reality of each country, at different moments, they started to construct and perform an autonomous political role that converted them, with a few exceptions, into a central actor of the respective national political systems. In this political context, and throughout the years, they developed and consolidated a type of civil–military relationship based on military dominance with respect to the civil authorities that in general was deactivated in different ways—due to collapse in some cases and consensus in others—with the general democratic restoration that developed with the democratic restoration that developed starting in the 1980s.

Also, when talking about these organizations that have an extensive and continuous institutional life, and that during the better part of this period have operated with significant levels of functional and political autonomy, they tend to carry the baggage of self-generated concepts and doctrines about their own role and about defense and security in general, methods of organization and function, ways of relating socially and institutionally, customs based on nonformal practices and formal norms, and their own mechanisms of reproduction that have accumulated and established themselves historically and that encourage and bolster a tendency to develop and sustain autonomous behavior as they have remained unscathed, including in spite of the political democratic consolidation that has developed in the region.

Thus, as has been mentioned, a defense policy should be planned, executed, and supervised from the highest political governmental institution, through a concrete state civil administrative structure. In this regard, it is important to indicate that in general the administration of the national states in South America has been marked by a significant institutional weakness. In this sense, there was a dominant historical development centered on criteria reflecting a historical particularism with a considerable dose of politicization. Also, their specialization and professionalization were limited and feeble. In general, they granted privileges through the distribution and assignment of positions in functions of political party interest and did not develop an effective professional administrative career hierarchy based on competence, technical qualifications, and specialized training. Generally, the central administrations maintained these characteristics of feebleness and institutional weakness aside from certain historical moments during which they tried to advance the construction of a more solid bureaucratic structure and public administration, and with the exception of the existence of some relatively restricted environments characterized by an elevated level of professionalism (O'Donnell, 2010).

Certainly, these features were accentuated during the course of the 1990s, under the protection of a neoliberal concept according to which the dominant idea was that it was necessary to liberate the market forces and alter the state-centric framework that had signaled the intervention and intermediation of the State with society during the previous decades under different methods. Thus, the State was the object of a drastic and sharp reduction in its administrative capacities (Garcia Delgado, 1998). In this framework of reduction and downsizing of the scale of the capacities and competencies of the administrations in this group, the Ministries of Defense were also impacted as they were authorities that have traditionally been weak, immature, and less than formal vis-à-vis the bureaucratic development and functional and political autonomy of the armed forces. In this sense, it is important to point out that the processes of democratization of the systems of defense and the construction of the capacity of the political government of defense that have been seen throughout recent years in the South American region go beyond the different national situations of these concrete conditions in matters of construction and State institutional capacity.[2]

---

2   With regards to civil control over armed forces in Latin America, one can cite in general two noticeable waves, the first linked to the processes of democratic restoration and consolidation in the 1980s, and a second currently in development, associated with the process of restoration of the "keeper of order" role during the course of the second half of the first decade of the millennium until the 2013.

On the one hand, there has been a bureaucratized military body, strong and well-structured, with a history of permanent existence of more than a century in most of the cases of the South American countries, and with a tradition of corporative behavior and carrying out important roles in the political sphere. On the other hand, it is a state-governmental organization that shows signs of weakness in its institutional capacities. The possibility of implementing an effective and sustained political government in command of military affairs and defense is associated with the existence of the political will directed at constructing, supporting, and strengthening the basic institutional capacities of the civil administration that allows for the realization of the exercise of the government. And in this context, the recent experience on the cases in which they are advancing with relative speed and effectiveness is signaled by the central—I would say indispensable—role that they play in terms of the civil human resources, both those that pertain to the administration as well as the political, to shape the political leadership of defense.

Rethinking the Conditions and Methods for Addressing and Implementing Defense from a South American Regional Perspective

In the context described, both in the sphere of internal political development and in the international, it is clearly stated that there exist a confluence of circumstances that can create relatively favorable conditions to start a process of reflection and action regarding defense from a regional perspective.

As we mentioned at the beginning, defense is a political-state action that assumes the existence of framework of concepts, institutions, and bureaucracies of significant complexity and has traditionally been addressed and considered from a perspective almost exclusively from the consolidation and armed protection of the national State. Indeed, historically the armed forces have predominantly been the organizations that have conceptually fostered these visions and those that have directed the State's efforts on these matters. For various reasons, the civil administrations and the political leadership have maintained themselves relatively distant from the knowledge and conduct of the armed forces and affairs of defense throughout the better part of the twentieth century. The process of democratic restoration that began to develop toward the end of the 1970s and that spilled over into the region in the following decade opened the door for the start of a process of democratization of the national defense.

In this sense, these favorable conditions are associated with the advance—certainly not linear and marked by protests, counter-protests, achievements, and setbacks—of the democratic policy about the formulation of a defense policy and the leadership of the armed forces and the concomitant commitment of the South American political leaders to the development of authority and a regional perspective in defense issues. There are also a number of relatively common circumstances for the entire region in this sense, that make it possible to create an agenda of themes about which it is possible to operate from a regional perspective, leaving aside those aspects with respect to which the characteristics of the region complicate effective advances.

In this sense, one can point to the development of the civil leadership capabilities and the emerging concepts of the field of the "defense politics", addressing the way that things should be organized; the general political subordination of the armed forces with the framework and distinct differences of the political circumstances of the each country; the still very immature development of the majority of the South American military organizations based on group criteria; the inclusion of the issue of natural resources in the arena of political discourse as related to security and defense; and the preservation of the political capacity to seal off and encapsulate military conflict situations.

Despite the conditions and advances mentioned, it is necessary to point out that these are still based on a vision of defense and the military organization in which traditional concepts anchored in the national and unilateral perspective are still very important, of numerous mutually conflictive and latent situations and interstate perceptions that should not be forgotten, and the maintenance of a bureaucratic capacity and a significant functional autonomous military, articulated with the persistence of marked weaknesses in the civil policy capacity to provide leadership in matters of defense in many of the countries of the region.

The possibility of consolidating the political concept of a regional "signature" that more effectively penetrates the military organizations, seeps more deeply into the political authorities, and permits better and clearer articulation of the actions of defense in South America is related to the feasibility of consolidating the regional political authorities related to matters of defense; that is to say, the South American Defense Council. And that in turn is strictly related to the possibility of consolidated the exercise of a political government of effective defense at the national level in each country or at least in the vast majority of the States of South America. It is difficult to think of the possibility that the democratic policies could appropriate the agenda of South American defense, if in those South American countries the democratic control of defense and the armed forces is still limited.

The current challenge of regionalism in matters of defense is not only in assuring the validity of the region as a "zone of peace", and directing and encouraging the processes of military cooperation and defense in this sense, but also (and fundamentally) to shore up the processes of the democratization of defense and the armed forces. This not only has to do with assuring the subordination of the Armed Forces to the democratic institutions of the region—something that is a reality based on the present—but rather developing the capacity of the civil management that allows the South American democratic authorities to define, implement, and supervise the political objectives in the arena of defense policy and the military.

Chapter 11

Trends, Strategic Tensions, and Cooperation in Security and Intelligence in the Andean Region

Fredy Rivera Vélez

Introduction

Since the 1980s, Latin America has not had significant armed conflicts or wars between nations, with the exception of that between Ecuador and Peru in 1995. Aside from that incident, bilateral disagreements and border tensions have not led to open hostilities, which is the reason why—compared with other continents— Latin America is considered an area of peace between nations and with emerging signs of its new functioning organizations of integration such as the Union of South American Nations (Unión de Naciones Suramericanas, UNASUR) that can replace the traditional Andean Community (Comunidad Andina, CAN) and, somewhat less so, the Common Market of the South (Mercado Comun del Sur, MERCOSUR). However, this situation, which indicates interstate tranquility, does not necessarily reflect the consolidation of a collective security regime, because tensions still persist and there are unresolved problems, such as those discussed here; for example, the conflict between Costa Rica and Nicaragua, or the permanent dispute and disagreement between Peru and Chile with regards to the maritime boundaries in the South Pacific. In fact, these four countries maintain judicial lawsuits in the International Court of Justice in The Hague.

The Andean region has not escaped from these tensions. While the last armed conflict was resolved in 1998 through peace talks and the establishment of definitive borders between Peru and Ecuador, the different interpretations of national security doctrines, internal security, or public security of the different countries, in addition to the incompatible political ideologies among the governments, represent factors that have repercussions in the new integration projects and accentuate the challenges to reaching their objective. One cannot disregard the complex, varied, and weak institutional development that paved the way for the attempts to establish integration mechanisms that can withstand the shifting politics of the region. Lastly, it is important to consider the interests and strategic political alignment of each one of the countries in relation to the cooperation of the USA in intelligence, security, and defense that in many cases results in the construction of national agendas.

These limitations have do not impeded the Andean countries from cooperating or trying to build bridges among themselves, as the region has signed several treaties that demonstrate the possibility that the states can harmonize their views regarding the struggle against drugs or ways to confront natural disasters; nevertheless, the majority of the agreements reached are bilateral in nature rather than having a multilateral character in which every country expresses its reservations or agreement.

We should keep in mind that in the past 15 years the Andean region has witnessed a displacement of strategic defense interests by internal security concerns dominated by prevailing drug-trafficking problems, all the while without abandoning recurrent plans for citizen safety. This last point—by means of ad-hoc conceptions, influences derived from health sciences and preestablished public policy formulas—has shown inefficiencies in combating organized international crime and its national connections;[1] thus some Andean governments have flirted with the intervention of armed forces for matters of internal security, although it implies undermining their doctrinaire nature, roles, and traditional notions.

In effect, the increase in transnational organized crime, especially that related to drug trafficking and its links to national crime, is reestablishing security agendas in Andean countries and promotes strong debates about the pertinence of existing intelligence to confront this phenomenon.

From that perspective, a series of questions arises that puts in doubt, on the one hand, the true significance and effectiveness of the old national security doctrines to combat the so-called new threats, and, on the other hand, questions whether sufficient forces exist for the cooperation in intelligence, because the declarations and discourses about the transnationality of organized crime is not sufficient to confront the reality due to the incremental impacts that this phenomenon has had on Andean countries.

This situation is complicated by the constitutional and normative changes that impact the inner workings of the military, police, and intelligence entities that are subject to democratic control on behalf of institutions that fulfill their obligation of defense, security, and intelligence activities.[2]

---

1   In principal, the indiscriminate use of epidemiological foci derived from the conceptual knowledge of public health to come up with technical answers to organized crime. These foci do not provide practical guarantees about the complex realities in the field of internal security that are so pressing in all the Andean countries. It is necessary to mention that the citizen security "packets" have broad support from multilaterals such as the Inter-American Development Bank (IDB) and the World Bank.

2   The more representative case of controls, investigations, and sanctions is Columbia, where they have created dramatic modifications in the intelligence system, with legal reforms and restructuring in the Administrative Security Department (Departamento Administrativo de Seguridad, DAS), which is now called the Columbian Central Intelligence Agency (Agencia Central de Inteligencia de Colombia, ACI).

Tendencies in the Regional Strategic Environment

The Andean region presents a complex and contradictory scenario with different opportunities and challenges. All the Andean countries possess their own concerns and areas of interest, but a true shared security and intelligence agenda that satisfies the differences and interests of the actors still does do not exist. While it is true that the states have demonstrated a disposition to have a dialogue and arrive at short-term agreements (some of which can be found in the UNASUR South American Defense Council), they fail to go any further and become concrete and binding medium-term policies. Instead, there exists a strong rhetoric about integration that could be considered in the plane of demagoguism and media politics.

An important element in the current moment for Andean security, defense, and intelligence is the varied reduction or increase in influence from the USA. This change is a result not only of the urgent and relevant concerns that Washington has in other regions of the world, but rather is related to the political and ideological changes produced in recent years in Bolivia, Ecuador, and Venezuela, in addition to the increased importance of an emerging Brazil that has become involved in the security interests of these countries; in fact, except for Venezuela, the countries mentioned are not seen as authentic threats to national security for the USA. Traditionally close to Columbia and Peru—who replicate the North American security doctrine with certain nuances—the governments of G.W. Bush and Barack Obama have been relatively open spaces for a new style of regional autonomy in the areas of security and defense, but to a lesser degree for that of intelligence that still remains without significant reforms.

This does do not mean lowering one's guard in terms of regional strategy because, after all, the USA reactivated the Fourth Fleet in 2009, they continue their costly and often criticized cooperation with Columbia in the antiguerrilla and terrorism struggle through the (not officially recognized) use of their military installations (WOLA, 2010: 5–6), and they still offer recurrent conditional help—except in Bolivia and Venezuela—for the war against drug trafficking that incorporates important intelligence cooperation through various programs and agreements with the different countries of the region (Tulchin, 2010: 5–6).

The tendency of the USA to have a cooperation that is more open to dialogue with some of the Andean countries includes the participation in the creation of new normative frameworks such as the Columbian Intelligence Law or the increase in support in military cooperation in the Peruvian war against drugs (US Embassy, 2011).[3] That is not the case for countries seen as reticent to Washington policies,

---

3   Of the US$65 million received by Peru as part of American cooperation in 2010, almost 50 percent was destined to the war against drugs, apart from the US$27.8 million destined exclusively to military assistance.

such as Venezuela, Bolivia, and Ecuador, which to date have not reestablished diplomatic relations following the expulsion of Ambassador Heather Hodges.[4]

From this perspective, the role adopted by the USA stands out because, throughout the previous decades, the doctrine of national security was a focal point for implementing policies of defense in the region that operationally introduced the concept of "defense of internal security". Currently, by opening thematic areas that include other security issues related to migration, terrorism, and organized crime, the notions of new threats create an opportune setting to refresh their presence and cooperation in the region.

When in 1989 the Andean Regional Initiative (IRA) was launched, the police and military presence increased significantly through assistance conditioned on the completion of objectives and programs aimed at combating drug trafficking that demanded military participation.[5] The countries that adopted the war on drugs received economic and political compensation, such as the *Andean Trade Promotion and Drug Eradication Act (*ATPDEA),[6] while those that resisted were made examples of with reductions, including commercial , military and police aid, as is currently happening with Bolivia, Ecuador, and Venezuela.

Table 11.1   US Military and Police Aid, 2005–2010

Country	2005	2006	2007	2008	2009	2010
Bolivia	45,156,590	41,306,546	37,293,624	27,844,589	22,639,640	22,765,690
Columbia	596,121,737	589,374,053	619,484,593	402,104,615	439,025,261	433,288,480
Ecuador	32,541,101	31,422,055	31,788,949	27,780,131	33,317,540	17,451,452
Peru	55,934,641	61,074,548	65,110,953	43,391,262	84,830,341	65,355,710
Venezuela	2,279,450	552,550	1,557,500	617,463	636,660	421,660

Source: Just the Facts http://justf.org/All_Grants_Country?year1=1996&year2=2012.

Faced with these dynamics, the possibility of influencing the conformation of multilateral groups and their politics in a better way has not gone unnoticed for the Andean States and their leaders. One of the most noticeable actors, Venezuelan president Hugo Chávez, has been precisely the figure that tried to position himself as a relevant actor through his critiques of the USA; questioning the legitimacy

---

4   Ecuador deported the American Ambassador and declared her a "persona non grata" as a result of a confidential diplomatic cable released by Wikileaks, and published by the newspaper *El País*, about supposed police corruption in Ecuador. http://www.elpais.com/articulo/internacional/Ecuador/expulsa/embajadora/EE/UU/cable/Wikileaks/elpepuint/20110405elpepuint_17/Tes.

5   The inclusion of drug trafficking as a national security threat can be seen in all the countries of the region. Since 2000, White Defense Books have been created that describe this situation.

6   Unilateral program for the promotion of development of exports and commerce.

of the Organization of the American States (OAS; Organización de los Estados Americanos, OEA), especially for its management of the crisis surrounding the Honduran coup d'état in 2009, during which the USA played a lukewarm role as the protagonist in defense of democracy; and, he has found political allies in Bolivia, Ecuador, Argentina, Nicaragua, and some Caribbean States.

The rejection of Chávez by the USA led to the formation of alliances and strategic relationships with Russia and China, whose interests have traditionally been distant from Andean affairs and matters of defense. China in particular has been able to link itself strongly with the countries of the region through economic and commercial relationships, leaving the door open for possible stronger ties in the areas of security and defense. In recent years, Venezuela has increased its military spending considerably—to US$3.106 billion in 2010—justifying it as a response to the possibility of an armed invasion by the USA or Columbia, which spent $9.191 billion for the same year (Sipri, 2010).

Along with Cuba, Chávez has tried to establish himself as an alternative to the old ties to the USA, although the real power of Venezuela is limited and his discourse is not well received in many sectors of the regions (Ildis, 2007: 27); however, he already has allies in the Andean region, one of whom, Bolivian president Evo Morales, dissolved his country's cooperation with the USA in the areas of defense, intelligence, and internal security (especially in the area of drug trafficking), and bilateral relations between the two countries have not been reestablished since 2008. Another of the countries close to Venezuela is Ecuador, whose relationship with the USA has also deteriorated, although to a lesser degree than Bolivia's, and whose rhetoric is less hostile than Venezuela's. The recent election of Ollanta Humala in Peru would seem to also align that country with the leftist tendency of the Andean region, although it is too early to make predictions one way or the other. The political ties between the countries could be the first step that allows for the formulation of common security and regional defense policies.

On the other side of the spectrum we find Columbia, whose cooperation with the USA continues to be one of the fundamental pillars in its struggle against illegal armed groups such as the Armed Forces of Colombia (FARC), the ELN, and paramilitaries, as well as its efforts to combat groups of drug traffickers.

Table 11.2   US Military and Police Aid to the Region, 2005–2010 (Us$ M. = Million US Dollars)

País	2005	2006	2007	2008	2009	2010
Bolivia	274	277	307	361	347	314
Colombia	6,541	6,909	7,431	8,323	8,569	9,191
Ecuador	1,146	1,108	1,493	1,628	1,915	2,116
Perú	1,434	1,476	1,416	1,387	1,712	1,992
Venezuela	4,558	6,014	5,021	5,562	4,273	3,106
Venezuela	4,558	6,014	5,021	5,562	4,273	3,106

Source: Sipri, 2010.

Cooperation between Columbia and the Unites States is the subject of constant criticism from Venezuela, who considers the USA as using its relationship and ties with Columbia to maintain its influence in the Andean region and in the south of the continent. Nevertheless, the new government of Juan Manuel Santos has managed to establish more solid relationships with its neighbors, leaving in the past the ruptures that have occurred during the administration of his predecessor, Álvaro Uribe Vélez. In this sense, he has cleared the way for potentially closer cooperation between the member countries of the region (El Carabobeño, 2011).[7]

Despite the improvement in bilateral relations initiated by Santos, Plan Columbia continues to be a tense and delicate subject in the regional affairs, with the existence of disparate views regarding its implications for Peru, Ecuador, and Venezuela. In effect, the development of Plan Columbia, along with its successes and failures, is directly related to the shifts of the security and defense policies taken up by the authorities of the neighboring countries, because the spaces of intervention of armed groups and Columbian criminal bands have expanded. This is a consequence of the "spillover" of intervention and infiltration operations into institutions by obtaining new areas of operation in ports and frontier zones that are vulnerable due to their remoteness, lack of attention by the public policies, or lack of coordination of control and monitoring.

The desires of the governments to set into motion their own defense, security, and intelligence initiatives are one fundamental piece that has a double edge. On the one hand, it confronts its own necessities as a function of the threats to neutralize; but on the other hand, these same agreements and promises can generate an imbalance of regional forces because the states are not necessarily inclined toward those options (Rojas, 2007: 15).

Venezuela, for example, for all its focus on the UNASUR, prefers to also develop efforts to politically position the Bolivian Alliance for America (Alianza Bolivariana para América, ALBA), which finds counterweights to initiatives such as the Pacific Accord, recently signed between Columbia, Peru, Mexico, and Chile. Both aspire to influence in the area of security and neither is purely Andean. The tendency of the Andean countries to get on board with different cooperation initiatives supersedes the traditional sphere of the community and aims for more appealing spaces and initiatives with possibilities in the subcontinent such as UNASUR.

The Political Economy of Organized Crime, Institutions, and the Use of Rationalities

Organized crime and drug trafficking generated in Columbia and Peru pass through Ecuador and Venezuela principally on their way to Mexico to then connect to the

---

7   An example of this change in the Columbian external politics is found in the reestablishment of diplomatic relations with Ecuador that were broken off due to the bombing in March 2008, and the rapprochement with president Chávez that settled tensions regarding the subject of the Venezuelan tolerance of the FARC.

USA or Europe via the west coast of Africa. Recently, Brazil has converted into a destination of the criminal operations due to its condition as an emerging power and the increase in internal demand for drugs, socioeconomic spaces to launder assets, and arms trafficking. In this incremental context, both legal and illegal businesses find fertile ground in a territory that operates with an elevated dose of informality in the economy and institutional controls. Also, let us remember that the drug dealer has the capacity to corrupt public officials, police, military personnel, border guards and customs agents, judges and public prosecutors, private businessmen, supervisors, and so on, which makes the crime more dynamic in the face of the pronounced debilitation of the state's ability to deal with them.

Transnational and local organized crime operates in the "gaps" not filled by the formal, modern economy with public and private institutional supervision. It employs financial agents where the markets permit great quantities of money to circulate without passing through controlled transactions; it utilizes the opportunities made possible by the imbalance in the market of land, work, and commerce; in general it takes advantage of the informal dynamics of the economy, the lack of employment, and it is harbored in NGOs and organisms such as churches and philanthropic entities.

In addition to that, the deficits in the management of the controls in institutions, the infiltration of supervisory entities, and the weakened legislation in the anti-asset laundering field tend to construct a panorama of vulnerability in the face of the intervention operations of organized crime. Recent investigations that use an interdisciplinary methodology and also redirect the object of the study toward the criminal activities before the criminal organizations have realized the diverse strategies of the actors in the same activity; that is to say, the "model" criminal explanation, looks at the environments and opportunities, the activities of the drug dealer, gas smuggling, and human trafficking as a function of the windows of opportunities, risks, and damages.

The role of the organizations, independent of their nature or functional structure, will be as rational agents that take advantage of these opportunities and convert them into ways to achieve high economic returns by committing illegal acts. The new focus also look at the level of criminal infiltration in institutional, state, and private spheres to demonstrate the level of social impact or damage, as it does do not seek to uncritically repeat methodologically obsolete approaches, based on epidemiological analyses of citizen security that have been legitimized in recent years and have become models or "formulas" for the design of public policies but that do not explain the real dynamics and unfolding of organized crime (Nuñez, 2011; Pontón and Rivera, 2011).[8]

---

8 Critical analyses warn about the conceptual and methodological limitations of the use of notions derived from citizen security to understand the politic economy of organized crime, its causes, motivations, and the sphere of intervention. What's curious about the case is that the design of several public policies and certain sectors of the academy continue using slogans as discursive media filler that legitimizes its role in the public opinion despite its demonstrated ineffectiveness.

Drug dealing is one of the transversal subjects of interest for the entire region because it presents an enveloping effect through the increase in violence and insecurity in all the countries where its operations of action and penetration are under way. This threat, however, does do not affect the state security understood as the possibility of conquest or the dismantling of the state or its territory, but rather expresses a more complex and interdependent problem due to the shared intersection of phenomena such as elevated indices of social and political violence, organized delinquency, illegal arms trafficking, among others, that negatively affect the population.

In this sense, the concerns of the states regarding the well-being of their habitants and territories are also expressed in the promulgation of new laws and regulations regarding security, defense, and intelligence. These legal bodies consist of important components directed at the distinct fields of security and defense that incorporate various dimensions and structures.

The Policies of Security and Intelligence Versus Organized Crime

For decades, the doctrine of national security was implemented in various South American countries like a reference guide on how to construct security, defense, and intelligence policies. In Ecuador and Bolivia, these doctrines have been revised and they have established new laws that seek to supersede the traditional laws. Columbia and Peru persist in continuing with the norms that give them results in the combat against internal and external threats, despite having initiated interesting reforms in the intelligence sector; nevertheless, the position of organized crime as an objective is not consistent and varies according to the particularity of each country and the moment in which they find themselves aligned with the respective intelligence community.

In effect, the discussion about intelligence communities, their operating environment, their sectorial application and, above all, the influence of and relationship with the intelligence police, continue to be topics rarely raised in the academic and public policy analyses, because the weight of the military sector in the intelligence systems of Andean countries persists and hinders the development of a strategic intelligence under civil democratic conduct (Rivera, 2011). This represents a limitation to confront the contingencies from the operations spread by the actions of criminal bands that have regional and extraregional connections. Without wanting to, it also favors the growth of specialized and professional criminal activity, that—from the view of intelligence—the institutional, doctrinaire, and regulatory changes in our countries are slow compared with the needs of a certain intelligence community. It is not strange then, that US national security views with apprehension the increasing closeness of Bolivia and Ecuador to the Venezuelan and Bolivarian communities that have opened important channels with China, Russia, Cuba, and Iran; in fact, these ups and downs with the traditional and hegemonic source of US cooperation have opened new intervention scenarios in light of reforms. While this happens in the rational game of trial and error, it increases the vulnerabilities of each one of the Andean countries that is connected interdependently by organized crime.

It is not enough in current times to define organized crime with the slogan or phrase "new threats" to distance it from the old perceptions of national security associated with realism, and try to combat it all at the same time. The complex and dynamic sector of economic rationality that unfolds and the capacity of infiltration that the international organized crime agencies have in the social fabric of our countries is not being addressed in an adequate manner by the national intelligence agencies. Greater dynamism is seen with regards to preparation, the use of the latest operations and communication technology, the analysis of strategic zones, as well as national and international markets that the criminal actors use, all related to preventive and neutralizing responses by intelligence systems of our countries. In this sense, the national discourses are anchored in nineteenth-century sovereignty and the application of failed security prescriptions in other regional contexts. Organized crime demonstrated its rationalities a long time ago by anticipating the changes that have existed in the countries of the Andean region.

Seen from this regional perspective, Andean intelligence is faced with distinct particularities, heterogeneities, and problems, the concerted efforts of national and international criminal bands that take advantage of, or operate under, the combination of various factors:

- The strategic geographic position of certain zones of the region that link with international crime activity, especially border areas as well as maritime and river ports.
- The economic rationality created by the differentiated insertion in globalization that modifies spaces, productive agents, and subregional commercial spheres that energized in their own ways the incontrollable circuits of financial informality and monetary circulation outside the formal, modern, and institutionalized organisms in the public and private spheres. In the Ecuadorian case, the existence of the dollarization and, in the case of Venezuela, the distinct bands for the type of exchange that produced black markets, constitute elements that facilitate money laundering. Peru is not far behind with its tolerance of casinos and game parlors, where millions of dollars and other currencies circulate.
- The gradual deinstitutionalization of justice entities, financial and police controls that have opened "breaches" or spaces for the infiltration of mafia operations through corrupt purchases, intimidation or threats in order to not do or "stop doing" through the omission of controls, which generally designate by action or omission.
- The interdependence that exists between the countries of the regions and the 50-plus-year unresolved internal conflict in Columbia that has involved neighboring territories through the use of armed state and non-state actors,

and the derivations and negative impact of Plan Columbia throughout these many years.

- The doctrinaire modifications in the national police and armed forces, and the constitutional changes that opened different public policy scenarios in security, defense, and intelligence sending the countries of the region on two paths: Peru and Columbia on one path, Ecuador, Bolivia, and Venezuela on the other. These modifications have created possibilities for a greater infiltration of organized crime in the state structures and the societies in general.

- The ups and downs, fluctuations, ruptures, and continuities of the external politics of each of the Andean countries in relation to the bilateral security and/or antidrug programs established with the USA. At this point, it is crucial to analyze the topic of cooperation, the system of controls of the receiving government, and the debates around the sovereignty of the "intelligence" of Ecuador and Bolivia is radically different from that of Peru and Columbia.

In general terms, the combined interaction of these six factors support a complex set of problems that centers on the operations and branching out of organized crime that links various dimensions, facets, spaces, actors, and interdependent dynamics between neighboring countries but that are articulated to territories as distant as Mexico, Brazil, and the European Union (Pontón and Rivera, 2011).

Conceptual Limitations and Practical Relations

The absence of a unifying perspective at the regional level is not the only challenge for the distinct initiatives from the Andean countries; there is also the conduct and particular concerns of each government that affects the practice and solidifying of regional relations. In this sense, the progress toward the real integration continues to be limited despite the desire to establish normative frameworks and conventions with relative ease.

One of the greatest challenges to overcome is the divergent security interests between the diverse states, because, if common areas exist that should be addressed in a joint manner such as international organized crime or drug trafficking, there are other tensions that debilitate a potential regional unity. This includes the new tendency of US cooperation to be expressed more in bilateral than multilateral terms.

The permeability of the borders has meant, for example, that Ecuador and Venezuela consider the Columbian conflict to be one of the most relevant matters in terms of national security and defense. This is because irregular combatants, state security forces, and Columbian intelligence entities carry out, openly or clandestinely, operations of a distinct nature in sovereign territories of neighboring countries. In this context, the actions of the FARC in Venezuela and Ecuador have found a decisive although questionable reply on behalf of the government of Columbia, exemplified by the fumigation of coca crops and the execution of Operation Phoenix in 2008, which violated the territorial sovereignty by bombarding a drug insurgent camp within the Ecuadorian national space.

These types of operations were condemned by Latin American countries and led to an increased mobilization of the armed forces in the borders of Venezuela and Ecuador, at the same time that they created tensions and diplomatic ruptures with various consequences. If this case in particular can be considered closed since the reestablishment of diplomatic relations between Ecuador and Columbia in 2010, the underlying problem remains dormant and demonstrates the inability of the states to generate coordinated—much less joint—responses to an important security problem on their borders. There are divergent views about who should confront the problem, how to go about it, and which mechanisms to use to create compromises and agreements on this topic, as well as which hierarchal structures are transparent and overcome the dialogue among the deaf among the countries; so, whichever way you look at it, one of the challenges to be addressed is to establish a zone of integration and peace such as that mentioned in the declaration of principle of UNASUR.

The region's border issues continue to be particularly delicate beyond the problems between Columbia and its neighbors. Currently, Peru and Chile still have a dispute regarding their maritime borders, and Bolivia persists with its historic demand for access to the sea that was lost to Chile during the Pacific War in the late nineteenth century; in effect these tensions hinder interstate relations between the concerned parties. Chile and Peru continue to wait for a resolution to their dispute in the tribunal of The Hague while maintaining a certain degree of military tension in the disputed zone; meanwhile, Chile refuses to address the Bolivian subject with any depth until the dispute with Peru is resolved.

With regard to the Bolivian complaint, the Chilean authorities have do not come up with options beyond the possibility of offering facilities to Bolivia to have nonsovereign access to the Pacific Ocean, an offer which is insufficient for the Bolivian government. While both Chile and Peru have promised to honor the verdict of tribunal, whatever that may be, their border relations will continue to be tense for the immediate future, and one cannot envision a resolution to the dispute in the near future.

Apart from its border issues, Peru has other concerns of an internal nature that are also related to problems in Columbia and the region. More than three years ago, operative cells of the Shining Path guerilla group began to reappear after a period of relative calm in several areas of the Peruvian sierra and the Amazon that are associated with coca growth and the production of cocaine; evidence of a connection with the regional drug traffic and international organized crime which lends it distinct characteristics to those activities seen in the 1980s and 1990s.

These new realities and situations, which bring with them new security and intelligence concerns, also present better opportunities to coordinate forces between the different states, not only in the Andean region but in the entire subcontinent. If indeed the threats of organized crime and drug trafficking are difficult to deal with and confront through state mechanisms, especially the military, they are recognized by all the states as a more-or-less homogeneous way of addressing common problems that allow for the possibility of interstate cooperation in the future in police and intelligence operations.

From this perspective, the countries of the Andean region have successfully promoted bilateral agreements among themselves with the goal of facilitating cooperation in the struggle against drug trafficking. Independently of their tensions and political visions, Columbia has reached cooperation agreements with Peru, Ecuador, and Venezuela, and there is a general tendency in the region to celebrate those types of conventions. In the multilateral environment, all the Andean states have adhered to the statute regarding the fight against drug trafficking signed in the framework of the UNASUR in mid-2010, an instrument that forms part of the central themes of the agenda of the South American Council on the World Drug Problem established the same year.

In areas related to peace, national defense, and military armament, the prospects are less encouraging for the Andean region, as in the last few years there has been a considerable increase in military spending and a propensity toward an arms race despite the existence of conventions and appeals to slow arms acquisitions, principally in the framework of the OAS and the UNASUR (Rivera, 2010).

The logic behind this increase corresponds as much to the legitimate right to the modernization of antiquated military equipment as to the security dilemmas that have been overcome in the continent (WOLA, 2010: 13). This situation then presents a challenge for the current and future measures of mutual trust, transparency, and other international instruments that seek to convert the region into a zone of peace and stability.

Challenges to Cooperation and National Realities

The particular conditions of internal security and defense that intersect all the Andean countries constitute an important challenge in and of itself that must be addressed. As mentioned, the strategic character of the region obliges the design of novel formulas to confront the set of new challenges and cooperation in terms of intelligence assumed as an empirical necessity; nevertheless, the CAN, weakened by the unilateralism of its four remaining members, would find it difficult to represent itself in a forum capable of constructing an common strategic Andean agenda, despite the fact that it does participate in the security regimes such as the Inter-American Defense Board (Junta Inter-Americana de Defensa, JID) and the South American Defense Council (Consejo de Defensa Sudamericano, CDS) (Leal, 2007: 3–4). This last group has already overcome one of its first difficulties by successfully incorporating Columbia in its framework despite the reservations and many of the other member states.

In fact, Columbia managed to reinforce its image as a committed state with the initiative of UNASUR to negotiate, along with Venezuela, the securing of the position of the secretary general of the organization after the death of the late secretary Néstor Kirchner. The certainty that this secretariat will be alternated with Venezuela is another positive sign of openness, as it indicates that both countries are capable of working together despite the political differences of their leaders (Vargas, 2011).

Beyond the conventional types of political discussions, the treatment of issues such as the struggle against drug trafficking in the framework of the UNASUR is positive; although there has existed a lot of rhetoric and little concreteness until now, because from its beginning there was a debate about the scope of the Council to go beyond matters of security, clearly established in the Bariloche Mandate of 2008, to include areas such as public health, justice, education, and development. If these areas were related to the subject of drugs, this would distort the character that the Council was originally founded upon. The issue, seen as a uniting priority in the government agendas, has the potential of converting itself into a relevant space for the formulation of the common policies in the future.

The additional space in which it is possible to make advances, and in which there already exists a normative framework, is the transparency of defense administration and spending, potentially with a view to limiting or even reversing the current tendency toward growth. While it is too early to talk about an arms race in Latin America, the possibility of one happening has not disappeared entirely. The Economic Commission for Latin America (ECLA; Comisión Economica para America Latina, CEPAL, in Spanish) and the OAS have designed mechanisms to be able to make these processes transparent, which could be adapted and improved for cases such as the UNASUR in search of better results than those which have been currently achieved. A higher degree of transparency in defense matters would considerably strengthen the measure of mutual confidence and could lead to instances of more effective cooperation through sharing knowledge about the strengths, possibilities, and limitations of the states.

It is important to note the relevance of the UNASUR and the CDS as spaces of integration. This is due to the initiative in particular that has been able to include difference actors of the region independent of their political perspectives, something that the CAN and ALBA have do not achieved, thereby generating at the same time the space and the opportunities for Brazil to attempt to consolidate its role as a regional power and an alternative to the USA. As opposed to the OAS, which has been the target of criticism from some states, the UNASUR and CDS have been conceived to function without the presence of the USA.

As a space of future cooperation the CDS offers some noticeable advantages. First of all, the organization already has the membership of almost all the South American countries, independently of their political posture, and it offers the possibility for all the members to influence its agenda. At least in its normative aspect, the CDS already integrates military and nonmilitary mechanisms, continues the achievements made possible with the CAN and MERCOSUR in defense and security, and aligns itself with the framework previously established by the UN and the OAS (Menezes Texeira, 2010: 51). While the organism is too new to evaluate its performance, it has very real possibilities of having an strategic importance in the future, not only in the formulation of common policies at the negotiating table, but also a possibility of establishing mechanisms that permit the completion of field operations. This last point depends a great deal on a continuous process of institutionalization and strengthening. Without this process, the CDS will remain just a forum for discussion or a place for the formulation of agreements, without really going beyond the other previous initiatives as has happened in previous years.

For its part, the Andean region would find it difficult to present itself as a space for integration and cooperation beyond the network of bilateral initiatives mentioned previously. The already established CAN has had little real success in its attempts to influence security matters, and the political divisions between the member states have more importance in this space than in others. Also, considering the exit of Chile and Venezuela from the organization, even successful initiatives within this framework would have a limited reach with only four countries. While it is possible that third-party alternatives to the OAS and the new UNASUR could reach the Andean region, the differences in policies between the states and their postures around the CAN make this a rather remote possibility, as there is no guarantee that a new Andean project would triumph in the face of a lack of willingness to start new binding initiatives.

Conclusions

The Andean region has little possibility of consolidating a situation of cooperation on its own. This should negate the possibility of constructing a viable space for the promotion of peace and security through two mechanisms. The first is the opportunity brought through permanent efforts and the willingness to create bilateral ties through the collaboration in areas such as fighting drug trafficking and organized crime which include important intentions of creating links between judicial systems. Secondly, in the multilateral plan, there is clearly an active participation of the Andean countries in extraregional initiatives such as the UNASUR; in this sense, it can be said that the Andean perspectives of establishing itself as an area of cooperation and security depend on the success of the South American initiatives more than on the Andean-only institutions that already exist.

As is the case in all of South America, the Andean region will have to continue pushing for clear and reliable mechanisms of dialogue and transparency in order to reduce tensions and eliminate barriers that impede the greater cooperation. The inclusion of preexisting frameworks in the UNASUR could be a good alternative to reach this objective, to create a system that articulates the achievements of the OAS and JID, as well as the multiple bilateral conventions and measures of mutual confidence that already exist to orient the practices and norms, bilateral as well as multilateral, in the future.

The elimination of the security dilemmas that the states generate mutually would have another important positive aspect if it allowed for greater cooperation on other important problems at the regional level: the disparity and heterogeneity of the intelligence services and their appointment to different communities, which hinders the increase of a fundamental resource to reach this objective: confidence.

Despite the multiplicity of bilateral initiatives, many of them managed at informal levels, there still does do not exist a functional regional group that can effectively confront this problem. In a multilateral environment, UNASUR has made some progress in this sense, but a more effective cooperation is necessary to deal with these interstate and domestic problems.

At the same time, it would be convenient for the states to continue promoting and strengthening initiatives that have already been handled with success in the past. Activities such as the humanitarian demining between Peru and Ecuador demonstrate the possibility of generating real tangible cooperation between countries, a possibility that would be worth exploring further and advancing, and potentially expanding to other areas. Latin America is not an example for the world in terms of cooperation in security and defense, but there are few reasons that it could do not be in the future, and many of them lie in the political sphere.

While it is possible to conceive of Latin America and the Andean region in particular as zones of peace due the absence of interstate conflict, the existence of some unresolved tensions and the continuation of traditional practices linked to doctrines of national security appear to be limiting factors for cooperation in the near future. This is an obstacle that can be overcome but just because of that it should not be underestimated. Without an efficient treatment that deals with the inclusion of shared strategic intelligence, the possibility for the Andean countries to deal with their disputes and their internal problems will remain stuck.

It is important to mention the importance of the series of legal, normative, structural, and police and military doctrine reforms that are underway in the Andean countries. This situation will open new areas for cooperation, but also will constitute a challenge to be overcome due to the enormous complexity that the exterior politics, the national interests, and the strategies of each of the governments represent.

Conclusion

The chapters of this book have analyzed, using different perspectives and methods, the contours of development and areas of new regional configurations within the Americas in a time of global regionalization. In doing so, this collective work has given life to a growing subregional and complex phenomenon evident in the configuration of the regional formation of South America. Accordingly, three characteristics distinguish this New South American regionalism (NSAR). Firstly, we speak of new regionalism, because it is part of the major trend of global regionalization that started after the Cold War, and it is a response to the shift of the world axis from the North Atlantic to the South Pacific since the 1980s. The second notable difference in the political–economic nature of this germinal regional configuration is political, as its focus lies in the regional reorientation of development on the basis of two paths: democratic stability, and a historical reduction of structural inequalities. The final feature is the redefinition of geopolitics, the role of social forces, and approaches to securities and national neighbors.

New South American Regionalism is thus the result of a complex process of regionalization from the bottom, and multiple regionalisms from the top, with new social forces. These forces are expressed in different but balancing regional projects, marked by the return of politics and state, which plays a strategic role in its development. In another way, a single look at the regional map shows that the relation between national entrances varied from an entrance to regional trade integration, social development, health cooperation, or organized crime, or politically even overcame democratic challenges. The NSAR incontestably exists, but does not mirror the European, North American, African, and Asian experiences. Rather, the NSAR reflects the heterogeneous economic, social, and political–economic configurations of social forces and political orders specific to South American capitalism and diverse political orders, all responding to a changing world order and, in doing so, it is oriented to its challenges, which define the political–economic nature of its of development. This central reflection brings us to the conclusion that what makes the NSAR stand out are the undeniably complex relations between development and regionalism. This research enterprise therefore challenges us to unpack these relationships by considering four analytical elements within this research agenda.

The first is that to study and critically reflect on the reality that surrounds us is to talk about an inherited order of development, a world overloaded with values, visions, political interests, and criticisms. There are two ways to approach this: One is by focusing academically on the normative and conceptual meanings, political projects, and debates around the concept. The other is by understanding development as determined inherited structures that define conditions and opportunities of human agency. As Philip Abrams states, "we can construct new worlds but only on the basis and within the framework of what our predecessors have constructed for us" (1983: 5). This idea is not new and has been central to the understanding of critical political economy and historical sociology, although expressed through a myriad of different heterodox approaches. From this perspective, a political economy of development is about how the reality comes about and is produced in a certain time and place by power, ideas, agency, and structure of the global, regional, and national realities. Accordingly, it is possible to identify a set of analytical issues which are theoretically and methodologically related and central to resolving further research questions concerning development and regionalism in the Americas.

The major historical framework of development in Latin America, globalization, with its complex multileveled, multifaceted, and contradictory reality, has been marked by the complex political economy between regionalism and regionalization (formal or informal). Starting with the twin dynamics of open regionalism and liberalization, and following on with the intertwined processes between heterodox political–economic regionalism and extension of its global reinsertion to the Asia-Pacific, the South American regional phenomenon follows a pattern of complex development responses to globalization. This process sped up following the Cold War and has gone beyond the traditional and formal dimensions of governmental and economic dimensions, above all widespread notions of regional integration, defined as the cession of sovereign powers in supranational organizations. The nature of the new Southern Cone regionalism is eminently political, even in the case of its most open and liberalized economies (Chile, Peru, and Colombia), with complementarity between its regional projects rather than an overlap of them. We can therefore define this as the first theoretical and methodological issue against the conceptual iron-cage of the regionalist concept.

In this sense, we conclude that concepts and approaches that we use to comprehend reality are often more related to inertia of dominant academic traditions and orientations of epistemic communities than the new realities we are challenged to understand. This is the case of the notion of regionalism and its relation to development and regionalization. We conclude in our interchanges how the conceptual iron-cage of regionalism has been nurtured by the European and North American experiences and their major epistemic communities, and is composed of four major paradigms or bars: The first is the idea that regionalism only occurs under the condition *sine qua non* that there is a cession of sovereign national power over to supranational organizations. Secondly is the notion that the economy follows a conventional wisdom of market-led integration (paralleling development) and where politics only underpin and reinforce natural and historical orientations, in its political–economic nature. Thirdly, it is the belief that regionalism is well-defined by a tendency of convergence toward regional standardization and homogeneity in its development strategies in relation to governmental action. The fourth element of the conceptual iron-cage is idea that it centrally concerns formal and top-down development from states and formal markets. Reality speaks, however, and it says that the history of regionalism does not begin in Latin America with the regional European process of the 1960s during the Cold War, but derives from the rise of North American power, giving the region a hemispheric framework found only in the Americas. Furthermore, the current regionalist processes in the Southern Cone are framed by the globalization of the post-Cold War, challenging us to rethink the political–economic nature of its approach and realities.

In terms of evidence, the structure of the development inherited by this regionalism lies in its different capitalist configurations, social forces, and political orders largely studied by Latin American and critical international political economy (IPE) of development scholars. There its agency manifestly rests today in its political nature, defined by the weight of politics and political regimes within democratic frameworks. As a result, three different political–economic dimensions seem to be structurally intertwined, shaping the developmental orientation of it regional historical process: the structure of its global reinsertion (primary sectors), and formal and informal structures of development. Within that, the most significant evidence is the shift in the process with Latin America giving way to South America Regionalism as a result of Mexico's detachment from the political of economy of Latin America and its final inclusion into the structures of North America since the early 1970s.

Perhaps the structure of global reinsertion has been the dimension of major change in the last decades, a change increasingly tied to the rise of the Asia-Pacific and in particular of China, with a profound impact in the new regional configuration. In fact, we can observe how the shift to the Pacific of this structural insertion has increased and is at the very base of the NSAR and of political leverage of the heterodox new political orders in the region that are based on democracy (Brazil, Argentina, Ecuador, and Venezuela). Nonetheless, the case goes beyond the national state focus. Accordingly, the relation between development and regionalism of the NSAR also needs to be grasped within the framework of what we can identify as the new global geopolitical triangle in the Asia-Pacific anchored in the political economy of development among South East Asia, North America, and South America. The process cannot be reduced to only a *reprimarizacion* of the South American economy within a long super-cycle (Erten and Ocampo, 2012). Instead, it represents a major analytical and methodological puzzle. We know about the economic weight and relation to trade and finance at national level of China, the USA, and Brazil, but the methodological national entrance for research makes it difficult to grasp the real developmental nature of this new global axis that frames the conditions, orientations, and opportunities of the NSAR. Here globalization and regionalism contain two dynamics in tension: On the one hand, the power and capacities of these nation states to rule, to an important extent, their economies within boundaries relating to one another. On the other hand, those economies are no longer confined within national frontiers and the center of their powers generally is based elsewhere. The Chinese economy, for instance, is mainly a regional economic network, as Wong demonstrates here, as are the North American and Brazilian economies. That imposes central methodological challenges that demand, in addition, the inclusion in all analyses of a focus on sectors and value chains of production, commerce, and finance. Similar trends can be identified concerning the informal economy of development, for instance in human rights, human traffic, organized crime, piracy, and the same informal economic sectors that go across national borders and even beyond the sea.

This is the central issue in any conceptual framework that seeks to grasp the new dynamics of regional development. For decades, the second major feature of Latin America, beyond its political democratic instability, has been the weight of its informal economy. In summary, the region is currently characterized by the highest percentage of informal economy in the world, around 50 percent on average, for instance, in Peru. This does not only include the economic sectors unregistered in the national accounts, but also organized crime, making its weight in development felt, and a key consideration for any research concerning development, political economy, and geopolitics. Informal sectors are an integral part of the social structures of development and regionalization of the region.

There are different viewpoints about the regional reconfigurations of Latin America, and most of them, from a top-down understanding, based on the European historical experience of state sovereign cession of powers to supranational structures combined with market-oriented development. The idea is that regionalism is about interstate integration, led by government, to increase gains in trade and finance. In other words, from many European perspectives, regionalism is what the states and governments do from the top in order to foster regions as formal entities to advance challenges of economic globalization. In the light of this, some scholars posit that the current Latin American trends simply represent a loose, rudimentary or typical false, populist reaction to the existent international order. For these scholars (e.g. Malamud, 2011), countries which have embarked on the path of regional cooperation are those which have been unable to consolidate the outsourcing processes of reforms of the 1990s, a path in which countries such as Chile, Mexico, Colombia, and recently Peru have shown evidence of the shared wisdom of global and regional options of development. Others, from more liberal and institutionalist lines of thought, contend that the new regionalisms in South America are defined by different and contradictory regional projects overlapping with one another in both scope and interest, a sort of spaghetti bowl unable to build a regional convergence with global tendencies. The argument then is that Latin American regionalism is caught in a sort of sovereignty trap–manifested in its deficient institutionality.

As demonstrated in the preceding chapters, ideas do not always fit reality and a time of crises and change in the world order as we have today; perhaps the attempt to measure realities in relation to preexistent ideas is not the most appropriate way to understand and address change. This book has taken another approach, which is to reflect, from current processes of change, the caveats of current realities and how these realities have come about, both in terms of well-being and conflict, concerning the old and new world powers. In this sense, we depart from the idea that the central issue underlying the discussion about regionalism was development in a changing world order. In other words, we questioned why and how the current realities of development, here and there, have come about in this and not in another way. Today there is an undeniable connection between regionalism and development, where the former has become a growing middle place, containing multiple formal and informal intersections between nation states and a global order in crisis and transformation. Recent evidence shows that once countries attend historical unsorted issues, the axis of development moves to new frontiers; hence regionalism not only shields states but also reshapes them, and, in doing so, regionalism becomes another dimension of development, which is the main conclusion of this collective academic work.

Bibliography

Abrams, P. (1983) *Historical Sociology.* (Ithaca: Cornell University Press).

Acosta, A. and Martínez, E. (2010) (eds) *Agua: Un Derecho Humano Fundamental.* (Quito: Abya-Yala).

Acosta, A., Martínez, E., and Falconi, F. (2005) *TLC: Más que un Tratado de Libre Comercio.* (Quito: FLACSO).

Adler, E. and Barnett, M. (1998) A Framework for the Study of Security Communities. In: E. Adler and M. Barnett (eds), *Security Communities.* (Cambridge: Cambridge University Press), pp. 29–65.

Agencia Latinoamericana de Informacion (2011) *Cooperación UNASUR-Haití: Hora de Hacer un Balance Completo, 13 July 2011.* Available at: http://alainet. org/active/48018 (Accessed 2 April 2012).

Agosin, M., Larrain, C., and Grau, N. (2010) Industrial Policy in Chile *IDB Working Papers,* no. IDB-WP-170.

Agüero, F. (1995) *Soldiers, Civilian and Democracy.* (Baltimore: The John Hopkins University Press).

Akamatzu, K. (1962) A Historical Pattern of Economic Growth in Developing Countries. *Developing Economies* Vol. 1, March/August.

Albanese, J. (2008) Risk Assessment in Organized Crime: Developing a Market and Product-Based Model to Determine Threat Levels. *Journal of Contemporary Criminal Justice* 24: 263. Available at: http://ccj.sagepub.com/cgi/content/abstract/24/3/263.

Albanese, J. (2010) *Assessing Risk, Harm, and Threat to Target Resources against Organized Crime: A Method to Identify the Nature and Severity of the Professional Activity of Organized Crime and Its Impacts (Economic, Social, Political).* Working Papers Series, no. 12, December, Global Consortium on Security Transformation (GCST). Available at: http://www. securitytransformation.org/gc_publications.php.

Altmann, J. and Rojas, F. (eds) (2008) *América Latina y el Caribe: ¿Fragmentación o convergencia? Experiencias recientes de la integración.* (Quito: FLACSO).

Amsden, A. (2001) *The Rise of "the Rest". Challenge to the West from Late-industrializing Economies.* (Oxford: Oxford University Press).

Arbix, G. and Martin, S. (2010) *State Activism without Statism.* Paper presented at the Workshop on States, Development, and Global Governance, University of Wisconsin-Madison, 12–13 March.

Bagley, B. (1990) América Latina y la Administración Bush. In: Arcos, R. (ed.) *Cuadernos de Política Exterior.* (Ecuador: AFESE—ILDIS).

Bagley, B. (2001) *Narcotráfico, Violencia Política y Política Exterior de Estados Unidos hacia Colombia in los Noventa*. (Bogotá, Colombia: Centro de Estudios Internacionales de la Universidad de los Andes).

Bagley, B., Bonilla, A., and Paez, A. (eds) (1991) *La Economía Política del Narcotráfico: El Caso Ecuatoriano*. (Miami/Quito: North-South Center, University of Miami–FLACSO Sede Ecuador).

Bagley, B., Bonilla, A., and Paez, A. (eds) (2003) La Globalización and la Delincuencia Organizada. *Revista Foreign Affairs* en Español. [Documento electrónico] Available at: http://www.foreignaffairs-esp.org/20030401faenespessay11295/bruce-bagley/la-globalizacion-y-la-delincuencia-organizada.html.

Balassa, B. (1961) *The Theory of Economic Integration*. (Homewood: Richard Irwin).

Balassa, B. (2011) *The Theory of Economic Integration*. (London: Routledge).

Barrios, J., Gandelman, N., and Michelin, G. (2010) Analysis of Several Productive Development Policies in Uruguay. *IDB Working Papers* no. IDB-WP-170.

Battaglino, J. (2011) La Política de Defensa y la Política Militar Durante el Kirchnerismo. In: Malamud, A. and De Luca, M. (eds), *La Política en Tiempo de los Kirchner*. (Buenos Aires, Eudeba).

Baumann, R. (2010a) Regional Trade and Growth in Asia and Latin America: The Importance of Productive Complementarity. *CEPAL* LC/BRS/R238, November.

Baumann, R. (2010b) The Geography of Brazilian External Trade: a BRIC with a limited regional focus. In: D. Nelson, B. Hoekman (eds) *Political Economy of Trade Policy in the BRICs*. World Bank Trade and Development Series.

Baumann, R. (2010c) Integración Regional: La Importancia de una Geometría Variable and de Pasos Paralelos. In: A.O. García (ed.), *Latinoamérica frente al Espejo de su Integración: 1810–2010*. (SRE/UNAM: Mexico).

Baumann, R. and Francis N. (2011) *Regional Productive Complementarity and Competitiveness*.

Bello, W. (2004) *Deglobalization: Ideas for a New World Economy*. (London: Zed).

Belmar, C. and Maggi, C. (2010) Políticas e instituciones de fomento de las PYMES en Chile. In: C. Ferraro and G. Stumpo (eds) *Políticas de Apoyo a las Pymes en América Latina. Entre Avances Innovadores y desafíos institucionales*. (Santiago: Economic Commission for Latin America and the Caribbean).

Bennett, J. (2008) The Union of South American Nations: The New (EST) Regionalism in Latin America. *Suffolk Transnational Law Review*, Academic One File, No 32 (Suffolk Transnational).

Biblioteca del Congreso Nacional de Chile (2002) Conceptualización del Plan de Acceso Universal con Garantías Explícitas (AUGE), Eje de la Actual Reforma de Salud. *Serie de Estudios de Anticipación/CEA/BCN* 1(1) (April). (Valparaíso: Biblioteca del Congreso Nacional de Chile). Available at: www.bcn.cl/histley/ historias-de-la-ley- ordenadas-por-materia. Birdsall, N. and Lodono, J. (1998) No Tradeoff: Efficient Growth via More Equal Human

Capital in Latin America. In: N. Birdsall, C. Graham, and R. Sabot (eds) *Beyond Tradeoffs: Market Reforms and Equitable Growth in Latin America.* (Washington, DC: Brookings Institution Press and IADB), pp. 111–45.

Birdsall, N., Lustig, N., and McLeod, D. (2011) Declining Inequality in Latin America: Sole Economics, Some Politics. *Working Paper* 251: 5.

Bøås, M., Marchand, M., and Shaw, T. (eds) (1999) New Regionalism in the New Millennium. Special Issue, *Third World Quarterly* 20: 5.

Bøås, Morten and McNeill, David (eds) (2004) *Global Institutions and Development: Framing the World.* (New York: Routledge).

Bøås, M., Marchand, M., and Shaw, T. (2005) *The Political Economy of Regions and Regionalism.* (London: Palgrave Macmillan).

Boniface, D. (2011) United States Multilateralism and the Unilateral Temptation Los Desafíos del Multilateralismo, en América Latina. *Revista "Pensamiento Propio"* 33: 100–104 (CRIES).

Bonilla, A. (1993) *Las Sorprendentes Virtudes de lo Perverso. Ecuador y Narcotráfico en los 90 en Colección de Ciencia Política.* (Quito: FLACSO– Sede Ecuador).

Bonilla, A. and Long, G. (2010) Un Nuevo Regionalismo Sudamericano. *Íconos Revista de Ciencias Sociales* 38: 23–8.

Bonilla, A. and Paez, A. (2006) Estados Unidos y la Región Andina: Distancia y Diversidad. *Revista Nueva Sociedad* 206: 126–39. Available at: http://www. nuso.org/upload/articulos/3399_1.pdf (Accessed 13 October 2013).

Borgia, F. (2010) Health in Uruguay: Progress and Challenges in the Right to Health Care Three Years after the First Progressive Government. *Social Medicina* 3(2): 110–125.

Bouzas, R. (2005) El "Nuevo Regionalismo" y el Área de Libre Comercio de las Américas: Un Enfoque Menos Indulgente. *Revista de la CEPAL*, April.

Bowles, P. (2002) Regionalism and Development after the Global Financial Crises. In: Rosamond, B., Breslin, S., Hughes, C., and Phillips, N. (eds), *New Regionalism in the Global Political Economy: Theories and Cases.* (London: Routledge).

Brennan, B. and Olivet, C. (2010) Regional Social Policy from Below: Reclaiming Regional Integration: Social Movements and Civil Society Organisations as Key Protagonists. In: Deacon, B., Macovei, M., van Langenhove, L., and Yeates, N. (eds) *World-Regional Social Policy And Global Governance: New Research And Policy Agendas in Africa, Asia, Europe and Latin America.* (London: Routledge).

Breslin, S. and Higgott, R. (2000) Studying Regions: Learning from the Old, Constructing the New. *New Political Economy* 5(3): 333–52.

Breslin, S., and Hook, G. (2003) *Microregionalism and World Order.* (Basingstoke: Palgrave).

Briceño, J. (2006) Regionalismo Estratégico e Interregionalismo en Las Relaciones Externas del MERCOSUR. *Revista Aportes para la Integración Latinoamericana* XII(15) December.

Briceño, J. (2010) From the South American Free Trade Area to the Union of South American Nations: The Transformations of a Rising Regional Process. *Latin American Policy* 1(2): 208–29.

Briceño Ruiz, J. (2011) *El ALBA como Propuesta de Integración Regional, en América Latina and el Caribe: ALBA ¿Una Nueva Forma de Integración Regional?* Altmann, J. (ed.) (Buenos Aires: TESEO; FLACSO, Fundación Carolina), pp. 19–84.

Buchs, M. (2007) The European Social Model. In: *New Governance in European Social Policy.* (Basingstoke: Palgrave/Macmillan).

Bulmer-Thomas, V. (ed.) (2001) *Regional Integration in Latin America and the Caribbean: The Political Economy of Open Regionalism.* (University of London: Institute of Latin American Studies).

Bulmer-Thomas, V. and Knight, A. (2003) *The Economic History of Latin America since Independence*, 2nd edition. (Cambridge: Cambridge University Press).

Burgess, R. (1982) The Role of Theory in Field Research. In: R. Burgess (ed.), *Field Research: A Sourcebook And Field Manual.* (London: Routledge), pp. 209–12.

Buss, P. (2011) Brazil: Structuring Cooperation for Health. *The Lancet* 377(9779): 1722–3.

Buss, P. and Carmo Leal, M. do (2009) Global Health and Health Diplomacy. *Cadernos da Saúde Pública* 25:12. Available at http://www.scielo.br/scielo.php?script=sci_arttext&pid=S0102-311X2009001200001&lng=en&nrm=iso&tlng=en (Accessed 2 February 2012).

Bustelos, G.P. (2003) El Enfoque de Regulación Económica y Economía Política Internacional. ¿Paradigmas Convergentes? *Revista de Economía Mundial* 8: 143–73 (Madrid). Available at: http://www.ucm.es/info/eid/pb/Bustelo%20-%20REM03.pdf.

Buzan, B. (1991) *People, States and Fear: An Agenda for International Security Studies in the Post-Cold War Era*, 2nd edition. (London: Longman).

Buzan, B.(2003) Regional Security Complex Theory in a Post-Cold War World. In: F. Söderbaum and T. Shaw (eds) *Theories of New Regionalism.* (Basingstoke: Palgrave Macmillan), pp. 140–59.

Cable, V. and Henderson, D. (eds) (1994) *Trade Blocs?: The Future of Regional Integration.* (London: The Royal Institute of International Affairs).

Cameron, M., and Hershberg, R. (eds) (2010) *Latin America's Left Turns. Politics, Policies and Trajectories of Change.* (London: Lynn Rienner).

Cardoso, F. (2000) O Brasil e uma Nova América do Sul. *Resenha de Política Exterior do Brasil* No. 87, 2nd semestre.

Casas, Á. (2002) El Nuevo Regionalismo Latinoamericano: Una Lectura Desde el Contexto Internacional. *Revista de Economía Mundial* 6: 138–57.

CEPAL (2011) *China: Direct foreign investment from China in Latina America and the Caribbean.* Annual Report Information Sheet.

Chasqueti, D. (2007) Uruguay 2006: Éxitos y Dilemas del Gobierno de Izquierdas. *Revista de Ciencia Política* 27: 249–63.

Cohen, B. (2011) *International Political Economy: An Intellectual History.* (Princeton: Princeton University Press).

Connell-Smith, G. (1977) *Los Estados Unidos y América Latina.* (México: Fondo de Cultura Económica).

Cornia, A. (2010) Income Distribution under Latin America's New Left Regimes. *Journal of Human Development and Capabilities* 11(1): 85–114.

Corporación Nuevo Arco Iris (2009) ¿*El Declive de la Seguridad Democrática?* Available at: http://www.fes-seguridadregional.org/images/stories/docs/5180-001_g.pdf.

Cox, R. (1981) Social Forces, States and World Orders: Beyond International Relations Theory. *Millennium Journal of International Studies* 10(2): 126–55.

Cox, R. (2002) *The Political Economy of a Plural World: Critical reflections on Power, Morals and Civilization.* (London: Routledge).

Cox, R. (2009) The "British School" in the Global Context. *New Political Economy* 14(3): 315–28.

Crocco, M. and Santos, F. (2010) El Sistema de Fomento de las Micro y Pequeñas Empresas en el Brasil. in Ferraro, C. and G. Stumpo (eds) *Políticas de Apoyo a las Pymes en América Latina. Entre Avances Innovadores y Desafíos Institucionales.* (Santiago: Economic Commission for Latin America and the Caribbean).

Cusco Declaration on the South American Community of Nations (*2004*) Third South American Presidential Summit. *Cusco*, 8 December.

Dabène, O. (2012) Consistency and Resilience through Cycles of Repoliticization. In: P. Riggirozzi and D. Tussie (eds), *The Rise of Post-Hegemonic Regionalism. The Case of Latin America.* Series: United Nations University Series on Regionalism.

Davila, M. (2005) *Health Reform in Contemporary Chile: Does Politics Matter?* Masters Thesis, University of North Carolina at Chapel Hill, Department of Political Science.

Deacon, B. and Macovei, M. (2010) Regional Social Policy from Above: International Organisations and Regional Social Policy. In: Deacon, B., Macovei, M., van Langenhove, L., and Yeates, N. (eds) *World-Regional Social Policy and Global Governance: New Research and Policy Agendas in Africa, Asia, Europe and Latin America.* (London: Routledge).

Deacon, B., Ortiz, I., and Zelenev, Z. (2007) Regional Social Policy, UN Department of Economic and Social Affairs *Working Paper No. 37*, ST/ESA/2007/DWP/37 (New York: UNDESA).

Deacon, B., Macovei, M., van Langenhove, L., and Yeates, N. (eds) (2010) *World-Regional Social Policy and Global Governance: New Research and Policy Agendas in Africa, Asia, Europe and Latin America.* (London: Routledge).

De Lombaerde, P. and Garay, L. (2006) *The New Regionalism in Latin America and the Role of the US.* OBREAL/EULARO Background Paper, presented at the International Symposium on *New Linkages in Latin America: Economic Integration and Regional Security*, Session 4: Challenges for the Economic

Integration in Latin America, Sophia University and the Japan Center for Area Studies, Tokyo, 28 March 2006. Disponible en dirección electrónica, visitada en Diciembre de 2011 http://www.iadb.org/intal/intalcdi/PE/2009/03385.pdf.

Deutsch, K., Burrell, S., and Kann, R. (1958) *Political Community in the North Atlantic.* (Princeton: Princeton University Press).

Diaz Alejandro, C. (1970) *Essays on the Economic History of the Argentine Republic.* (London: Yale University Press).

Diaz Alejandro, C. (1989) Comment on Two (or More) Peronisms. In: G. Di Tella and R. Dornbush (eds), *The Political Economy of Argentina, 1946–1983.* (London: Macmillan and Saint Antony's College), pp. 86–8.

Diaz Alejandro, C. (2000) Latin America in the 1930s. In:R. Thorp (ed.), *An Economic History of Twentieth-Century Latin America, Vol. 2: Latin America in the 1930s: The Role of the Periphery in World Crisis.* (London: Palgrave), pp. 15–42.

Di Pietro L. (2003) *La Dimensión Social del Mercosur. Recorrido Institucional and Perspectivas*, Paper presented at workshop: Integración Regional and la Agenda Social. (Buenos Aires: BID-INTAL), pp. 12–13.

Doctor, M. (2009) *Furthering Industrial Development in Brazil: Globalization and the National Innovation System*, Paper prepared for delivery at the 2009 Congress of the Latin American Studies Association, 11–14 June, Rio de Janeiro, Brazil.

Duffield, M. (2001) *Global Governance and the New Wars: The Merging of Development and Security.* (London: Zed Books).

Duncan, G. (2005) *Del Campo a la Ciudad en Colombia. Infiltración Urbana de los Señores de la Guerra.* (Universidad de los Andes, Colombia) [Documento electrónico] Available at: http://scholar.googleusercontent.com/scholar?q=cac he:qyNwPxXFhUwJ:scholar.google.com/&hl=es&as_sdt=0,5.

ECLAC (2002) *Globalization and Development.* (Santiago, Chile: Economic Commission for Latin America and the Caribbean).

ECLAC (2010) *Social Panorama of Latin America, 2010.* (Santiago: Economic Commission for Latin America and the Caribbean).

El-Agraa Ali, M. (1982) *International Economic Integration.* (London: Macmillan Press).

El Carabobeño (2011) "Ban elogia a Santos por normalizar relaciones con Venezuela". 12 June. Available at: http://www.el-carabobeno.com/portada/articulo/15256/ban-elogia-a-santos-por-normalizar-relaciones-con-venezuela. (Accessed 16 July 2011).

Erten, B. and Ocampo, J. (2012) Super-cycles of Commodity Prices since the Mid-nineteenth Century. *DESA Working Paper 110.*

Esping-Andersen, G. (1990) *The Three Worlds of Welfare Capitalism.* (Princeton, NJ: Princeton University Press).

Espinosa, C. (2010) Ecuador se Inserta en el Sistema de Estados: Las Relaciones Internacionales de Ecuador entre 1830 y 1870. In: Zepeda, B. (ed.), *Ecuador: Relaciones Exteriores a la Luz del Bicentenario.* (Serie: Colección Bicentenario).

Estevadeordal, A., and Suominen, K. (2007) *Sequencing Regional Trade and Cooperation Agreements.* Internal paper. Integration and Regional Programs Department, Inter-American Development Bank.

Ewig, C. (2008) Reproduction, Re-reform, and the Reconfigured State: Feminists and Neoliberal Health Reforms in Chile. In: Bakker, I. and Silvey, R. (eds) *Beyond States and Markets: The Challenges of Social Reproduction.* (New York: Routledge), pp. 143–58.

Ewig, C. and Kay, S. (2011) Post-Retrenchment Politics: Policy Feedbacks in Health and Pension Reforms in Chile. *LAPS*, Winter.

Falconi, F. (2005) La Construccion de Una Economia con Cimientos Ecologicos. In: Acosta, A. and Falconi, F. (eds) *Asedios a lo Imposible. Propuestas Economicas en Construccion.* (Quito: FLACSO e ILDIS).

Fawcett, L. (2009) The Origins and Development of the Regional Idea in the Americas. In: L. Fawcett and M. Serrano (eds), *Regionalism and Governance in the Americas.* (London: Palgrave/Macmillan).

Fawn R. (2009) Regions and their Study: Where from, What for and Where to? *Review of International Studies* 35(1): 5–34.

Filgueira, F. (2005) *Welfare and Democracy in Latin America: The Development, Crises and Aftermath of Universal, Dual and Exclusionary Social States.* Paper prepared for the UNRISD Project on Social Policy and Democratization, Geneva.

Franco, M. (2002) *Fases and momento actual de la estructura social Argentina,* (Mendoza: Universidad Nacional de Cuyo).

French-Davis, R. (2010) *Macroeconomía para el empleo decente en América Latina and el Caribe,* (Santiago de Chile: Oficina Internacional del Trabajo).

French-Davis, R., Muñoz, O., and Palma, G. (1995) The Latin American Economies, 1950–1990. In: Bethell, L. (ed.) *The Cambridge History of Latin America, Vol. 6: Latin America since 1930: Economy, Society and Politics.* (Cambridge, UK: Cambridge University Press).

Frenkel, R. (2003) Globalization and financial crisis in Latin America. *Cepal Review* 80.

Frieden J., and Lake D. (eds) (2000) *International Political Economy: Perspectives on Global Power and Wealth,* 4th edition. (Boston, New York: St. Martin's Press).

Fuentes, C. (2008) Fronteras Calientes. *Foreign Affairs Latinoamérica* 8: 3.

Gambetta, D. (2007) *La Mafia Siciliana. El Negocio de la Protección Privada.* (Mexico D.F: Fondo de Cultura Económica).

Gamble, A. and Payne, A. (eds) (1996) *Regionalism and World Order.* (London: Palgrave Macmillan).

García Delgado, D. (1998) *Estado–Nación y Globalización. Fortalezas y Debilidades en el Umbral del Tercer Milenio.* (Buenos Aires: Editorial Ariel).

Gasparini, L., and Lustig, N. (2011) The Rise and Fall of Income Inequality in Latin America. *Documento de Trabajo* 118, May.

Gilpin, R. (2001) *Global Political Economy: Understanding the International Political Economy*. (Princeton: Princeton University Press).

Gomez, E. (2009) Brazil's Blessing in Disguise. *Foreign Policy*, July. Available at: http://www.foreignpolicy.com/articles/2009/07/22/brazils_blessing_in_disguise (28 March 2012).

Gomez-Mera, L. (2008) How "New" Is the "New Regionalism" in the Americas? The Case of MERCOSUR. *Journal of International Relations and Development* 11: 279–308.

Grabebdroff, W. (1979) La Política Exterior del Brasil, Entre el Primer y Tercer Mundo. *Nueva Sociedad* 41, March to April, pp. 108–19.

Grieco, J. (1997) Systemic Sources of Variation in Regional Institutionalization in Western Europe, East Asia and the Americas. In: E. Mansfield and H. Milner (eds) *The Political Economy of Regionalism*. (New York: Colombia University Press), pp. 164–88.

Griffith-Jones, S. (1984) *International Finance and Latin America* (New York: St. Martin's Press).

Griffith-Jones, S. (ed.) (1988) *Managing World Debt* (London: Harvester Wheatsheaf).

Grugel, J. (2002) *Democratization: A critical introduction* (New York: Palgrave).

Grugel, J. (2004) New Regionalism and Modes of Governance: Comparing US and EU Strategies in Latin America, *in European Journal of International Relations*, 10:4, 603–26, 605.

Grugel, J. (2005) Citizenship and Governance in MERCOSUR: Arguments for a Social Agenda. *Third World Quarterly* 26(7): 1061–76.

Grugel, J. and Piper, C. (2009) Do Rights Promote Development? *Global Social Policy* 9(1): 79–98.

Grugel, J. and Riggirozzi, M.P. (2007) The Return of the State in Argentina. *International Affairs* 83(1): 87–107.

Grugel, J. and Riggirozzi, P. (2012) Post-neoliberalism in Latin America: Rebuilding and Reclaiming the State after Crisis. *Development and Change* 43(1): 1–21.

Guangsheng, L. (2006) Assessment on Performance of ASEAN Economic Integration *International Review*, Autumn, Vol. 44.

Gwynne, R. and Kay, C. (2000) Views from the Periphery: Futures of Neoliberalism in Latin America. *Third World Quarterly* 21(1): pp. 141–56.

Haas, E. (1958) *The Uniting of Europe: Political, Social and International Organization*. (Stanford: Stanford University Press).

Haggard, S. (1997) Regionalism in Asia and the Americas. In: D. Mansfield and H. Milner (eds) *The Political Economy of Regionalism*. (New York: Columbia University Press).

Halperin Donghi, T. (1993) *The Contemporary History of Latin America*, 3rd edition. (Durham, NC: Duke University Press).

Hameiri, S. (2012) Theorising Regions through Changes in Statehood: Rethinking the Theory and Method of Comparative Regionalism. *Review of International Studies*, FirstView Articles, pp. 1–23.

Herbas, G. and Molina, S. (2005) IIRSA y la Integración Regional. *FOBOMADE– Foro Boliviano sobre Medio Ambiente y Desarrollo*. VI(17) May–August.

Hermann, J. (2010) Development Banks in the Financial-Liberalization Era: The Case of BNDES in Brazil. *CEPAL Review* 100: 189–204.

Hettne, B. (1993) Neo-Mercantilism: The Pursuit of Regionness. *Cooperation and Conflict* 28(3): 211–32.

Hettne, B. (1997) *The Double Movement: Global Market versus Regionalism*. In: R. Cox (ed.) *The New Realism: Perspectives on Multilateralism and World Order*. (Tokyo: United Nations University Press).

Hettne, B. (1999) Globalisation and the New Regionalism: The Second Great Transformation. In: B. Hettne, A. Inotai, and O. Sunkel (eds) *Globalism and the New Regionalism*. (London: Macmillan), pp. 1–24.

Hettne, B. (2003) *The New Regionalism Revisited*. In: F. Söderbaum and T. Shaw (eds) *Theories of New Regionalism*. (Basingstoke: Macmillan), pp. 22–42.

Hettne, B. (2005a) *Global Politics of Regionalism: Theory and Practice*. London. Pluto Press.

Hettne, B. (2005b) Beyond the "New" Regionalism *New Political Economy* 10(4): 543–71.

Hettne, B. (2006) Beyond the 'New' Regionalism. In: Payne, A. (ed.), *Key Debates in Political Economy*. London: Taylor and Francis.

Hettne, B. (2008) *Regional Actorship and Regional Agency: Comparative Perspectives*, presented at the 6th GARNET PhD School Global Governance and Regionalism, Brussels, 9–13 June.

Hettne, B. and Söderbaum, F. (1999) Rethinking Development Theory: Guest Editors Introduction. *Journal of International Relations and Development* 2(4): 354–7.

Hettne, B. and Söderbaum F. (2000) Theorising the Rise of Regionness. *New Political Economy* 5(3): 457–74.

Hettne, B., Inotai, A., and Sunkel (eds) (1999) *Globalism and the New Regionalism*. (London: Macmillan).

Hettne, B., Inotai, A., and Sunkel (eds) (2000) *National Perspectives on the New Regionalism*. (London: Macmillan).

Hettne, B., Inotai, A., and Sunkel (eds) (2001) *Comparing Regionalisms: Implications for Global Development*. (Basingstoke: Palgrave Macmillan).

Hook, G. and Kearns, I. (1999) *Subregionalism and World Order*. (New York: St. Martin's Press).

Hunter, W. and Sugiyama, N. (2009) Democracy and Social Policy in Brazil: Advancing Basic Needs, Preserving Privileged Interests. *Latin American Politics and Society* 51(2): 29–58.

Hurrel, A. (1995) Regionalism in Theoretical Perspective. In: L. Fawcett and A. Hurrell (eds) *Regionalism in World Politics: Regional Organization and International Order.* (Oxford: Oxford University Press), pp. 9–73.

ILDIS-FES (2007) Tendencias de Seguridad en América del Sur e Impactos en la Región Andina. In: ILDIS-FES (ed.), *Integración, Seguridad y Conflictos en la subregión Andina.* (Quito: ILDIS-FES), pp. 13–30.

ILO (2010) *Panorama Laboral 2010, América Latina.* (Lima: International Labour Organization).

Information of the State Council in China (2011) White paper. *People's Daily Online* 6 September.

International Meeting (2010) Palacio del Congreso Nacional Argentina. Buenos Aires, 4 October.

Isacson, A. (2009) *After Plan Colombia. Evaluating Integrated Actions, the Next Phase of U.S. Assistance.* Center for International Policy. Available at: http:// justf.org/files/pubs/091203_col.pdf.

Jayasuriya, K. (2003) Introduction: Governing the Asia-Pacific: Beyond the "New Regionalism." *Third World Quarterly* 24(2): 199–215.

Jayasuriya, K. (2009) Regulatory Regionalism in the Asia-Pacific: Drivers, Instruments and Actors, *in Australian Journal of International Affairs*, 63:3, 335–47.

Kahhat, F. (2008) Guerra Fría en los Andes. *Revista Foreign Affairs* 8(3). Available at: http://www.flacsoandes.org/internacional/publi_acade/peru/05farid_kahhat. pdf (Accessed 13 October 2013).

Katzenstein, P. (2000) *Asian Regionalism.* (Cornell University: East Asia Program).

Katzenstein P. (2005) *A World of Regions: Asia and Europe in the American Imperium.* (Cornell: Cornell University Press).

Katzenstein, P. (2010) *Civilizations in World Politics: Plural and Pluralist Perspectives.* (New York: Routledge).

Kaup, B. (2010) *A Neoliberal Nationalization?* The Constraints on Natural Gas-Led Development in Bolivia. *Latin American Perspective* 37(3): 123–38.

Keet, D. and Bello, W. (2004) *Linking Alternative Regionalisms for Equitable and Sustainable Development.* (Amsterdam: Transnational Institute).

Kellogg, P. (2007) Regional Integration in Latin America: Dawn of an Alternative to Neoliberalism? *New Political Science* 29(2): 187–209.

Kelly, P. (1997) *Checkerboards and Shatterbelts: The Geopolitics of South America.* (Austin: Texas: University of Texas Press).

Keohane, R. (1984) *After Hegemony: Cooperation and Discord in the World Political Economy.* (Cambridge: Cambridge University Press).

Keohane, R. (2002) *Power and Interdependence in a Partially Globalized World.* (New York: Routledge).

Kickbusch, I., Silberschmidt, G., and Buss, P. (2010) *Global Health Diplomacy: the Need for New Perspectives, Strategic Approaches and Skills in Global*

Health, Bulletin of the World Health Organization. Available at http://www. who.int/bulletin/volumes/85/3/06-039222/en (12 July 2010).

Kohl, B. (2010) Bolivia under Morales: A Work in Progress. *Latin American Perspectives* 37(3): 107–22.

Krasner, S. (1976) State Power and the International Trade Structure. *World Politics* 28: 317–47.

Krasner, S. (2000) *State Power and the Structure of International Trade*. In: Frieden J., and Lake D. (eds) *International Political Economy: Perspectives on Global Power and Wealth*, 4th edition. (Boston) pp. 19–36.

Krasner, S. (2009) *Power, state, and sovereignty: essays on international relations*, (New York: Routledge).

Kucinski, B. (1978) La Amazonia y la Geopolítica del Brasil. *Nueva Sociedad* No. 37, July to August, pp. 26–30.

Kuwayama, M. (2005) Latin America South–South Integration and Cooperation: From a Regional Public Goods Perspective. *CEPAL, Serie Comercio Internacional* 50.

Lake, D. (2009a) Open Economy Politics: A Critical Review. *International Organization* 4: 219–44.

Lake, D. (2009b) Regional Hierarchy: Authority and Local International Order, *Review of International Studies* 35(1): 35–58.

Leal Buitrago, F. (2007) *Una Mirada a la Seguridad en la Región Andina* Informativo UMNG IEGAP No. 22. (Universidad Militar Nueva Granada).

Lee Kuan Yew (2010) The Straits Times, (Singapore, December 9), p. A31.

Leftwich, A. (2006) Politics in Command: Development Studies and the Rediscovery of Social Science. In: A. Payne (ed.) *Key Debates in Political Economy*. (London: Taylor & Francis).

Legler, T. and Santa Cruz, A. (2011) El Patrón Contemporáneo del Multilateralismo Latinoamericano. *Revista Pensamiento Propio* 33: 18–20. January to June (CRIES, Mexico).

Lemke, D. (2002) *Regions of War and Peace* (Cambridge/New York: Cambridge University Press.

López, H.C. (2010) *Y Refundaron la Patria. De Cómo Mafiosos y Políticos Reconfiguraron el Estado Colombiano*. (Bogotá, Colombia: Corporación Nuevo Arco Iris).

Lugar, R. (2009) Discurso ante la XIII Conferencia Anual de la CAF sobre Comercio en las Américas; September 2009. Available at: http://lugar.senate. gov/news/record.cfm?id=317616&&.

McMillan, M., and Rodrik, D. (2011) Globalization, Structural Change and Productivity Growth, *NBER Working Paper*, no 17143.

Malamud, A. (2005) MERCOSUR Turns 15: Between Rising Rhetoric and Declining Achievement. *Cambridge Review of International Affairs* 18(3): 421–36.

Malamud, A. (2011) A Leader without Followers? The Growing Divergence Between the Regional and Global Performance of Brazilian Foreign Policy, *Latin American Politics and Society* 53(3): 1–24.

Malamud, A. (2013) Overlapping Regionalism, No Integration: Conceptual Issues and the Latin American Experiences. *EUI Working Papers RSCAS* 20.

Mansfield, E. and Milner, H. (eds) (1997) *The Political Economy of Regionalism.* (New York: Columbia University Press).

Mansfield, E. and Milner, H. (eds) (2010) Regionalism. *Annual Review of Political Sciences* 13: 145–63.

Mansfield, E. and Solingen, E. (2010) Regionalism. *Annual Review of Political Sciences* 13: 145–63.

Marchand, M., Bøås, M., and Shaw, T. (1999) The Political Economy of New Regionalism. *Third World Quarterly* 20(5): 897–910.

Marchand, M., Bøås, M., and Shaw, T. (2005) *The Political Economy of Regions and Regionalisms.* (Basingstoke, Palgrave/Macmillan).

Martínez Franzoni, J. (2008) Welfare Regimes in Latin America: Capturing Constellations of Markets, Families and Policies, *in Latin American Politics and Society*, 50(2): 67–100.

Martínez Franzoni, J. and Sanchez-Ancochea, D. (2013a) Can Latin American Production Regimes Complement Universalistic Welfare Regimes? Implications from the Costa Rican Case. *Latin American Research Review* 2013.

Martínez Franzoni, J. and Sánchez Ancochea, D. (2013b) *Good Jobs and Social Services. How Costa Rica Achieved the Elusive Double Incorporation.* (London: Palgrave McMillan).

Massi, E. and Singh, J. (2011) *The Politics of Natural Resources: A Critical Appraisal on the Return of the State in Brazil.* Paper presented at the Workshop Post-Neoliberalism: Towards a New Political Economy of Development for Latin America? University of Sheffield, October.

Mattli, W. (1999) *The Logic of Regional Integration: Europe and Beyond.* (Cambridge: Cambridge University Press).

Mejía Londoño, D. (2011) Introducción. In: G. Uribe, A. and D. Mejía Londoño (eds). *Políticas antidrogas en Colombia: éxitos, fracasos, and extravíos.* (Bogota: Universidad de los Andes).

Méndez, G., Senatore, L., and Traversa, F. (2010) *La política laboral de un proyecto socialdemócrata periférico: un análisis de los cambios institucionales en Uruguay 2005–2009* (Montevideo: Friedich Ebert Foundation).

Menezes Texeira, A. (2010) Regionalismo y Seguridad Sudamericana. ¿Son Relevantes el MERCOSUR y la UNASUR? Íconos. *Revista de Ciencias Sociales* 38: 41–53.

Mesa-Lago, C. (2007) *Reassembling Social Security: A Survey of Pensions and Health Care Reforms in Latin America.* (Oxford: Oxford University Press).

Mesa-Lago, C. and Muller, K. (2004) *La Política de las Reformas de Pensión en América Latina Después de dos Décadas.* (Caracas: Nueva Sociedad).

Mignolo, W. (1991) *The Idea of Latin America.* London: Wiley-Blackwell.

Mitrany, D. (1966) *A Working Peace System.* (Chicago: Quadrangle Books).

Mittelman, J. (1996) Rethinking the New Regionalism in the Context of Globalization. *Global Governance* 2: 189–213.

Mittelman, J. (2000) *The Globalisation Syndrome: Transformation and Resistance.* (Princeton: Princeton University Press).

Mkandawire, T. (2001) Social Policy in a Development Context. In: *Programme on Social Policy and Development*, Paper No. 7. (UNRISD: Geneva).

Mkandawire, T. (2006a) Targeting and Universalism in Poverty Reduction. *UNRISD Social Policy and Development Programme,* Paper no 23, Geneva.

Mkandawire, T. (ed.) (2006b) *Social Policy in a Development Context.* (Geneva: United Nations Research Institution for Social Development).

Mohammeddinov, M. (2006) Consideraciones Geoestratégicas de la Integración Europea y Sudamericana: Una Confirmación de Supuestos Neorrealistas. *Red de Revistas Científicas de América Latina y el Caribe, España y Portugal* 2(2): 113–33.

Montenegro, G. (2006) Desafíos y Oportunidades para la Defensa Nacional. In: Trotta, N. (ed.), *Argentina 2020. 20 Propuestas para Profundizar la Transformación.* (Buenos Aires, Editorial Lumier).

Montenegro, G. (2011) Desafíos y Límites del Gobierno Político de la Defensa y su Incidencia en el Desarrollo del Consejo de Defensa Suramericano. In: X Congreso de Ciencia Política de la República Argentina, *Democracia, Integración y Crisis en el Nuevo Orden Global. Tensiones y Desafíos para el Análisis Político,* Ciudad de Córdoba, July 27–30.

Müller, K. (2009) Contested Universalism: From Bonasol to Renta Dignidad in Bolivia. *International Journal of Social Welfare* 18: 163–72.

Neild, R. (2005) Asistencia Policial y Políticas de Control de Drogas de Estados Unidos. In: C.A. Youngers and E. Rosin (eds). *Drogas y Democracia in América Latina.* (Washington DC: Editorial Biblos), pp. 85–130.

Nel, P. and Nolte, D. (2010) Introduction: Special Section on Regional Powers in a Changing Global Order. *Review of International Studies* 36:(4): 877–9.

Nesadurai, H. (2008) The Association of Southeast Asian Nations (ASEAN). *New Political Economy* 13(2).

North, D. (1990) *Institutions and Their Consequences for Economic Performance.* In: K. Cook and M. Levi (eds) *The Limits of Rationality.* (Chicago: Chicago University Press), pp. 383–401.

North, D. (2002) Institutions and Economic Growth: A historical Introduction. *World Development* 17(9): 47–59, 1319–32.

Nuñez, J. (2006) *Cacería de Brujos.* Serie Tesis, FLACSO Sede Ecuador–Abya Yala. (Quito, Ecuador).

Nuñez, J. (2011) *Crítica a la Ideología de la Seguridad Ciudadana en Ecuador. 91 Estrategias Contra la Violencia.* (FLACSO, Quito).

Nunn A., Da Fonseca, E., and Gruskin, S. (2009) Changing Global Essential Medicines Norms to Improve Access to AIDS treatment: Lessons from Brazil, in *Global Public Health: An International Journal for Research*, Policy and Practice, 4: 131.

Nye, J. (1965) *Pan-African and the East African Integration*. (Cambridge: Cambridge University Press).

Nye, J. (2004) *Soft Power: The Means to Succeed in World Politics*. (New York: Public Affairs).

Ocampo, J.A. and Nef, L. (1994) The political economy of inter-American relations: A structural and historical overview. In: R. Stubbs and G. Underhill (eds), *Political Economy and the Changing Global Order*. (New York: Oxford University Press), pp. 404–18.

Ocampo, J., Rada, C., and. Taylor, L. (2004) Latin America's Growth and Equity Frustrations during Structural Reforms. *Journal of Economic Perspectives* 18(2): 67–88.

Ocampo, J., Rada, C., and. Taylor, L. (2009) *Growth and Policy in Developing Countries: A Structuralist Approach* (New York, NY: Columbia University Press).

O'Connor, E. (2010) El Nodesarrollismo Brasileño como Propuesta de Desarrollo para Argentina. *Economic Studies of International Development* 10: 2.

O'Donnell, G. (1973) *Modernization and Bureaucratic-Authoritarianism: Studies in South America Politics* (Berkeley: Institute for International Studies).

O'Donnell, G. (2010) *Democracia, Agencia y Estado. Teoría con Intención Comparativa*, Capítulo VIII. (Buenos Aires, Prometeo Libros).

Ortiz, I. (2007) *Social Policy. National Development Strategies.* (United Nations).

Pacini. M., and Siow Yue Chia. (1997) *ASEAN in the new Asia* (Singapore. Institute of Southeast Asian Studies).

PAHO (2010) UNASUR's Role in the Vaccination Against Pandemic Influenza. *Pan-American Health Organisation, Immunisation Newsletter*, 32:4. Available at http://new.paho.org/hq/dmdocuments/2011/SNE3204.pdf (12 March 2012).

Paladines, J. (2011) *La Sociedad del Riesgo en el Discurso Criminalizador de las Drogas*. Tesis de grado para la obtención del grado de Master in Ciencias Políticas. (Quito: FLACSO Sede Ecuador).

Panizza, F. (2009) *Contemporary Latin America: Development and Democracy beyond the Washington Consensus*. (New York: Zed).

Paus, E. (2012) "Confronting the Middle Income Trap: Insights from Latecomers", *Studies in International Comparative Development* 47(2): 115–38.

Payne, A. (1996) The United States and its Enterprise for the Americas. In: A. Payne and Gamble (eds), *Regionalism and World Order*. (London: Macmillan), pp. 93–129.

Payne, A. (2004) *The New Regional Politics of Development*. (New York: Palgrave).

Payne, A. (2005) *The Global Politics of Unequal Development*. (London: Palgrave).

Payne, A. and Gamble, A. (eds) (1996) *Regionalism and World Order.* (London: Macmillan).

Payne, A. and Phillips, N. (eds) (2010) *Development: Key Concepts.* (Cambridge: Polity Press).

Pécaut, D. (2008) *Las Farc. ¿Una Guerrilla sin fin o sin fines?* (Bogotá: Grupo Editorial Norma).

Peña, F. (2009) La Integración del Espacio Sudamericano ¿La Unasur y el Mercosur Pueden Complementarse? *Nueva Sociedad* No 219, January to February.

Perez, C. (2010) Technological Dynamism and Social Inclusion in Latin America: A Resource-Based Production Development Strategy. *CEPAL Review* 100: 121–42.

Pérez, M. (2009) *La Reforma del Sistema de Salud en el Primer Gobierno de Izquierda en la Historia del Uruguay: los Desafíos del Cambio,* Tesis de Licenciatura, Instituto de Ciencia Política, Facultad de Ciencias Sociales, Universidad de la República.

Pérez Caldentey, E. (2012) Income Convergence, Capability Divergence, and the Middle Income Trap: An Analysis of the Case of Chile, *Studies in International Comparative Development* 47(2): 185–207.

Phillips, N. (1999) *Global and regional links,* in N. Phillips and J. Buxton (eds), *Development in* Latin American Political Economy: states, markets and actors, (Manchester: Manchester University Press), 72–92.

Phillips, N. (2003a) Hemispheric Integration and Subregionalism in the Americas. *International Affairs* 79(2): 327–49.

Phillips, N. (2003b) The Rise and Fall of Open Regionalism? Comparative Reflections on Regional Governance in the Southern Cone of Latin America. *Third World Quarterly* 24(2): 217–34.

Phillips, N. (2004) The Southern Cone. In: A. Payne (ed.) *The New Regional Politics of Development.* (New York: Palgrave).

Phillips, N. and Prieto Corredor, G. (2011) The Demise of New Regionalism: Reframing the Study of Contemporary Regional Integration in Latin America. In: A. Warleigh-Lack, N. Robinson, and B. Rosamond (eds) *New Regionalisms and the EU Studies: Dialogues and New Research Directions.* (London, Routledge).

Pontón, D. and Rivera, F. (2011) *El Asenso Estratégico: Lógicas y Despliegues del Crimen Organizado en Ecuador.* (Quito: FLACSO-Ecuador).

Pribble, J. (2010) *Protecting the Poor: Welfare Politics in Latin America's Free Market Era.* Doctoral thesis defended at the Department of Political Science, North Carolina (The University of North Carolina at Chapel Hill).

Rada, C. and Taylor, L. (2009) *Growth and Policy in Developing Countries: A Structuralist Aprroach.* (New York, NY: Columbia University Press).

Ramirez, F. (2006) Mucho más que dos Izquierdas. *Nueva Sociedad* 205, September/October.

Ramírez, M., Staton, K. and Walsh, J. (2005) Colombia un Círculo Vicioso de Drogas y Guerra. In: Coletta A. Youngers and Eileen Rosin (eds) *Drogas and Democracia in América Latina.* WOLA. (Washington DC: Editorial Biblos), pp. 131–84.

Rapoport, M. and Cervo, A. (eds) (2002) *El Cono Sur: Una historia común.* (Buenos Aires: Fondo de Cultura Económica).

Rapoport, M. and Madrid, E. (2002) Los países del Cono Sur and las grandes potencias. In: M. Rapoport and A. Cervo (eds), *El Cono Sur: Una historia común.* (Buenos Aires: Fondo de Cultura Económica), pp. 225–80.

Reinhart, N., and Peres, W. (2000) Model: Micro Latin America's New Economic Responses and Economic Results. *World Development* 28(9): 1543–66.

Reygadas, L., and Filgueira, F. (2010) Inequality and the Incorporation Crisis: The Left's Social Policy Toolkit. In: M. Cameron and R. Hershberg (eds) (2010) *Latin America's Left Turns. Politics, Policies and Trajectories of Change.* (London: Lynn Rienner).

Rick, F. (2009) Regions and their Study: Wherefrom, What for and Whereto? *Review of International Studies* 35(1): 5–34.

Riesco, M. (2010) Regional Social Policies in Latin America: Binding Material for a Young Giant? In: Deacon, B., Macovei, M., van Langenhove, L., and Yeates, N. (eds) *World-Regional Social Policy and Global Governance: New Research and Policy Agendas in Africa, Asia, Europe and Latin America.* (London: Routledge).

Riggirozzi, P. (2010) Region, Regionness and Regionalism in Latin America: Towards a New Synthesis. *Latin American Trade Network Working Paper 130,* April.

Riggirozzi, P. (2012) Region, Regionness, and Regionalism: Towards a New Synthesis. *New Political Economy* 17(4): 421–43.

Rivera, F. (2005) Ecuador los Bemoles de la Guerra Contra las Drogas. In: Youngers C. and E. Rosin (eds) *Drogas y Democracia en América Latina.* (Washington DC: WOLA, Editorial Biblos), pp. 287–324.

Rivera, F. (2010) *Perspectivas Analíticas para la Paz, Seguridad y Desarme.* Documento de Trabajo. Secretaría Nacional de Planificación y Desarrollo. (Quito: SENPLADES).

Rivera, F. (2011) *Inteligencia Estratégica y Prospectiva.* FLACSO, Secretaría Nacional de Inteligencia. (Quito: SENAIN).

Robson P. (1980) *The Economics of International Integration.* (London: Allen & Unwin).

Robson P. (1993) The New Regionalism and Developing Countries. *Journal of Common Markets Studies* 31(3): 329–84.

Rodrik, D. (1995) Why is there Multilateral Lending? *Working Paper* no. 5160, National Bureau of Economic Research, June.

Rodrik, D. (2007) *Normalizing Industrial Policy.* Paper prepared for the Commission on Growth and Development.

Rodrik, D. (2011) *The Future of Economic Convergence*. Paper prepared for the 2011 Jackson Hole Symposium of the Federal Reserve Bank of Kansas City, August, pp. 25–7.

Rodrik, D. and McMillan M. (2011) Globalization, Structural Change and Productivity Growth. *NBER Working Paper*, no. 17143.

Rojas Aravena, F. (2003) Nuevos Contextos de Seguridad Internacional: Nuevos Desafíos, ¿Nuevas Oportunidades? In: F. Rojas Aravena (ed.), *La Seguridad en América Latina pos 11 de Septiembre*. (Caracas, Nueva Sociedad).

Rojas Aravena, F. (2007) Crimen Organizado Internacional: Una Amenaza a la Estabilidad Democrática. *Pensamiento Propio* 12(26): 155–75.

Romero V. (2007) América latina, defensa and seguridad en el siglo XXI. In: *Cuadernos de Defensa No. 1. Modernización de los Ministerios de Defensa*. Consejo de Defensa Sudamericano, pp. 11–19.

Romero, V.M. (2011) *La Economía de los Paramilitares. Redes de Corrupción, Negocio y Política*. (Colombia: Corporación Nuevo Arco Iris).

Rosenau, J. (1997) *Along the Domestic–Foreign Frontier: Exploring Governance in a Turbulent World*. (Cambridge: Cambridge University Press).

Rosenau, J. (1999) *Alfonsín, Menem and las Relaciones Cívico Militares. La Construcción del Control Civil Sobre las Fuerzas Armadas en la Argentina Democrática (1983–1995)*. Doctoral Thesis presented to the Department of Social Sciences of the Institute of Philosophy and Human Sciences of the State University of Campinas.

Rotberg, R. (2003) *When States Fail*. (Princeton University Press). Available at: http://press.princeton.edu/chapters/s7666.pdf.

Saguier, M. (2007) The Hemispheric Social Alliance and the Free Trade Area of the Americas Process: The Challenges and Opportunities of Transnational Coalitions against Neo-liberalism. *Globalisations* 4(2): 251–65.

Sain, M. (2002) *Reflexiones Acerca de las Relaciones Civil Militares en las Democracias Latinoamericanas de Principios de Siglo*. Ponencia Seminario Políticas de Seguridad y Defensa, Quito, May.

Sain, M. (2003) *Los Civiles y la Defensa Nacional en la Argentina*. (Buenos Aires: Mimeo).

Sanchez, D. (2007) Health Integration Processes: Challenges for MERCOSUR in the Health Field. *Cad. Saúde Pública* 23: 2. Available at: http://www.scielosp. org/scielo.php?script=sci_arttext&pid=S0102-311X2007001400005&lng=en &nrm=iso (Accessed 22March 2012).

Sandbrook, R., Edelaman, M., Heller, P., and Teichman, J. (2002) *Social Democracy in the Periphery: Origins, Challenges, Prospects*. (Cambridge: Cambridge University Press).

Sansó, D. (2011) *Conferencia dictada en el programa de capacitación para el análisis de inteligencia criminal estratégica aplicada a la criminalidad organizada*. (Quito: FLACSO-SENAIN).

Santos V. (2009) *Estados Fallidos: Definiciones Conceptuales. (México D.F.: Centro de Documentación, Investigación y Análisis, Subdirección de Política*

Exterior, Cámara de Diputados). Available at: http://www.diputados.gob.mx/cedia/sia/spe/SPE-ISS-07-09.pdf.

Scharpf, F. (2007) The European Social Model. In: M. Buchs (ed.) *New Governance in European Social Policy.* (Basingstoke: Palgrave/ Macmillan, 2007).

Scharpf, F. (2010) The Asymmetry of European Integration, or Why the EU Cannot Be a "Social Market Economy". *Socio-Economic Review* 8(2): 211–50.

Schirm, S. (2010) Leaders in Need of Followers: Emerging Powers in Global Governance. *European Journal of International Relations* 16(2): 197–221.

Schmitt-Egner P. (2002) The Concept of "Region": Theoretical and Methodological Notes on its Reconstruction. *Journal of European Integration* 24(3): 179–200, 191.

Schrank, A., and Kurtz, M. (2005) Credit Where Credit Is Due: Open Economy Industrial Policy and Export Diversification in Latin America and the Caribbean. *Politics & Society* 33(4): 671–702.

Seekings, J. (2008) Welfare Regimes and Redistribution in the South. In: Shapiro, I. (ed.) *Divide and Deal: The Politics of Distribution in Democracies.* (New York: New York University Press), pp. 19–42.

Sennes, R. and Tomazini, C. (2006) Agenda Sudamericana de Brasil. ¿Proyecto Diplomático, Sectorial o Estratégico? *De Foreign Affairs*, January to March.

Serbin A. (2012) New Regionalism and Civil Society: Bridging the Democratic Gap? In: P. Riggirozzi and D. Tussie (eds) *The Rise of Post-Hegemonic Regionalism The Case of Latin America.* (Netherlands: Springer/United Nations University), pp. 147–65.

Serrano, M. (2005) Regionalism and Governance: A Critique. In: L. Fawcett and M. Serrano (eds) *Regionalism and Governance in the Americas: Continental Drift.* (Basingstoke: Palgrave/Macmillan), pp. 1–24, 13.

Setaro, M. (2010) La Creación del Sistema Nacional Integrado de Salud and el nuevo Estado para la Performance. In: M.E. Mancebo and P. Narbondo (eds) *Reforma del Estado and Políticas Públicas en la Administración Vázquez: Acumulaciones, Conflictos and Desafíos.* (Montevideo Fin de Siglo – CLACSO–ICP).

Shahar, H. (2012) Theorising Regions through Changes in Statehood: Rethinking the Theory and Method of Comparative Regionalism. *Review of International Studies*, FirstView Articles, pp. 1–23.

Shaw, T. (1988) Africa Renaissance/African Alliance: Towards New Regionalism and New Realism in the Great Lakes a the Start of the Twenty-First Century. *Politeia* 17(3): 60–74.

Shaw, T. (2000) New Regionalism in Africa in the New Millennium: Comparative Perspectives on Renaissance, Realism and/or Regressions. *New Political Economy* 5(3): 399–414.

Sheahan, J. (2002) Alternative Models of Capitalism in Latin America. In: Huber, E. (ed.) *Models of Capitalism. Lessons for Latin America.* (Park: Pennsylvania State University Press).

Sil, R. and Katzenstein, P. (2010) *Beyond Paradigms: Analytic Eclecticism in the Study of World Politics.* (London: Palgrave Macmillan).

Singh, J., and Massi, E. (2011) *The Politics of Natural Resources: A Critical Appraisal on the Return of the State in Brazil,* paper presented at the Workshop *Post-Neoliberalism: Towards a New Political Economy of Development for Latin America?,* University of Sheffield, October.

Smith, P. (1986) *Talons of the Eagle: Dynamics of U.S.–Latin American Relations.* (New York: Oxford University Press).

Soares de Lima, M.R. and Hirst, M. (2009) Brazil as an Intermediate State and Regional Power Action, Choice and Responsibilities. *International Affairs* 82: 1, 21–40.

Söderbaum, F. (2003) Introduction: Theories of new regionalism. In: F. Söderbaum and T. Shaw (eds), *Theories of New Regionalism.* (Houndmills: Palgrave Macmillan), pp. 1–21.

Söderbaum, F. (2005) The International Political Economy of Regionalism. In: N. Phillips (ed.) *Globalizing International Political Economy.* (New York: Palgrave Macmillan), pp. 221–45.

Söderbaum, Fredrik (2012) *Conceptualizing Region, Regionalism and Regionalizatio.* (Unpublished).

Söderbaum, F. and Shaw T. (eds) (2003) *Theories of New Regionalism.* (Houndmills: Palgrave Macmillan).

Sorj, B. and Fausto, S. (eds) (2011) *Brasil y América del Sur: Miradas Cruzadas.* Primera Edición Argentina. (Centro Edelstein de Pesquisas Sociais/Instituto Fernando Henrique Cardoso).

Strange, S. (1986) *Casino Capitalism.* New York: Manchester University Press.

Strange, S. (1988) *States and Markets.* (New York: Continuum).

Stockholm International Peace Research Institute SIPRI (2011) *Background Paper on SIPRI Military Expendiure Data, 2010.* Available at: http://www.sipri.org/research/armaments/milex/factsheet2010 (Accessed 15 July 2011).

Stockholm International Peace Research Institute SIPRI (2011) *Military Expendiure of Venezuela.* Available at: http://milexdata.sipri.org/ (Accessed 15 July 2011).

Tanaka, M. and Vera, S. (2008) El "Neodualismo" de la Política Peruana. *Revista de Ciencias Políticas* 28(1): 347–65.

Tavara, J. (2010) Política Industrial y Desarrollo en el Perú. In: J. Rodríguez and M. Tello, M. (eds) *En Opciones De Política Económica In El Perú, 2011–2015.* (Lima: Fondo Editorial de la Pontifica Universidad Católica de Perú), pp. 15–44.

Taylor, L., and R. Vos (2002) Balance of Payments Liberalization in Latin America: Effects on Growth, Distribution and Poverty. In: R. Vos; L. Taylor, L., and

R. Páez de Barros (eds) *Economic Liberalization, Distribution and Poverty: Latin America in the 1990s.* (Cheltenham: Edward Elgar).

Tello, M. and Tavara, J. (2010) Productive Development Policies in Latin American Countries: The Case of Peru, 1990–2007. *IDB Working Papers* no. IDB-WP-129.

Thorp, R. (1998) *Progress, Poverty and Exclusion: An Economic History of Latin America in the 20th century.* (Washington, DC: IDB).

Thoumi, F. (2009) La Normativa Internacional de Drogas como Camisa de Fuerza. *Revista Nueva Sociedad* No. 222, pp. 42–59. Available at. www.nuso.org/upload/articulos/3620_1.pdf.

Tockman, J. (2010) *Varieties of Post-neoliberalism: Ecuador and Bolivia's Divergent Paths of Citizenship, Participation and Natural Resource Policy.* Paper presented at the Latin American Studies Association Congress, Toronto, Canada (6–9 October 2010). Available at: http://lasa.international.pitt.edu/members/congres–papers/lasa2010/files/3867.pdf (Accessed 1 February 2011).

Tokatlian, J. (2010) La Guerra Antidrogas y el Comando Sur. Una Combinación Perfecta. *Revista Foreign Affairs* 10(1), January to March.

Touraine, A. (2006) América Latina en Tiempos de Chávez. *Nueva Sociedad* No. 205, September/October.

Tulchin, J. (2010) *La Política y los Intereses de Seguridad de Estados Unidos en América Latina.* (Bogotá: Friedrich Ebert Stiftung).

Turcotte, S. and Mostajo, F. (2008) La Política de Brasil hacia Sudamérica: Entre Voluntarismo y Resistencias. *Foro Internacional* 48(4) (October to December), pp. 785–806.

Tussie, D. (1995) *The Inter-American Development Bank.* Series: The Multilateral Development Banks. (Ottawa: North-South Institute).

Tussie, D. (2003a) Regionalism: Providing a Substance to Multilateralism? In: F. Söderbaum and T. Shaw (eds) *Theories of the New Regionalism.* (Basingstoke: Palgrave Macmillan).

Tussie, D. (2003b) Latin America: Contrasting Motivations in The Rise and Fall of Open Regionalism? Comparative Reflections on Regional Governance in the Southern Cone of Latin America. *Third World Quarterly* 24(2): 217–34.

Tussie, D. (2009) Latin America: Contrasting Motivations for Regional Projects. *Review of International Studies* 35(1): 169–88.

Tussie, D. and Riggirozzi, P. (2011) *The Rise of Post-Hegemonic Regionalism in Latin America.* UNU/CRIS Series on Comparative Regionalism.

Tussie, D. and Trucco, P. (2009) *La Economía Política del Regionalismo Sudamericano.* (Buenos Aires: FLACSO).

UN (2005) *In Larger Freedom. Towards Security, Development and Human Rights for All.* Report of the Secretary-General of the United Nations for Decision by Heads of State and Government in September 2005, A/59/2005. Available at: http://daccessdds.un.org/doc/UNDOC/GEN/N05/270/78/PDF/NO527078.pdf?OpenElement.

UN (2006) *Delivering as One: Report of the Secretary-General's High Level Panel*. (New York: UN).

UN Office on Drugs and Crime (2011) *World Drugs Report 2011*. (New York: UN).

UNASUR (2009) *Declaración Presidencial de Quito, 10 August 2009*. Available at: http://www.comunidadandina.org/unasur/10-8-09Dec_quito.htm (Accessed 16 September 2011).

UNASUR (2009) Agreement 01/09-21/04/2009. Available at: http://www.ocai.cl/unasur-english.pdf. (Accessed 29 March 2012).

UNASUR Bulletin (2010) *Ecuador and Domenican Republic Agree to Cooperate in the Reconstruction of Haiti* (*Ecuador y Republica Domenicana subscriben convenio para reconstruccion de Haiti*), 4 November 2010. Available at: http://www.pptunasur.com/contenidos.php?id=1100&tipo=27&idiom=1website (Accessed 28 March 2012).

UNASUR Plan Quinquenal, 2010-2015. Available at: http://www.ins.gob.pe/repositorioaps/0/0/jer/rins_documentosunasur/PQ%20UNASUR%20Salud.pdf (Accessed 20 March 2012).

UNASUR Salud (2011) *Report of the Pro Tempore Secretariat*. Available at: http://ISAGSs-unasul.org/site/wp-content/uploads/2011/12/Informe-2011.pdf (Accessed 28 March 2012).

UNDP (2011) *Regional Integration and Human Development: A Pathway for Africa*. (New York, UNDP).

UNESCO (2006) *Buenos Aires Declaration calling for a New Approach to the Social Science Policy Nexus*. Online: http://portal.unesco.org/shs/en/ (Accessed March 2008).

UNSC (2011) *Recognizing Interconnected Nature of Haiti's Long-Term Development Challenges, Security Council Reiterates Need for Sustained International Support*. UN Security Council 6510th Meeting, April 2011. Available at: http://www.un.org/News/Press/docs/2011/sc10218.doc.htm (Accessed 28 March 2012).

US Embassy, Lima, Peru (2011) *US Cooperation with Peru (Cooperación de Estados Unidos al Perú)*. Available at: http://spanish.peru.usembassy.gov/cooperacion.html (Accessed 15 July 2011).

Valenzuela, A. (2011) *Estados Unidos Destaca el Papel de UNASUR para Evitar Conflictos Regionales*. Informe 21.com, 11 enero 2011. Available at: http://informe21.com/arturo-valenzuela.

Varas, A. (1992) From Coercion to Partnership: A New Paradigm for Security in the Western Hemisphere? In: H. Schoultz and A. Varas (eds), *The United States and Latin America in the 1990s*. (London and Chapel Hill: University of North Carolina Press), pp. 46–65.

Varas, A. (1995) Latin America: toward a new reliance on the market. In: B. Stalling (ed.), *Global Change, Regional Response: The New International Context of Development* (New York: Cambridge University Press), 273–308.

Vargas, A. (2011) Política Exterior Colombiana y Unasur. *El Colombiano.com*, March. Available at: http://www.elcolombiano.com/BancoConocimiento/P/politica_exterior_colombiana_y_unasur/politica_exterior_colombiana_y_unasur.asp (Accessed 8 July 2011).

Väyrynen, R.(2003) Regionalism: Old and New. *International Studies Review* 5(1): 25–51.

Vieira, E. (2005) Evolución de las Teorías Sobre Integración en el Contexto de las Teorías de Relaciones Internacionales. *Papel Político* No. 18, December, pp. 235–90.

Villarán, F. (2010) Políticas e Instituciones de Apoyo a la Micro y Pequeña (MYPE) Empresa en Perú. In: Ferraro, C., and G. Stumpo (eds) *Políticas de Apoyo a las Pymes en América Latina. Entre Avances Innovadores y Desafíos Institucionales.* (Santiago: Economic Commission for Latin America and the Caribbean).

Wagner, A. (2010) Regionalismo y Seguridad Sudamericana: ¿Son Relevantes el Mercosur y la Unasur? Iconos. *Revista de Ciencias Sociales* no. 38, September, pp. 41–53.

Waltz, K. (2001) *Man, the State and War.* (New York: Columbia University Press).

Warleigh-Lack, A. and Rosamond, B. (2010) Across the EU Studies-New Regionalism Frontier: Invitation to a Dialogue. *Journal of Common Market Studies*, 48:4, 993–1013.

Washington Office on Latin America (2010) *Sudamérica Sale de Compras: Informe WOLA Sobre el Gasto de Defensa en Amrérica del Sur.* (Washington: WOLA).

World Commission for the Social Dimension of Globalization (WCSDG) (2004) *A Fair Globalization: Creating Opportunities for All.* (Geneva: International Labour Office–World Commission on the Social Dimension of Globalization).

Weaver, F. (2000) *Latin America in the World Economy: Mercantile Colonialism to Global Capitalism.* (Boulder, CO: Westview Press).

Webber, J. (2009) From Naked Barbarism to Barbarism with Benefits: Neoliberal Capitalism, Natural Gas Policy and the Evo Morales Government in Bolivia. In: McDonald, L., and Ruckert, A. (eds) *Post-Neoliberalism in the Americas.* (London: Palgrave).

Wendt, A. (1999) *Social Theory of International Politics.* (Cambridge: Cambridge University Press).

Weyland, K., de la Madrid, R., and Hunter, W. (2010) *Leftist Governments in Latin America.* (Cambridge: Cambridge University Press).

The White House Office of the Press Secretary (2009) www.whitehouse.gov/the-press-office/background-briefing-senior-administration-officials-presidents-meeting-with-unasur.

The World Bank (1994) *The East Asian Miracle.* (New York, Oxford University).

Wong, J. (1979) *ASEAN Economies in Perspective: A Comparative Study of Indonesia, Malaysia, the Philippines, Singapore & Thailand.* (London, Macmillan Press).

Wong, J. (1985) ASEAN's Experience in Regional Economic Cooperation. *Asian Development Review* 3(1).

Wong, J. (1996) The East Asian Phenomenon and the Implications for Economic Development. In: Basant K. Kapur etc. (eds), *Development, Trade and the Asia-Pacific, Essays in honour of Professor Lim Chong Yah.* (Singapore, Prentice Hall).

Wylde, C. (2011) State, Society and Markets in Argentina: The Political Economy of Neodesarrollismo under Nestor Kirchner, 2003–2007. *Bulletin of Latin American Research*, 30(4): 436–45.

Yañez, E., RojasArvenas, F., and D. Silva (2011) *The Juancito Pinto Conditional Cash Transfer Program in Bolivia: Analyzing the Impact on Primary Education.* FOCAL Policy Brief, Canadian Foundation for the Americas.

Yeates, N. (2001) *Globalisation and Social Policy.* (London: Sage).

Yeates, N. (2002) Globalisation and Social Policy: From Global Neoliberal Hegemony to Global Political Pluralism. *Journal of Global Social Policy* 2(1): 69–91.

Yeates, N. (2005) *Globalisation and Social Policy in a Development Context: Regional Responses, Social Policy and Development Programme.* Paper No. 18. (Geneva: UN Research Institute for Social Development).

Yeates, N. (2010) The Globalization of Nurse Migration: Policy Issues and Responses. *International Labour Review* 149(4): 423–40.

Yeates, N. and Deacon, B. (2006) *Globalism, Regionalism and Social Policy: Framing the Debate.* UNU-CRIS Occasional Papers (O-2006/6). Available at: www.cris.unu.edu/fileadmin/workingpapers/20060418154630.O-2006–6.pdf.

Yeates, N. and Deacon, B. (2010) Globalization, Regional Integration and Social Policy. In: Deacon, B., Macovei, M., van Langenhove, L., and Yeates, N. (eds) *World-Regional Social Policy And Global Governance: New Research And Policy Agendas in Africa, Asia, Europe and Latin America.* (London: Routledge).

Yeates, N., Macovei, M., and van Langenhove, L. (2010) The evolving context of world- regional social policy. In: Deacon, B., Macovei, M., van Langenhove, L., and Yeates, N. (eds) *World-Regional Social Policy and Global Governance: New Research and Policy Agendas in Africa, Asia, Europe and Latin America.* (London: Routledge).

Youngers, C. and Rosin, E. (2005) La Guerra Contra las Drogas Impulsada por Estados Unidos su Impacto en América Latina y el Caribe. In: C.A. Youngers and E. Rosin (eds) *Drogas y Democracia in América Latina.* (Washington D.C: WOLA, Editorial Biblos), pp. 13–28.

Yue, C.S. and Pacini, M. (eds) (1997) *ASEAN in the new Asia.* (Singapore: Institute of Southeast Asian Studies).

Index

9/11 attack, 60

Abrams, Philip, 214
Afghanistan, 57
agricultural insurance, 151
ALBA. *See* Bolivian Alliance for the
　　Peoples of Our America (ALBA)
ALCSA. *See* South American Association
　　of Free Commerce (ALCSA)
Alliance for Progress, 34–5
Al Qaeda, 57
Amazon, 39, 207
Andean Community of Nations (CAN),
　　35–6, 49, 51–2, 91, 135, 137, 152,
　　178, 197
　　Andres Bello Convention, 135
　　Fixed Gross Capital Formation, 108
　　Hipólitio Unanúe agreement, 135
　　Social Humanitarian Fund and Integral
　　　Plan for Social Development, 154
Andean Pact. *See* Andean Community of
　　Nations (CAN)
Andean Regional Initiative (IRA), 200
Andean Trade Promotion and Drug
　　Eradication Act (ATPDEA), 200
Andean Tribunal of Justice, 35
Andres Bello Convention, 135
anticrime strategic intelligence community,
　　180
"anti-imperialist" bias, 53
Argentina, 1, 34, 39, 41–3, 46, 51, 54,
　　57–9, 98, 115, 126–7, 171, 180,
　　186–7, 201, 215
　　Integration Act, 36
　　Operation Emanuel (2007), 45
　　Pro-Huerta program, 142
Armed Forces of Colombia (FARC). *See*
　　Revolutionary Armed Forces of
　　Colombia (FARC)
arms trafficking, 164, 203–4

ASEAN Framework Agreement on
　　Services (AFAS), 79
ASEAN Free Trade Area (AFTA), 79
ASEAN Investment Area (AIA), 79
ASEAN plus Three (APT), 83
ASEAN Regional Forum (ARF), 83
ASEAN Way, 78, 84–6
Asian financial crisis (1997), 71, 80, 83
Asian regionalism, 31
Association of Southeast Asian Nations
　　(ASEAN), 65, 67, 71, 152
　　Declaration of ASEAN Concord II, 79
　　Economic Community (AEC), 79
　　humble beginning, 79–81
　　Post Ministerial Conference (PMC),
　　　83
　　progress in regional economic
　　　cooperation, 81–3
　　regional economic cooperation, 78
　　"Ten Minus X", principle of, 86
　　Treaty of Amity and Cooperation
　　　(TAC, 1976), 85
　　"Two plus X", principle of, 86
　　Vision 2015, 79, 86
　　way of organizing regional
　　　cooperation, 84–6
　　wide-ranging extraregional activities,
　　　83–4
Australia and New Zealand Closer
　　Economic Relations Trade
　　Agreement (ANZCERTA), 152,
　　154

Bacrims (armed criminal groups), 176
balance of power politics, 9, 36, 64, 138,
　　165, 185
Balassa model of regionalism, 21
Bangkok Declaration, 79–80
Bolivia
　　Bolivian crisis (2008), 2

Bonasol universal pension program "Renta Dignidad", 124
Bono Juana Azurduy (cash transfer programs), 124
Bono Juancito Pinto (cash transfer programs), 124
cash transfer programs, 124
infant mortality, 124
Bolivian Alliance for the Peoples of Our America (ALBA), 41, 49, 52–3, 202
Venezuelan leadership in, 53
Bolivian crisis (2008), 2
Brasilia 2000 summit, 40–41
Brazil
1964 coup, 35
acceptance of Pan-Americanism, 34
ALADI, 39
bid for permanent seat in the UN Security Council, 38
Brazilian Development Bank (BNDES), 39, 119
"concentric circle" of influence, 38
conquest of the Amazon, 39
economic and geopolitical interests, 36
entry into SELA, 35
foreign policy, 35
geopolitical definition of South American space, 39
geopolitical discourse, 39
industrial policy, 119
Integration Act, 36
knowledge-intensive sectors, 119
leadership in South America, 58
military strategists, 38
Nuclear Nonproliferation Treaty, 35
Partido dos Trabalhadores (Labour Party, PT), 121
Programa de Aceleração do Crescimento (PAC), 119
road-infrastructure projects, 59
special relationship with the USA, 34–5, 37
transnational corporations, 39, 43
Bretton Woods institutions, 9, 15, 25, 149
International Financial Institutions (IFIs), 41

BRICS (Brazil, Russia, India, China, and South Africa) countries, 40–41
Bush, George W., 1, 58, 199
doctrine of preemptive war, 46
Buzan, Barry, 19

Caldentey, Perez, 120
CAN. *See* Andean Community of Nations (CAN)
Cardoso, Fernando Enrique, 38, 40, 138
Caribbean Community, 80, 155
cross-border social security, 150
Caribbean Community and Common Market (CARICOM), 49, 150, 152, 154–6
Managed Migration Program (MMP), 155–6
Caribbean Community Single Market and Economy (CSME), 155
Carillo Fuentes Organization, 175
Central African Customs Union (CACEU), 80
Central American Integration System (SICA), 49, 52
ceteris paribus factor, 14
Chavez, Hugo, 40–41, 43–5, 44–5, 52, 59, 200
Chiang Mai Initiative (CMI), 83
child labor, 154
Chile, 5, 33–4, 45, 61–2, 115, 117, 124, 126, 142, 156, 186, 197, 202, 207, 214, 216
AUGE plan, 123
Corporation for the Promotion of Production (CORFO), 120
industrial policy, 120
National Council of Innovation for Competitiveness (NCIC), 120
pension reform, 123
Plan for Universal Access with Explicit Guarantees, 122
China, 70, 87, 184
Asian financial crisis, 71
demand for primary goods, 125
economic growth and inflation, 73
economic orbit, 77
economic rise, 71–5
gross domestic product (GDP) of, 78

versus Japan-led East Asia, 75–7
regional economic order, 77–8
regional growth and integration,
    pattern of, 74
trade balance with selected economies,
    74
as world's second largest economy, 73
civil society organizations, 132–3, 144,
    149
Clinton, Hillary, 58, 61
cocaine trafficking, 164, 171–3, 175
Cold War, 11, 34, 50, 80, 86, 184–5
    Inter-American Treaty of Reciprocal
        Assistance, 30
Colombian imbroglio, 39, 45–6
Columbian Intelligence Law, 199
Common Effective Preferential Tariff
    (CEPT), 79, 83
Common Market of the Southern Cone
    (MERCOSUR). *See* Southern
    Common Market (MERCOSUR)
Community of South American Nations
    (CSAN), 41, 43
Comunidad Andina de Naciones (CAN),
    29, 210
Comunidad de Estados Latinoamericanos
    and Caribeños (CELAC), 47, 49
conditional cash transfers (CCTs), 115
Constitutive Treaty (2008), 41
Corporation for the Promotion of
    Production (CORFO), Chile, 120
Costa Rica, 113, 115–16, 197
    conflict with Nicaragua, 197
Cox, Robert, 2, 22
criminal financial infiltration, 180
criminal organizations, 164, 166, 174–5,
    203
    economic power of, 181
cross-border social security, 150, 152
Cuba, 53, 56–7, 59, 63, 157, 201, 204
Cuban Revolution, 58

defense in South America, perspectives on
    civil–military relationship, 193
    conditions and methods for addressing
        and implementing, 195–6
    defense and the armed forces,
        consideration of, 189–95

defense politics, 196
inter-American institutionalism, 184
political government and defense
    institutionalism, 183–9
political leadership of the armed forces,
    189, 192
political–military tension, 187
power politics, use of, 184
South American Defense Council. *See*
    South American Defense Council
    (SADC)
"Southern Cross" Binational Peace
    Force, 186
zone of peace, 196
defense of internal security, concept of,
    200
division of labour, 151
Dominican Republic, 52, 56, 142
drug trafficking and organized crime
    "all-out war" against drugs, 167–8,
        171, 175, 199
    analysis of, 166
    Andean Trade Promotion and Drug
        Eradication Act (ATPDEA), 200
    antidrug policies' balloon effect, 170,
        174
    Carillo Fuentes Organization, 175
    and challenges for South American
        regional cooperation, 177–80
    cocaine. *See* cocaine trafficking
    drug trafficking cartels, 168, 172,
        175–7
    economic revenue of, 164
    financial importance of, 165
    global effect, 173–4
    hegemonic drug policy model, 167–70
    illegal drug market and its impact on
        the region, 170–72
    international regulations on, 167
    new criminal actors, 175–7
    new criminal rationalities, 174–5
    new problematic scenario, 170–80
    Organization of the Michoacana
        Family, 175
    political economy of, 164–7, 170,
        202–4
    power of economic production of,
        173

risk diversification of criminal
  economies, 174
security and intelligence *versus*, 204–6
Self Defense Forces, 176
Shanghai Opium Commission (1909),
  167
Sinaloa Cartel, 175
Single Convention on Narcotic Drugs
  (1961), 167
social vulnerability and exclusion, 180
South American Council for the Fight
  against Drug Trafficking, 177
transnational criminal groups, 177
transnationality of, 198

East African Community (EAC), 80–81
East Asia (EA)
  China-centric regional economic order,
    77–8
  China's economic rise, 71–5
  comparison of economies, 76–7
  composition of regional trade, 105–6
  distinguishing features of cooperation,
    86–7
  as dynamic economic region, 65–7
  Export Concentration Index, 100–101
  gross domestic product (GDP) of, 78
  Herfindahl–Hirschman Index (HHI),
    102
  institutional structure of, 71
  intraregional trade, origins and
    destinations of, 68–9
  Japan-led EA-I *versus* China-led EA-
    II, 75–7
  Japan-led "flying geese" pattern, 67–71
  performance indicators, 66
  regionalism in, 4
  Relative Entropy Indexes of GDP, 110
  socioeconomic development indicators,
    72
  trade in producer goods and other
    goods with Latin America, 97
  Trade Intensity Index (ITI), 98–9
"East Asia Developmental State" model,
  71
East Asian Economic Community, 77
East Asian Miracle, 71
East–West conflict, 58

Economic Commission for Latin America
  (ECLA), 124, 126, 150, 209
Economic Community of West African
  States (ECOWAS), 81, 152, 154
Ecuador–Colombia dispute, 46, 187
Ecuador crisis (2010), 2
Ecuador–Peru war (1995), 197
"Enterprise for the Americas" project, 1,
  37
European Union (EU), 2, 9, 11, 19, 60, 73,
  127, 206
Export Concentration Index, 100–101

Failed States, 165
Falkland Islands War (1982), 57, 59
FARC. *See* Revolutionary Armed Forces of
  Colombia (FARC)
First World-led internationalization
  initiatives, 39
Flying Geese model, for economic growth,
  67–71
food security, 141, 147, 154
foreign direct investment (FDI), 40, 67, 79,
  115, 120
foreign-exchange revenue, 92
Four Little Dragons, 65
Franco, Itamar, 38
free trade areas, 21, 29, 91, 95, 156
Free Trade Association of the Americas
  (FTAA), 37–8, 52, 54, 58, 60, 95,
  132–3, 156

Germany, 78
Gini coefficient, 116
global financial crisis, 73, 76, 80–81, 86,
  184
globalization, notion of, 11
"Good Neighbor" policy, 56, 80
governance, right-based models of, 130
Granada, 56
gross domestic product (GDP), 78, 102
  relative entropy indexes of, 109–10
Guatemala, 56

Haiti, 56, 141–2
healthcare services, 117
Herfindahl–Hirschman Index (HHI), 102
Hipólitio Unanúe agreement, 135

Hispanic American Regionalism
   (1820s–1870s), 32–3
Hodges, Heather, 200
human capital, 71, 113
human trafficking, 164, 203
hyper-presidentialism, tradition of, 133

import substitution industrialization (ISI),
   34–6, 42, 71
income distribution, 2, 113, 115
India, 40, 57, 79, 83, 98, 184
Initiative for the Integration of the South
   American Regional Infrastructure
   (IIRSA), 40–41, 43
Integration Act, 36
intellectual property rights (IPR), 37, 141
Inter-American Defense Board (JID), 208,
   210
inter-American institutionalism, 184
Inter-American Reciprocity Treaty (IART),
   34
Inter-American Treaty of Reciprocal
   Assistance (1947), 30, 56, 62
intergovernmental social policy
   cooperation, 152
International Court of Justice, The Hague,
   197
International Governmental Organizations,
   150
International Labor Organization, 149
International Opium Convention, 167
international political economy (IPE), 10,
   22, 215
   concept of, 13–14
   future aspects of, 15–16
   major perspectives in, 18
   pluralist school of, 14–15
   rationalist–reflectivist classifications,
      17
   of South American Regionalism, 16–17
international relations (IR), 26, 30, 53–4,
   130, 163, 165
International Union for American
   Republics, 56
interstate integration, 11–12, 216
Iran, 57, 63, 187, 204
   development of nuclear energy, 59
Iraq, 57

ISAGS. *See* South American Institute of
   Health Governance (ISAGS)
Italian–American mafia, 164

Japan, 67, 87
   versus China-led East Asia, 75–7
   Flying Geese model, for economic
      growth, 67–71
   gross domestic product (GDP) of, 78
   Plaza Accord (1985), 75

Katzenstein, Peter, 31, 131
Keynesian welfare politics and socialism,
   137
Kirchner, Néstor, 60, 209
Korean War, 86

labor mobility rights, 154–5
Latin America, 9
   Cepalismo, 34
   composition of regional trade, 107–8
   double incorporation, 114–16
   Export Concentration Index, 100–101
   exports, 125
   Gini coefficient, 116
   Herfindahl–Hirschman Index (HHI),
      102
   and homogeneity of regional growth,
      102–11
   integration and regionalism in, 50–55
   market and social incorporation,
      116–26
   neighbors and nonneighbors, 92–6
   notion of, 33
   open regionalism in, 36
   political economy, 136
   public social spending, 122
   public spending in health, 123
   reasons for more regionalism, 94–6
   redistributive benefit program, 123
   regionalism. *See* South American
      regionalism
   regional multiplier effect, 96
   regional social policy, 149
   regional trade preferences, 93, 96, 98
   tariff wall-jumping strategies, 35
   trade in producer goods and other
      goods with Asia, 97

Trade Intensity Index (ITI), 98–9
trade liberalization, 37
United States of America and, 55–7
unity, 32
US military and police aid, 200–201
Latin American Economic System, 49
Latin American Free Trade Association
    (LAFTA). *See* Latin American
    Integration Association
Latin American Integration Association,
    35, 49, 80
liberal institutionalism, 14, 19–21, 23, 25

Maastricht Treaty (1991), 37
Mexico, 1, 32, 35, 37, 45, 57, 98, 115, 132,
    134, 175, 178–9, 206, 215
migration, issue of, 58
Millennium Development Goals, 159
money-laundering, 174, 180
Monroe Doctrine, 33, 56
Morales, Evo, 44–5, 61, 120, 124, 201
multiform citizen movements, 149

Napoleon III (1850–1870), 33
national security, doctrine of, 6, 16, 19,
    168, 183, 197–200, 204–6, 211
Nations Commerce Treaty (2006), 52–3
neoliberal institutionalism, 14, 20, 25
    central weaknesses of, 21
newly industrialized economies (NIEs),
    65, 67
New South American Regionalism
    (NSAR), 3–5, 10, 213
    challenges of, 16
    distinctive feature of, 27
    future prospects of, 14–15
    Washington and, 58–64
    See also South American regionalism
Nicaragua, 56, 157, 197, 201
Nixon, Richard, 167
Non-Aligned Movement, 60
North American Free Trade Agreement
    (NAFTA), 1, 29–30, 36–7, 132,
    134, 157
North American regionalism, 11
    and actor-oriented regional
        perspectives, 19–21
Nuclear Nonproliferation Treaty, 35

Obama, President, 60–61, 199
open method of coordination (OMC), 129
Operation Emanuel (2007), 45
Operation Phoenix (2008), 207
Organization of American States (OAS), 2,
    30, 34, 37, 63, 178, 201, 209–10
Organization of the Michoacana Family,
    175
organized crime. *See* drug trafficking and
    organized crime

Panama, 56, 177
Pan-American Health Organization
    (PAHO), 141–2
Pan-Americanism (1870s–1930s), 33–4
    Brazil's acceptance of, 34
Pan-American Union of 1910, 56
Phillips, Nicolas, 12, 23, 41
Plan Colombia, 37, 39, 202, 206
Plaza Accord (1985), 75
Political Economy of International
    Relations, 165
postneoliberalism, notion of, 137
poverty reduction, policy of, 58, 136
Pro Huerta project, Argentina, 142
public–private infrastructure ventures, 43
public social spending, 122
purchasing power parity (PPP), 73

Reagan, Ronald, 167
regional development banks, 21, 30, 41,
    150
regional governance, of social policy, 5,
    16, 129–30, 132–3, 137–8, 143–5,
    148–9, 157–9
regional integration agreements, 136
regionalism
    Balassa model of, 21
    concept of, 21
    contours of the framework for, 25–8
    critical-oriented perspectives on, 22–5
    for interstate integration, 11
    new realist/regionalism approach (NR/
        RA) for, 22
    new regionalist approach (NRA) for,
        22
    North American and actor-oriented
        regional perspectives, 19–21

political–economic thought on, 13–15, 27

political economy (PE) of, 10, 18

in regional development banks, 21

world order approach (WOA) for, 22–4

Regionalism and Asia (Peter Katzenstein), 31

regionalism–globalization relationship, 144

regionalization, political–economic thought on, 13–15, 21

regional security complex, concept of, 19, 32

regional social policy
  concept of, 149
  expressions of, 152–7
  in practice on four continents, 153
  principles of, 150–52

regional trade agreements, 20

regionness, notion of, 134

regulatory regionalism, 140

rest of the world (ROW), 97–8, 100, 104–5

Revolutionary Armed Forces of Colombia (FARC), 45–6, 176–7, 187, 201

Roosevelt Corollary (1905), 33

Russia, 40, 57, 59, 83, 177, 184, 201, 204

Shanghai Opium Commission (1909), 167

Singapore, 71, 74, 77, 79–80

Single Convention on Narcotic Drugs (1961), 167

Sistema Económico Latinoamericano and del Caribe (SELA), 35

small and medium enterprises (SMEs), 119

social incorporation, 5, 113–18, 125–6, 127

social insurance, 115, 117, 124–6, 151

Söderbaum, Fredrik, 16–17, 23, 131, 134

South American Association of Free Commerce (ALCSA), 38

South American citizenship, 40

South American Council for the Fight against Drug Trafficking, 177

South American Council on the Global Drug Problem, 177

South American Council on the World Drug Problem, 208

South American Defense Council (SADC), 30, 57, 62, 185–8, 196, 199, 208

South American Health Council, 5, 130, 139
  health care programmes, 142
  Pro Huerta project, 142
  Scholarship Program, 140
  South–South cooperation, 141

South American Institute of Health Governance (ISAGS), 140, 144

South American regionalism, 2, 36, 41
  conceptual limitations and practical relations, 206–8
  contribution to enhanced positive change, 126–7
  cooperation and national realities, challenges to, 208–10
  cycles of, 32–5
  Hispanic American Regionalism (1820s–1870s), 32–3
  Inter-American System and Developmentalism (1945–1980), 34–5
  Pan-Americanism (1870s–1930s), 33–4
  political economy of, 16–17
  recasting the social in, 134–7
  regional economic integration, 21
  regional integration agreements, 136
  regional strategic environment, tendencies in, 199–202
  social purpose of, 142–4
  See also New South American Regionalism (NSAR); North American regionalism

South Asia
  composition of regional trade, 105–6
  Relative Entropy Indexes of GDP, 110

South Asian Association for Regional Cooperation (SAARC), 152, 154
  Social Charter, 154

Southern African Development Community (SADC), 30, 42, 46, 152, 154

Southern Common Market (MERCOSUR), 29, 30, 36–7, 39, 49, 51–2, 91, 108, 110, 135, 137, 152, 197
  establishment of, 134
  functionality and identity crisis of, 54

Southern Cone regionalism, 214

"Southern Cross" Binational Peace Force, 186
South Korea, 65, 78, 83, 98
South–South regional integration projects, 126, 141
Summit of South American Presidents, 40–41, 138
Summit of the Ministers of the Defense of the Americas, 186
sustainable development, 52–3, 156

tariff barriers, 79, 83
Trade Intensity Index (ITI), 98–9
transnational criminal groups, 177
transnational organized crime, 175, 198
Treaty of Amazonian Cooperation, 39
Treaty of Amity and Cooperation (TAC, 1976), 85
"twenty-first century socialism", 59, 157

Union of American Republics, 33
Union of South American Nations (UNASUR), 2, 4, 32, 35, 43, 47, 49, 177–8, 184, 197, 202, 211
    Brazil's structural weight and soft power, 31
    democratic clause of, 45
    formation of, 30, 40
    funding for health and food security programs, 141
    membership of, 29
    origins of, 35–43
    postneoliberal development models, 31
    presidential summit, 30
    recasting region as space for policy and action, 130–34
    regional defense integration, 6
    regional Health Council. *See* South American Health Council
    regional health governance, 137–42

security dynamics and political instability in formation of, 44–6
social policy, 157
social purpose of, 142–4
South American Council on the Global Drug Problem, 177
South American Defense Council, 57
United Nations, 9, 24, 141, 167
    Security Council, 38
United States of America (USA)
    Alliance for Progress, 34–5
    gross domestic product (GDP) of, 78
    hemispheric integration, 31
    "hyperliberal" projects of continental reach, 132
    military and police aid to Latin America, 200–201
Uruguay, 5, 36, 39, 42, 114–18, 121–6, 134, 156, 187
    Equity Plan, 122
    Integrated National Healthcare System, 124
    National Healthcare Fund, 124

Venezuela, 1, 40–46, 51–4, 59–62, 122, 138, 142, 157, 169, 173, 177–8, 186–7, 199–210, 215
Vietnam War (1967), 80, 86

war on terrorism, 57
Washington Consensus, 115, 136, 184
"Western hemisphere", 33
World Bank, 71, 150
    regional migration policy, 156
World Commission on the Social Dimension of Globalization, 150
World Health Organization, 141
World Institute for Development Economics and Research, 24
World Trade Organization (WTO), 37, 141
World War II, 33, 86, 184

THE INTERNATIONAL POLITICAL ECONOMY OF NEW REGIONALISMS SERIES

Other titles in the series

The EU and the Eurozone Crisis
Policy Challenges and Strategic Choices
Edited by Finn Laursen

China-Africa Relations in an Era of Great
Transformations
*Edited by Li Xing with Abdulkadir
Osman Farah*

The European Union Neighbourhood
Challenges and Opportunities
Edited by Teresa Cierco

The New Democracy Wars
The Politics of North American
Democracy Promotion in the Americas
Neil A. Burron

The European Union after Lisbon
Polity, Politics, Policy
Edited by Søren Dosenrode

Roads to Regionalism
Genesis, Design, and Effects of
Regional Organizations
*Edited by Tanja A. Börzel,
Lukas Goltermann, Mathis Lohaus
and Kai Striebinger*

New Regionalism or No Regionalism?
Emerging Regionalism in the
Black Sea Area
Edited by Ruxandra Ivan

Our North America
Social and Political Issues beyond NAFTA
Edited by Julián Castro-Rea

Community of Insecurity
SADC's Struggle for Peace and Security
in Southern Africa
Laurie Nathan

Global and Regional Problems
Towards an Interdisciplinary Study
*Edited by Pami Aalto, Vilho Harle
and Sami Moisio*

The Ashgate Research Companion
to Regionalisms
*Edited by Timothy M. Shaw, J. Andrew Grant
and Scarlett Cornelissen*

Asymmetric Trade Negotiations
*Sanoussi Bilal, Philippe De Lombaerde
and Diana Tussie*

The Rise of the Networking Region
The Challenges of Regional Collaboration
in a Globalized World
*Edited by Harald Baldersheim,
Are Vegard Haug and Morten Øgård*

Shifting Geo-Economic Power of the
Gulf Oil, Finance and Institutions
*Edited by Matteo Legrenzi
and Bessma Momani*

Building Regions
The Regionalization of the World Order
Luk Van Langenhove

National Solutions to
Trans-Border Problems?
The Governance of Security and Risk
in a Post-NAFTA North America
Edited by Isidro Morales

The Euro in the 21st Century
Economic Crisis and Financial Uproar
María Lorca-Susino

Crafting an African Security Architecture
Addressing Regional Peace and Conflict
in the 21st Century
Edited by Hany Besada

Comparative Regional Integration
Europe and Beyond
Edited by Finn Laursen

The Rise of China
and the Capitalist World Order
Edited by Li Xing

The EU and World Regionalism
The Makability of Regions
in the 21st Century
*Edited by Philippe De Lombaerde
and Michael Schulz*

The Role of the European Union in Asia
China and India as Strategic Partners
*Edited by Bart Gaens, Juha Jokela
and Eija Limnell*

China and the Global Politics
of Regionalization
Edited by Emilian Kavalski

Clash or Cooperation of Civilizations?
Overlapping Integration and Identities
Edited by Wolfgang Zank

New Perspectives on Globalization
and Antiglobalization: Prospects for a
New World Order?
Edited by Henry Veltmeyer

Governing Regional Integration for
Development: Monitoring Experiences,
Methods and Prospects
*Edited by Philippe De Lombaerde,
Antoni Estevadeordal and Kati Suominen*

Europe-Asia Interregional Relations
A Decade of ASEM
Edited by Bart Gaens

Cruising in the Global Economy
Profits, Pleasure and Work at Sea
Christine B.N. Chin

Beyond Regionalism?
Regional Cooperation, Regionalism and
Regionalization in the Middle East
*Edited by Cilja Harders
and Matteo Legrenzi*

The EU-Russian Energy Dialogue
Europe's Future Energy Security
Edited by Pami Aalto

Regionalism, Globalisation
and International Order
Europe and Southeast Asia
Jens-Uwe Wunderlich

EU Development Policy
and Poverty Reduction
Enhancing Effectiveness
Edited by Wil Hout

An East Asian Model for Latin
American Success
The New Path
Anil Hira

European Union and New Regionalism
Regional Actors and Global Governance
in a Post-Hegemonic Era
Second Edition
Edited by Mario Telò

Regional Integration and Poverty
*Edited by Dirk Willem te Velde
and the Overseas Development Institute*

Redefining the Pacific?
Regionalism Past, Present and Future
*Edited by Jenny Bryant-Tokalau
and Ian Frazer*

Latin America's Quest for Globalization
The Role of Spanish Firms
*Edited by Félix E. Martín
and Pablo Toral*

Exchange Rate Crises
in Developing Countries
The Political Role of the Banking Sector
Michael G. Hall

Globalization and Antiglobalization
Dynamics of Change in the
New World Order
Edited by Henry Veltmeyer

Twisting Arms and Flexing Muscles
Humanitarian Intervention and
Peacebuilding in Perspective
*Edited by Natalie Mychajlyszyn
and Timothy M. Shaw*

Asia Pacific and Human Rights
A Global Political Economy Perspective
Paul Close and David Askew

Demilitarisation and Peace-Building
in Southern Africa
Volume I – Concepts and Processes
*Edited by Peter Batchelor
and Kees Kingma*

Demilitarisation and Peace-Building
in Southern Africa
Volume II – National and
Regional Experiences
*Edited by Peter Batchelor
and Kees Kingma*

Persistent Permeability?
Regionalism, Localism, and Globalization
in the Middle East
*Edited by Bassel F. Salloukh
and Rex Brynen*

The New Political Economy of
United States-Caribbean Relations
The Apparel Industry and the
Politics of NAFTA Parity
Tony Heron

The Nordic Regions and the European Union
*Edited by Søren Dosenrode
and Henrik Halkier*

9 781138 270497